The Purposeful Argument:
A Practical Guide

The Purposeful Argument:

A Practical Guide

Brief Second Edition

Harry R. Phillips

Patricia Bostian

Central Piedmont Community College

All Illustrations by iStockphoto.com/A-digit

CENGAGE
Learning·

Australia • Brazil • Mexico • Singapore • United Kingdom • United States

The Purposeful Argument:
   A Practical Guide
Brief Second Edition
Harry Phillips, Patricia Bostian

Product Director: Monica Eckman

Product Manager: Kate Derrick

Senior Content Developer: Leslie Taggart

Development Editor: Stephanie Pelkowski
   Carpenter

Managing Developer: Megan Garvey

Product Assistant: Cailin Barrett-Bressack

Media Developer: Janine Tangney

Marketing Brand Manager: Lydia LeStar

Senior Content Project Manager:
   Aimee Chevrette Bear

Art Director: Hannah Wellman

Manufacturing Planner: Betsy Donaghey

Rights Acquisition Specialist: Ann Hoffman

Production Service: Q2A/Bill Smith

Text Designer: Shawn Girsberger

Cover Designer: Wing Ngan

Cover Image: © ZUMA Press, Inc. / Alamy

Compositor: Q2A/Bill Smith

For product information and technology assistance, contact us at
Cengage Learning Customer & Sales Support, 1-800-354-9706

For permission to use material from this text or product,
submit all requests online at **www.cengage.com/permissions.**
Further permissions questions can be emailed to
permissionrequest@cengage.com.

Library of Congress Control Number:

Brief Student Edition

ISBN-978-1-285-43808-5

ISBN-1-285-43808-6

Cengage Learning
200 First Stamford Place, 4th Floor
Stamford, CT 06902
USA

Cengage Learning is a leading provider of customized learning solutions with office locations around the globe, including Singapore, the United Kingdom, Australia, Mexico, Brazil and Japan. Locate your local office at **international.cengage.com/region.**

Cengage Learning products are represented in Canada by Nelson Education, Ltd.

For your course and learning solutions, visit **www.cengage.com.**

Purchase any of our products at your local college store or at our preferred online store **www.cengagebrain.com.**

Instructors: Please visit **login.cengage.com** and log in to access instructor-specific resources.

Printed in the United States of America
1 2 3 4 5 6 7 17 16 15 14 13

BRIEF CONTENTS

TABLE OF CONTENTS

© iStockphoto.com/A-digit

10 Build Arguments 239

11 Support an Argument with Fact (*Logos*), Credibility (*Ethos*), And Emotion (*Pathos*) 271

PART 5   MLA and APA Documentation Systems   353

PREFACE

Purpose

Since our department first offered a course in argumentative writing in 1998, teachers at our community college have expressed frustration with the range of textbooks available for the course. This second edition of *The Purposeful Argument* continues to respond to this concern. Our textbook—aimed at freshman writers at two- and four-year colleges—delivers the essentials of argumentative writing in accessible, student-friendly language. The textbook allows writers to recognize where argument fits in their lives and how it can be a practical response both to the issues in everyday life and to academic and intellectual problems encountered in the classroom. In this way, the text meets student writers on their own terms, in their own lives, and demands that they determine what they argue about. Changes to this new edition reflect the suggestions of our students and those of veteran teachers of argument, who are sensitive to what makes a textbook genuinely useful.

The philosophical center of *The Purposeful Argument* rests with John Dewey's notion that public education can best serve a democratic culture when it connects classroom with community and by thinking of the classroom as a laboratory for intelligent democratic activity. Building on this idea, those who argue competently can become the lifeblood of local action and change. Put another way, a nation, state, or community that does not engage purposefully in regular discussion and informed argument cannot fulfill itself.

Accessibility is central to the purpose of this project, and this second edition includes a streamlining of many features of the textbook. From many students' perspectives, some current argument texts are dense and filled with examples apart from their worlds. In response to these concerns, *The Purposeful Argument* relies less on discussion via traditional academic language to get across a concept and more on cogent definition, explicit example, and practical exercises that guide student writers through the process of assembling an argument. Examples of student, local, and professional writing are in many cases annotated and color-coded so as to identify elements of argument structure.

From another perspective, *The Purposeful Argument* puts in place the groundwork for student writers to create possibilities for themselves in a culture that demands more and more from its citizens. When so much of what we encounter has to do with the lure of consumption, and when so much of our national discourse is riveted to economic conditions, job security, and terror and intervention, it can be tough for freshman writers to think of themselves as agents capable of meaningful change. But at its core, *The Purposeful Argument* argues this very position. In its purest moment, this guide enables student writers to establish rhetorical places for themselves that ideally can reinvigorate our democracy via responsible citizenship. Because communication is less local in advanced industrial nations, this project invites a return to a more traditional form of democratic participation with its attention to local engagement. And local engagement can begin with a writer's commitment to the idea that the private responsibility to argue is essential to the public good.

With this emphasis on local engagement, we have noticed stronger, more focused arguments in the past several years. In general, when students are encouraged to honor and respond to issues that matter to them, their investment becomes evident and the writing, purposeful. This kind of ownership, we believe, results from an approach that steers writers into issues originating in the larger worlds of political, economic, and social issues as well as into their own worlds and concerns. With some students, this means arguing on issues that are solidly academic and intellectual in nature; with others, it means tackling issues of immediate concern in everyday life. Thus, compelling writing has emerged on issues as varied as the U. S. Supreme Court's ruling on corporate personhood, student loan requirements, China's behavior at the climate change conference in Copenhagen, favoritism in the workplace, recent health care reform and its implications for students, social networking and employment, religious values and curriculum design in Texas, and American consumers' role in the mining of "conflict minerals" in the Republic of the Congo.

A central focus of *The Purposeful Argument* is our intention to write to our specific audience—first-year writers—and this means delivering the fundamentals of argument to many nontraditional students, to nonnative speakers of English, to parents, to students who work one or more jobs, often in excess of the traditional work week, and to students who may or may not have experience with conceptual material and its application in their academic careers. This book is structured to accommodate our students and the diverse life experience they bring to our classrooms. Following are features of *The Purposeful Argument* that, in our view, distinguish it from the many excellent argument textbooks currently on the market—textbooks that may, however, fall outside the lines of accessibility and usefulness to many college students.

Organization and Chapter Flow

Part One of this guide attends to how effective arguments work. Chapter 1 introduces readers to essential features of argument and their interrelatedness. The chapter's sections move students into thinking about argument as a practical response to both everyday and academic issues and briefly introduce them to the types of argument found in the book. In Chapter 2, the crucial need to separate issue from topic is treated early. As a way to recognize issues and where they arise, this chapter identifies communities we belong to and some issues within these communities. The chapter offers numerous prompts and strategies for exploring an issue, such as prewriting activities that help students make a topic they might initially see as "boring" interesting to them and their readers. Audience focus, emphasized throughout the chapters, is introduced here, and students are presented with practical ways to determine appropriate audiences for their arguments. Arguing at the right time and establishing credibility fill out this chapter.

Part Two begins with the essential work of building clear context for an issue, the focus of Chapter 3. It is here that students are introduced to sources and how to access and use them. We choose to bring in the research process earlier rather than later because building a knowledge base often can enlarge the way we think about an issue, and this can influence what a writer claims and the way an argument is structured. Chapter 4 is geared toward the important work of using resources and how to read and evaluate them critically. As well, this chapter is a primer for working responsibly with borrowed material and ideas. Learning how to recognize and avoid fallacies is the center of Chapter 5. This chapter organizes fallacies—common in advertising and politics—into categories of choice, support, emotion, and inconsistency. Chapter 6 is devoted to the opposition, why it matters, how to work responsibly with it, and finding points of overlap. This chapter, we feel, adds to conventional approaches to opposing points of view.

Part Three treats the how-to of argument building. Chapter 7 helps students develop their argument strategies based on definitions, causes or consequences, comparisons, solution proposals, and evaluations, concluding with a rubric for preparing an exploratory essay. Discussion of Toulmin-based argument makes up Chapter 8. Chapter 9 introduces Rogerian argument, in addition to two less traditional approaches to argument in American classrooms: Middle Ground and Microhistory. We are enthusiastic about students learning to argue from a middle-ground perspective, as this approach insists on a close knowledge of audience and opposition. The middle-ground approach has, in the past few years, been popular among writers looking to escape either–or thinking and instead craft practical positions on complex issues. We are equally enthusiastic about a fourth kind of argument discussed in this chapter—an argument based on a microhistory—where writers work with primary documents and then forge a position apart from conventional understanding of the period in which these documents originate. Chapter 10 is about building arguments. It is example-rich and orients writers to the building blocks of argument—claims, reasons, qualifiers, support, the warrant, backing, and audience reservations. We view this chapter as one writers will use frequently during the drafting process. We elaborate in Chapter 11 on how to use support effectively, and this involves establishing writer credibility, specific appeals to audience, and a rubric for evaluating support brought to an argument.

Part Five is centered in the ideal of ownership, that is, in ways writers can make arguments distinctly their own. Chapter 12 is a discussion of tactics—visual argument and humor, among others—that let writers vary their approaches to an audience. And Chapter 13 is devoted to writing style and editing. While material in this final chapter is typically relegated to textbooks designed for earlier writing courses, we present this material in the context of argument writing as what we feel are necessary refreshers.

All chapters in Parts One through Four begin with a narrative that describes a real-life issue and conclude with a "Keeping It Local" exercise, pointing out that argument is a practical way to negotiate purposefully issues in everyday and academic life.

Part Five is devoted to MLA and APA documentation systems. For each system, guidelines and examples are provided. The important work of documenting carefully material borrowed from other writers and sources is addressed in this section.

New Features

- New examples illustrate each of the four types of argument *The Purposeful Argument* covers. These argument types are now spread over two chapters, with Chapter 8 devoted to Toulmin-based argument and Chapter 9 focused on Middle Ground argument, Rogerian argument, and argument based on a Microhistory.
- New assignments in Keeping It Local boxes at the end of each chapter prompt students to try out the chapter's strategies on an issue relevant to their own communities.
- New checklists throughout consolidate for students the key features of particular kinds of argumentative writing and research.
- Research is now consolidated in Part Two, making it easier for instructors to assign whenever they prefer.
- Part Four, "How to Take Ownership of Your Argument: A Style Guide," now includes a guide for obtaining peer reviews of one's writing.
- Part Five, MLA and APA Documentation Systems, now contains a complete APA student essay to accompany the annotated MLA student essay.

Key Features

- Writers are encouraged to argue in response to issues in their everyday and academic environments—school, the workplace, family, neighborhood, social-cultural, consumer, and concerned citizen—and thus learn how argument can become an essential negotiating skill in their lives. This book emphasizes local and intellectual issues throughout and provides a methodology for connecting the local with global trends. Importantly, this allows writers to build a strong understanding of an issue by generating broad context.
- Argument structure is presented in practical, how-to ways, complete with exercises, charts, and real-life examples. Ways to organize an argument—Toulmin-based, Rogerian, Middle Ground, and Microhistory options—are fully defined and demonstrated.
- Simplified text format and page layout improve upon conventional argument textbook design by making information direct and accessible.
- Checklists throughout *The Purposeful Argument* provide support for writers as they craft their own arguments.
- Annotated examples of effective arguments illustrate strengths and weaknesses.
- "Your Turn" exercises consist of questions and prompts so that writers can apply argument structure to arguments they are building. "Internet Activity" prompts direct writers to online investigations that connect to the research process.
- "Tips" panels typically are clues for ways of thinking about a feature of argument during the planning process.
- Key terms are bolded throughout the text. A Glossary related to practical argument provides an alphabetized reference for these and other terms found in *The Purposeful Argument*. A term is defined with regard to its function and placement in an argument.

Teaching and Learning Aids

The supplements listed here accompany *The Purposeful Argument*. They have been created with the diverse needs of today's students and instructors in mind.

- MindTap for *The Purposeful Argument*, 2/e, is a personalized, fully online digital learning platform of authoritative Cengage Learning content, assignments, and services that engages your students with interactivity while also offering you choice in the configuration of coursework and enhancement of the curriculum via complimentary web apps known as MindApps. MindTap is well beyond an ebook, a homework solution or digital supplement, a resource center website, a course delivery platform or a Learning Management System. It is the first in a new category—the Personal Learning Experience.

- The instructor's manual provides course-specific organization tools and classroom strategies, including sample syllabi, designs for mapping the course, assignment flow, ways to utilize the book, suggestions for teaching the course online, and ways to best use electronic resources. The center of the guide is a series of rubrics and exercises that can be adapted to an instructor's work with each chapter.

In sum, *The Purposeful Argument* is a student-centered approach to argument. It is a guide that lets students determine how they can use argument in life and equips them with a concrete, how-to approach. It lets instructors play to their strengths by letting writers work with their strengths—their investment in issues that matter to them in daily and classroom life. From the beginning, the text presents argument in ways that can empower and enable writers to publicly validate what most concerns them.

The Purposeful Argument is designed to complement and not overwhelm. The language of *The Purposeful Argument* is friendly and direct. Short, concise paragraphs are the rule; paragraphs are followed immediately by real-life examples, checklists, charts, rubrics, exercises, and sample student writings.

Competent, informed argument is as important today in American life as it was during other crucial periods in our history. It was and is a way to be heard and, when conditions permit, to be granted a seat at the discussion table. While public memory has shaped the way we view extraordinary moments in our past—indigenous peoples' fate at the hands of colonizers and an aggressive government, debates over sacred and secular ideals, arguments for political independence, the rhetoric of abolition and women's rights movements, the voice of labor, and the Civil Rights Movement—it is crucial to remember that, in addition to the arguments of accomplished writers, activists, and orators associated with these moments, a turbulence of voices was audible. These were the sounds of everyday people moving the culture forward. Without their contributions, the figures we celebrate now would be footnotes only. The voice of the individual *does* matter. If we choose not to speak up, others will make decisions for us.

ACKNOWLEDGMENTS

We are grateful to many individuals for their help creating this edition. Development Editor Stephanie Pelkowski Carpenter has shown Olympian patience with this current edition. She's also offered dozens of insightful suggestions regarding changes and new features. Her grasp of the project's vision from the beginning has guided the revision process. We are grateful in no small way for her professionalism.

Margaret Leslie, Senior Product Manager, deserves special recognition for her continued encouragement and good cheer and her ability to steer the project in very positive directions. Leslie Taggart, Senior Content Developer, Lydia LeStar, Brand Manager, and Aimee Bear, Senior Content Project Manager have our gratitude for their expert guidance throughout the process. Cailin Barrett-Bressack, Editorial Assistant, also provided timely and useful assistance.

The astute reviewers for this second edition helped us to identify ways to reach first-year writing students more effectively. We are grateful for their advice and ideas:

James Allen
College of DuPage

Marsha Anderson
Wharton County Jr. College

Lynnette Beers-McCormick
Santiago Canyon College

Laura Black
Volunteer State Community
  College

Mary Chen
Tacoma Community College

Kathleen Doherty
Middlesex Community College

Cassie Falke
East Texas Baptist University

Karen Golightly
Christian Brothers University

Nate Gordon
Kishwaukee College

Lauren Hahn
DePaul University

Betty Hart
The University of Southern
  Indiana

Erik Juergensmeyer
Fort Lewis College

Lindsay Lewan
Arapahoe Community College

Theodore Matula
University of San Francisco

Mandy McDougal
Volunteer State CC

Gary Montano
Tarrant County College

Elizabeth Oldfield
Southeastern Community
College

M. Whitney Olsen
Arizona State University

Amy Ratto Park
University of Montana

Deborah Ruth
Owensboro Community and
Technical College

Dan Sullivan
Davenport University

Robert Williams
Grossmont College

We also wish to thank members of the Advisory Review Board and the more than 65 reviewers and focus group participants who contributed steadily to the first edition. Their thoughtful feedback allowed us to refine and improve a range of chapter-specific features of this textbook.

Susan Achziger
Community College of Aurora

Kara Alexander
Baylor University

Steve Anderson
Normandale Community College

Sonja Andrus
Collin College

Joseph Antinarella
Tidewater Community College

Brad Beachy
Butler Community College

Evelyn Beck
Piedmont Technical College

Jeff Birkenstein
Saint Martin's University

Carol Bledsoe
Florida Gulf Coast University

David Bockoven
Linn-Benton Community College

Ashley Bourne
J Sargeant Reynolds Community
College

Michael Boyd
Illinois Central College

Marty Brooks
John Tyler Community College

Shanti Bruce
Nova Southeastern University

JoAnn Buck
Guilford Technical Community
College

Carol Burnell
Clackamas Community College

Anthony Cavaluzzi
Adirondack Community College

Mary Chen-Johnson
Tacoma Community College

Scott Clements
Keiser College, Melbourne
Campus

Jennifer Courtney
University of North Carolina at
Charlotte

Susan Davis
Arizona State University

James Decker
Illinois Central College

Tamra DiBenedetto
Riverside Community College

Connie Duke
Keiser University

Keri Dutkiewicz
Davenport University

Sarah M. Eichelman
Walters State Community College

Gareth Euridge
Tallahassee Community College

Jane Focht-Hansen
San Antonio College

MacGregor Frank
Guilford Technical Community
  College

Richard Gilbert
Benedictine University of Illinois

Nate Gordon
Kishwaukee College

Virginia Grant
Gaston College

Valerie Grey
Portland Community College

Annette Hale
Motlow State Community College
  (McMinnville Center)

Pamela Herring
Southwest Texas Junior College

Cheryl Huff
Germanna Community College

Sue Hum
University of Texas at San
  Antonio

Rachel Key
Grayson County College

Jill Lahnstein
Cape Fear Community College

Charlotte Laughlin
McLennan Community College

Gordon Lee
Lee College

Michael Lueker
Our Lady of the Lake University

Anna Maheshwari
Schoolcraft College

Jodie Marion
Mt Hood Community College

Sarah Markgraf
Bergen Community College

Melinda McBee
Grayson County College

Randall McClure
Florida Gulf Coast University

Jeanne McDonald
Waubonsee Community College

Jim McKeown
McLennan Community College

Richard Middleton-Kaplan
Harper College

Gary Montano
Tarrant County College

Jennifer Mooney
Wharton County Junior College

Vicki Moulson
College of the Albemarle

Andrea Muldoon
University of Wisconsin-Stout

Mary Huyck Mulka
Minnesota State University
  Moorhead

Lana Myers
Lone Star College

Marguerite Newcomb
University of Texas–San Antonio

Troy Nordman
Butler Community College

Eden Pearson
Des Moines Area Community
College

Jason Pickavance
Salt Lake Community College

Paula Porter
Keiser University

Jeff Pruchnic
Wayne State University

Esther Quantrill
Blinn College

Maria Ramos
J. Sargeant Reynolds Community
College

Arthur Rankin
Louisiana State University at
Alexandria

Simone Rieck
Lone Star College

Jeffrey Roessner
Mercyhurst College

Ron Ross
Portland Community College

Jennifer Rosti
Roanoke College

Karin Russell
Keiser University

Debbie Ruth
Owensboro Community &
Technical College

Jamie Sadler
Richmond Community College

John Schaffer
Blinn College

Dixie Shaw-Tillmon
The University of Texas at San
Antonio

Suba Subbarao
Oakland Community College

Daniel Sullivan
Davenport University

Susan Swanson
Owensboro Community and
Technical College

Paul Van Heuklom
Lincoln Land Community College

Angie Williams-Chehmani
Davenport University

Will Zhang
Des Moines Area Community
College

Traci Zimmerman
James Madison University

Harry Phillips would like to thank Aron Keesbury, formerly acquisitions editor at Thomson Publishing and now with National Geographic Learning, for his steady encouragement and insightful feedback during the early stages of this project.

Patricia K. Bostian would like to thank her wonderful family for their generous support, particularly her husband Brad for his many wonderful textbook ideas, and her children Wyndham and Rhiannon for allowing her to talk about her ideas with them.

Finally, we want to acknowledge the steady interest our students have shown in argumentative writing over the last 15 years. In truth, it was their authentic interest in the course and their recognition that argument could serve them in daily life that fueled original interest in this project. As teachers, the course inspired us to regularly refine our approaches and, mostly, to listen closely to student writers who sensed, perhaps for the first time, that their private concerns could influence public thinking and decision making. In particular, we are grateful to Linda Gonzalez, Blaine Schmidt, and Ben Szany, among other students, for their willingness to contribute arguments to this textbook.

Harry R. Phillips

Patricia Bostian

PART ONE

How to Approach Argument in Real Life

CHAPTER 1

Argue With a Purpose

This text introduces you to argument and how to use it in response to everyday issues—at school, in the workplace, at home, in your neighborhood, with people who matter to you, in the swirl of community politics, and on a national or global scale. You will be able to use the tools in the following chapters to build practical arguments that make your voice clear and direct on issues in which you have a stake. Skills in argument will help you in your life as a student, a member of the local labor force, a consumer, a concerned citizen, and perhaps a parent and homeowner; in fact, argument can help you address all of the many issues associated with life in these communities.

This chapter is an overview of the nature and purpose of argument. Later chapters address the apparatus of argument—how to craft a claim, build support, work with the opposition, and build other structural elements. Think about argument as a set of tools that lets you negotiate your world with clarity and purpose. The skills you take away from this text, and the work required to complete a class in argument, can transfer to the real world. You may simply be responding to short-term assignments, but in doing so, you will learn to build sound arguments—a skill that will be useful long after your final class project is turned in.

In the sections that follow, you'll get a sense of what argument is and what argument is not, and you'll learn how to:

- Recognize where argument is appropriate in real life.
- Argue about issues that matter to you.
- Establish local context for an issue through the research process.
- Recognize why arguments break down.
- Match argument with purpose.

What Argument Is and What Argument Is Not

You are arguing when you claim a point of view on an issue, defend your claim with different kinds of support, and respond fairly to those with differing points of view. Argument is useful when you want to persuade others (decision-makers, fellow classmates, coworkers, a community agency or organization, a special interest group, elected representatives, business leaders, or an individual) to take seriously your point of view; when you want to find out more about something that matters to you; and when you want to establish areas of common interest among different positions. With nearly all arguments, it is essential to establish a clear context for your issue and to have a target audience.

Argument is not about putting yourself in uncomfortable, win–lose, either–or situations. It is not about fighting or trying to shame someone who holds a different point of view. Some people associate argument with anger, raised voices, and emotional outbursts. But when these people behave in competitive, angry, and overly emotional ways, communication is often sealed off and the people involved become alienated from one another. This is not the aim of argument. Argument creates a space where we can listen to each other.

The following essay by Thomas Frank is excerpted from "The Price of Admission." The full essay appears in the June 2012 issue of *Harper's*, a magazine that began publication in 1850 and today treats a wide range of issues in literature, politics, culture, finance, and the arts. In the essay, Frank includes a claim, various levels of support, and efforts to build his credibility as one taking a position on the issue of college tuition. Missing from the excerpt, but present in the longer essay, are attention to the opposition, reasons that support the claim, and a warrant, that is, attention to the values that motivate the writer to argue on this issue. The essay is accompanied by an editorial cartoon by R.J. Matson (see Figure 1.1).

Excerpt from "The Price of Admission"

by Thomas Frank

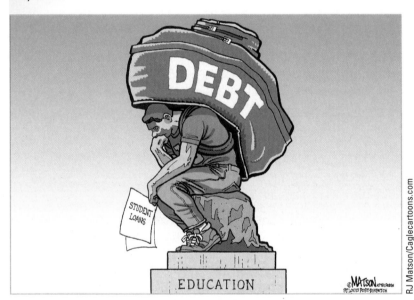

Figure 1.1 Editorial cartoon by R.J. Matson

Massive indebtedness changes a person, maybe even more than a college education does, and it's reasonable to suspect that the politicos who have allowed the tuition disaster to take its course know this. To saddle young people with enormous, inescapable debt — total student debt is now more than one trillion dollars — is ultimately to transform them into profit-maximizing machines. I mean, working as a schoolteacher or an editorial assistant at a publishing house isn't going to help you chip away at that forty grand you owe. You can't get out of it by bankruptcy, either. And our political leaders, lost in a fantasy of punitive individualism, certainly won't propose the bailout measures they could take to rescue the young from the crushing burden.

What will happen to the young debtors instead is that they will become *Homo economicus*, whether or not they studied that noble creature. David Graeber, the anthropologist who wrote the soon-to-be-classic *Debt: The First 5,000 Years*, likens the process to a horror movie, in which the zombies or the vampires attack the humans as a kind of recruitment policy. "They turn you into one of them," as Graeber told me.

Actually, they do worse than that. Graeber relates the story of a woman he met who got a Ph.D. from Columbia University, but whose $80,000 debt load put an academic career off-limits, since adjuncts earn close to nothing. Instead, the woman wound up working as an escort for Wall Street types. "Here's someone who ought to be a professor," Graeber explains, "doing sexual services for the guys who lent her the money."

The story hit home for me, because I, too, wanted to be a professor once. I remember the waves of enlightenment that washed over me in my first few years in college, the ecstasy of finally beginning to understand what moved human affairs this way or that, the exciting sense of a generation arriving at a shared sensibility. Oh, I might have gone on doing that kind of work forever, whether or not it made me rich, if journalism had not intervened.

It's hard to find that kind of ecstasy among the current crop of college graduates. The sensibility shared by their generation seems to revolve around student debt, which has been clamped onto them like some sort of interest-bearing iron maiden. They've been screwed — that's what their moment of enlightenment has taught them.

As for my own cohort, or at least the members of it who struggled through and made it to one of the coveted positions in the knowledge factory, the new generational feeling seems to be one of disgust. Our enthusiasm for learning, which we trumpeted to the world, merely led the nation's children into debt bondage. Consider the remarks of Nicholas Mirzoeff, a professor of media at New York University, who sums up the diminishing returns of the profession on his blog: "I used to say that in academia one at least did very little harm. Now I feel like a pimp for loan sharks."

Analyze this Reading

1. What is the writer's claim, the position the writer takes in response to the issue of student debt?
2. Identify examples the writer uses to support his claim.
3. How does the writer establish his credibility; that is, how does he build trust with readers regarding his competence to take a stand on this issue?

Respond to this Reading

1. The writer contends that political leaders won't make the effort to bail out today's college students from debt. Do you favor a legislative bailout? Explain, and if you don't favor such a bailout, what claim would you make to address the student debt problem?

2. What is your relationship to education and debt? What examples would you use to demonstrate this relationship?

3. If you were to argue on this issue, at what target audience would you aim? Would your audience be officials at your college, your state legislators, your peers, or the members of your community? Explain.

Recognize Where Argument Is Appropriate in Real Life

You'll get to know this guide as a student in a class, one class among many that you need to complete as you move toward your degree, but there is another, equally important way to think about your work with argument—the set of skills you'll acquire and take with you when class is over. Make these skills serve what matters to you, in and beyond the classroom. Whether it's a small group of coworkers, the author of a scholarly article, your local parent–teacher organization, the editor of an online magazine, a car mechanic, or the billing agency for your cell phone or broadband service, you'll have a better chance of being taken seriously when you support your point of view with credible information delivered through a variety of logical, ethical, and emotional appeals.

Vital issues in our lives occur both in the academic world and in the swirl of everyday life. When you have a clear point of view (a claim) about the quality of cafeteria food at your child's school and then justify your claim with effective support, thereby establishing your credibility as a concerned parent, your audience will listen. Similarly, if a teacher in one of your classes asks you to claim a position on the status of immigration reform in your state and you respond by drafting a claim based on thorough research, your argument is likely to fare well when it is evaluated. This is especially true when you come across as well informed and sensitive to those who might differ from you. And if conditions at work start to resemble positions that were recently outsourced, you're more likely to get the attention of your boss or coworkers when you present a balanced, fair-minded argument that takes into account those who view the issue differently.

In your life as a student, are there issues that involve tuition, lodging, the accessibility of your teachers, course policies, conflicts with your job, and loan opportunities? Are there also intellectual issues in your life as a student that you are asked to respond to, such as genetically engineered food, climate change, and representative government as practiced in our country? And outside the classroom, if your street lacks adequate storm-water facilities, if earlier public-school start times are proposed by the school board and you know that this will affect your family's schedule, or if a family member has a contrary idea about what makes a sensible budget, a well-crafted argument allows you to move away from emotional arguments (a trap for many) and into the realm of reason, common sense, and community. An emotional argument, on the other hand, lacks the support of a rational approach to an issue and puts in jeopardy your credibility with your target audience. The exact change you want is never a guaranteed outcome of a good argument, but at the very least you will have made your voice audible before an audience that matters to you.

From another perspective, you affect and diversify the particular community you address with an argument. A well-organized argument gets you a seat at the discussion table, whether in the classroom or before your city council. This means that your position on an issue can matter in the local decision-making process (see Figure 1.2). If we say nothing, others will speak for us or make assumptions about us that may conflict with who we are and what we value.

Argue About Issues That Matter to You

Argue about what matters to you as a student and in everyday life. Some people associate argument with dry, abstract issues that may or may not directly affect their lives, but this is an attitude to stay away from. Good writing, and similarly, good argument, spring from the same place—from the effort of everyday people struggling to define and solve problems. A good argument will touch the reader in many ways: logically, because you provide real-life support for your point of view; emotionally, because you touch on something that the reader cares about; and ethically, because you establish your credibility as an informed community member whom your audience can trust.

One way to think about argument is as a practical tool for the regular challenges we face. For example, would it be helpful to know how to present your

Auremar/Shutterstock.com

Figure 1.2 Speaking up in response to issues that matter to us is the heart of argument. In this photo, the figure speaking is responding to a workplace issue and delivering her ideas to coworkers.

point of view to city and county politicians when repairs on your street are neglected while streets in other areas are taken care of much sooner? Might it be helpful to compose an argument in the form of a letter to a son, daughter, parent, or in-law regarding an important family matter? Do you have an idea about how certain parts of your job can be improved, and would a logical, well-researched proposal directed to a supervisor be a reasonable first step? Do parking problems and a smoking ban at school disturb you, and do you want to find out more about these issues and formulate a claim that is reinforced by careful research? If you answer "yes" to these or similar everyday issues, then this guide can be useful as a way to represent yourself with integrity.

Let's look, for example, at the issue that begins this chapter and one that nearly all college students contend with these days—increasing tuition rates. Some of us may be compelled to argue on this issue because we're forced to work more hours during the week to pay for this semester's tuition, forced to take out loans that mean years of debt after college, and disturbed that our college seems to endorse lending practices that unfairly burden students heading into the world after graduation. A carefully arranged argument gives us the chance to claim a strong position on tuition rates, conduct research on the nature and history of the problem, listen to other points of view, and then propose a way to address the problem reasonably. After choosing to argue on this issue, a reasonable first step would be to establish context and determine your target audience, tasks discussed in the next section.

Another way to think about argument is as a practical tool for the intellectual and academic work you are asked to complete as a student. The steps in developing a good argument are the same, whether you are writing for a class assignment or about an issue in daily life. In both contexts you will need to evolve a precise point of view and then defend it. Successful arguments about the origins of our national debt, same-sex marriage, interpreting constitutional amendments, health-care policy, and the federal government's relationship with the banking industry are built on the same foundations as arguments responding to the everyday issues of life.

In fact, one measure of good arguments on issues like these is their ability to connect local and global contexts. So much of what comes to us through mainstream news—issues in the fields of medicine, technology, health care, and geopolitics, for example—has its origins beyond our immediate lives and communities. You can of course apply the tools of argument to these issues, and with good success, but argument on these issues can and should be connected to local contexts, too. The list below is a small sampling of large issues that have local impact.

Standardized testing	Bullying in schools and in the workplace
Gun laws	
Video cameras and public schools	Choice and public schools
Promotion practices in the nursing profession	Benefits for same-sex partners
	Taser guns in public schools

Immigration reform and local business

Big box construction and local business

Cell phone use while driving

Living wage proposals

High school dropout rates

Probation and oversight

Local job outsourcing

Local transit

The elderly and nursing home care

Crowded classrooms

Eminent domain and home owners

Sex offenders in the community

Fossil fuels

Climate change

Local road repairs

Photo-ID voting requirements

Campaign Finance Reform

Locally grown food

Returning veterans and health care

Energy rate hikes

Health care and non-native speakers

Teen crime and sentencing

Medicare and Social Security

Payday lending

In today's world, we all face multiple demands as we move through our day. Combine this busyness with the sheer scale of many of the issues we face—the economic recession, global warming, health care, security, terror, and military intervention—and it can be tough to believe that articulating our point of view on an issue is worth the effort or makes any difference. But it *can* make a difference, and building a good argument is a way to exercise some control over your life and establish your influence in the community. When your well-planned argument articulates your view on an issue in a thorough and compelling manner, you can generate confidence in yourself and respect from your audience. A sound argument does not, of course, guarantee that your issue will be resolved or that substantial change will result, but you can define for yourself exactly where you stand. For a democracy to remain healthy, it must function in large part by individuals responding to the forces that global environments put in our way.

Well-crafted argument is a way to represent yourself publicly with dignity and in an informed, fair, and open-minded way. Learn these skills now, and you'll have them forever.

your turn 1a ▶ **GET STARTED Acknowledge Issues That Matter to You**

Make a list of issues that concern you today. Include issues in your personal life, your workplace, your school, your church, a group you belong to, your neighborhood, and your town or city. As you make your list, consider also national and global issues that affect your life, such as conflicts in other countries, environmental concerns, or fuel costs. As a way to narrow your focus to issues most important to you, respond to the following questions.

1. Identify a major issue in your life or a position a teacher asks you to take in response to an academic issue.
2. When did this issue begin, and why does it continue to be a problem?
3. Identify a second issue that concerns you. If in question 1 you identified an academic issue, identify a more personal issue here.
4. When did this issue begin, and why does it continue to be a problem?

Establish Local Context via the Research Process

The important work of establishing local context for an issue involves aiming your argument at an appropriate audience, conducting research so as to generate a history for your issue, and when possible, connecting your local issue to broader, even global, conditions. These essential features of building local context are described in the following section.

Determine Your Audience

Recognize a practical audience for your argument; that is, direct your argument to those you most want to inform and persuade. Once you identify your audience, make a close study of them. An audience can be as small as one person, especially appropriate for an argument in a letter format, or your audience can be as large as your community or a block of undecided voters in a statewide election. Other audiences can include the following:

- Your class or certain members of a class
- Members of your church or parents in your neighborhood or school district
- The local school board, city council, county commission, or state legislators
- Family members, friends, or a partner
- A teacher or school administrator
- A supervisor at work or coworkers
- Readers of a zine, blog, listserv, special interest newsletter, or your local or school newspaper

Your audience may or may not agree with your point of view. In addition, an audience may not be as fully aware of the issue as you are, and in these cases you'll need to inform readers in order to get your claim across. Your job is to persuade an audience to think seriously about your point of view, and this means that you must know what your readers value. It's vital that you listen closely and get a sense of *why* they feel the way they do. What is it about their histories and values that make them see the issue differently from you? While you may deviate from your audience on a given issue, your argument will be much stronger and more concrete if you take the time to listen charitably—that is, without judgment and with an open mind—as you attempt to understand their viewpoints.

With regard to the tuition issue, one practical approach might be to target your city or town council and ask members to approve a resolution that you and other students have drawn up calling for a moratorium on tuition hikes.

Your argument will become more persuasive as you find overlapping points of view with your audience. Determine what you have in common with your audience—what values, beliefs, expectations, and fears you share. Move away from oppositional thinking, the "I'm right/you're wrong" approach. In the real world, when you work to identify common ground, you're more likely to get others to listen to you and move toward consensus.

your turn 1b ▶ **GET STARTED Identify a Target Audience**

Begin thinking about a practical audience for an argument by responding to the following questions.

1. Who might be interested in hearing what you have to say about the issues in your life today? Why?
2. Is there a specific person or group who could benefit from your perspective, affect an issue, or resolve it or modify it in some way? Explain.
3. How will you learn more about this target audience?
4. What tempting assumptions about this audience may prove inaccurate?

Establish Local Context for Your Issue

No man is an island! When English poet John Donne delivered this idea in a 1624 meditation, he claimed that, while isolation may be a part of living, we are all connected to the continent, to a community. We do not live separately from our communities, although sometimes it may feel as if we're living on their margins. The point is that when you decide to claim a position on an issue that matters to you, gather plenty of information so that you're fully aware of the **context**, the past and present, of your issue. An issue materializes in the swirl of local events and occurs because folks disagree—about its cause, what should be done about it, the terms that define it, whether or not it actually exists, and/or how it should be evaluated. So if you feel hemmed in by an issue, find out through research what others think and how they're responding.

You have many ways to find out where your issue originates. For an issue occurring at work, look into what created it. You may already know the answer, but asking fellow workers their understanding of the issue can fill in gaps. You may also want to gather information about your employer's past to get a sense of how the issue evolved. If you work in a large industry, you can read up on the deeper roots of this issue and how it is handled elsewhere in the state, country, or world. If your English teacher requires that you develop an argument in response to a character's behavior in a short story or poem, or if your history teacher asks you to evaluate the term *American exceptionalism*, plan to gather online and print sources as a way to inform yourself of the context in which your issue occurs and what scholars have to say about it.

When you argue in response to an issue on local or neighborhood politics, access the archives of your local newspaper and study the history of your issue. Newspapers often are available for free via online databases. For issues involving a family member and a health problem, for example, there are a number of databases available that house articles and essays on healthcare issues, and your school may subscribe to these databases. Building local context can also involve interviews with knowledgeable professionals or those who have been invested in the issue over time. You can also design and administer a survey that will add to your information base.

Returning to the tuition issue, this problem has a significant and well-documented local and national history. Scores of students, faculty, and social justice activists have responded to regular tuition hikes since they began. From the perspective of your school's administration, funding priorities may prevent immediate action, but during an interview you may learn a great deal from a school official who defends the hikes but is sympathetic with your desire to succeed with your education. And often you can count on there being a knowledgeable reporter in local media who can provide a larger frame for this issue as well as links to factual information. These are resources that can help you build local context for this issue.

Creating this kind of context does two important things for your final argument: It lets you argue with a strong sense of local history, and it sends a direct message to your readers that you've done your homework, that you've thought deeply about your issue, and most importantly, that you should be taken seriously.

Facundo Arrizabalaga/EPA/Newscom

Figure 1.3 Protestors respond to tuition hikes and other issues important to their local context.

internet activity 1a Exploring

Conduct an informal Internet search to look for general background information on an issue, perhaps one that you identified in the Your Turn 1a activity. Begin by accessing the online archives of your local newspaper; continue by using the academic databases your school provides and other online sites that your teacher recommends. Answer the following questions:

1. Has your search produced answers to some of your questions? Explain.
2. What kind of additional information do you want to gather?
3. As you begin to gather information, is your perspective changing; that is, does learning more about your issue let you see the issue in different and perhaps broader terms? Explain.

Connect Local and Global Contexts

When you write specifically about a local issue, like tuition hikes, plan to connect the issue with a context beyond your community. This makes a positive impression on readers because it shows that you're able to frame your issue in broad terms. It reveals that through your research you recognize that your issue is influenced by trends in regional, national, or global cultures. This will also allow your audience to think more critically about the issue, and it will likely make your argument more persuasive.

For example, escalating tuition rates in this country, Canada, and England, among other countries, reflect economic realities and corporate decision-making outside our communities (see Figure 1.4). When you argue about having to pay more for your education, you must bring to your argument a broad context for tuition hikes so as to orient readers to the origins of this issue. Similarly, when the outsourcing of certain jobs—like those in manufacturing, web design, accounting, and customer support—affects the local economy, trace this outsourcing to the global economic climate in order to form a larger picture for your

Figure 1.4 Editorial cartoon by Jeff Parker

Figure 1.5 Connecting a local issue to a broader context can be powerful.

audience. In addition, issues associated with food in local markets—the conditions in which it's produced and harvested, transportation, health concerns, pricing, and availability of certain items—typically lead to issues in another part of the country or world. Standardized testing, according to some researchers, can be traced to the presence of a business model in many of our public schools; learning about this aspect of the issue—and about the values and motives for this kind of testing—can fill in important background for this arguable issue. If you are motivated to write on local environmental matters like air and water quality, you'll want to read up on the influence of local development and regional energy production to get a sense of what causes these problems.

Whether the local issue that concerns you is in the area of health care, education, politics, work, family, or a retail industry, there likely are larger, often global, forces shaping the issue. When it's a trend you can trace beyond our national borders, we might use the term **glocal** to connect local and global contexts. When you look at what sustains us—air, water, food, transportation, education, and electronic communication—it won't be difficult to connect local issues with broader contexts. And when you look at what we desire materially—dwellings, cars, fashion, and so on—and begin examining American consumer culture, you should be able to make some revealing connections that will enlighten readers and move your argument along.

The key to connecting local and global contexts is found both in your own good sense of how things work and in your ability to research thoroughly in order to familiarize yourself with the history surrounding an issue. Your research process is vital to the success of your argument.

your turn 1c GET STARTED Connect the Local and Global

Answer the following questions to get a sense of how local issues can have global effects.

1. Identify a single *glocal* issue that concerns you, and describe its local effects.
2. How do these effects have an impact on your life and the lives of others?
3. In general terms, explain how economic and political ripples from a global or national issue may spread and affect the lives of others across your region, state, and community.

Recognize Why Arguments Break Down

Arguments can succeed when a writer has something to say, knows to whom it should be said, and knows how to present supporting information in persuasive ways. But arguments can also fail, especially when the essential steps needed to build good arguments are not given thorough treatment. Following are some of the major reasons why arguments don't succeed.

Arguments Break Down When They Do Not Persuade an Audience

Sometimes writers summarize and explain rather than argue. This can occur when a discernable issue is not separated from the larger topic. For example, by deciding you want to write on problems in your workplace, you've identified a good *topic* but not an arguable *issue*. There are numerous issues under this big topic—hiring practices, the politics of promotion, compensation, environmental impact, benefits, working within a hierarchy, discrimination, communication, and so forth—and it is vital that you choose a single issue on which to argue. When you fail to narrow and instead stay with the big topic, your writing lapses into summary and general statements, and this is death to persuasive writing. By focusing on the big topic, problems in your workplace, you'd be treating important issues only superficially. Each of these sub-issues is worthy of a full argument. Narrow your topic to a single issue that affects you, and you will be able to dig deeply and avoid spreading out generally.

Arguments Break Down When There Is a Lack of Balance in the Support

By loading body paragraphs with facts and logical appeals only, your argument will lack a cooperative, humanizing feel. The idea is to place ethical appeals (in which you establish your credibility through personal experience and the testimony of experts) and emotional appeals (in which you touch readers with emotionally charged examples) in balance with logical support. When you tilt too much in the direction on one kind of appeal, readers lose interest. After all, we're complex beings, and we want to be convinced in a variety of ways. Experts tell us that logical appeals should dominate in most arguments, comprising some 60–70 percent of an argument's support. When you focus your arguments in this way, you earn the opportunity to address your readers ethically and emotionally. They must know that you've done your research and that you write from experience; then, you can broaden your argument with different types of appeals.

Arguments Break Down When the Audience Is Poorly Defined

Nearly 2,500 years ago, Aristotle explained that a target audience is essential to competent argument. Early in the writing process, you should decide precisely whom you want to persuade. This will allow you to focus closely on

 tip 1a

Embrace the Glocal!
Remember that you are a local resident *and* a global citizen. Things are so interconnected today that it's hard to define ourselves and the conditions we live in without recognizing forces—economic, political, and environmental—that originate beyond our communities.

an audience whose values you understand. Knowing these values lets you build a bridge to the audience, which is necessary if you are to persuade them. This is what warrant and backing are about. You can design a good argument when you know what an audience expects, what touches it, and what kinds of appeals are likely to be effective. For example, if you want to argue for a moratorium on tuition hikes in your school or in all public colleges in your state, consider your target audience. To rally immediate support, your audience might be students, but to work toward real change, your target audience might be state lawmakers who have the decision-making capacity to enact legislation.

Arguments Break Down When They Contain Fallacies

Fallacies, often found in an argument's claims and reasons, weaken an argument because there are mistakes in logic and can involve unfair treatment of others. Fallacies are common in the many advertisements we take in every day. For example, ads for a certain brand of car, clothing, food, or medication, may promise that if we purchase the product, prestige, attractiveness, taste satisfaction, and health will be ours. These ads contain fallacies because the promise cannot be kept. In an argument, fallacies are statements that mislead due to poor or deceptive reasoning. For example, if you claim that third parties are the only way to restore true democracy to our political system, you have committed a fallacy based on a hasty generalization. Some readers of your argument may agree that third parties are needed to restore democracy, but some may claim that campaign finance reform, term limits, and citizen activism are also needed. The hasty generalization backs you into a corner.

Arguments Break Down When They Do Not Fairly Represent Opposing Views

The rebuttals and differing views you bring to your argument should not be brief and superficial: They should attend to what the opposition claims, how it supports a position, and what it values. This easily can require several full paragraphs in an arguments. When you respond to a rebuttal after having treated the other side fairly, you are in a position to thoroughly counter or build on another view. When full treatment of another view is neglected, however, writers tend to profile and stereotype, and this can offend perceptive members of an audience.

Match Argument with Purpose

After you decide what you want to accomplish with an argument, you can choose the kind of argument that fits your purpose. This guide helps you choose from four kinds of argument, all of which are treated in detail in Chapter 8, "Consider Toulmin-Based Argument" and Chapter 9, "Consider Middle Ground and Rogerian Argument, and Argument based on Microhistory."

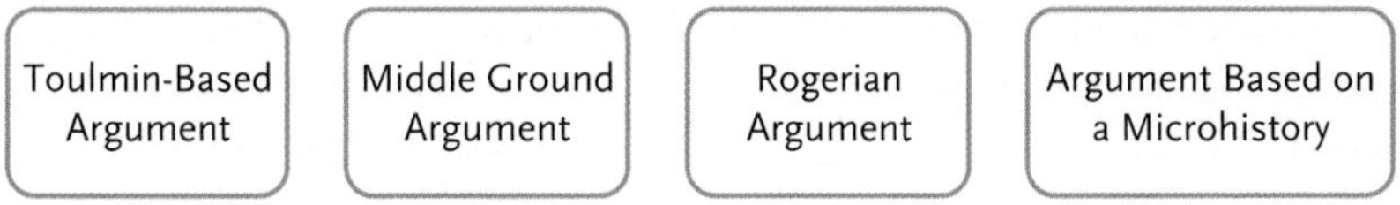

Toulmin-Based Argument	Middle Ground Argument	Rogerian Argument	Argument Based on a Microhistory

Figure 1.6 Four Kinds of Arguments

For example, an issue that received a lot of attention in North Carolina a few years ago concerned the attorney general's recommendation that children of illegal immigrants be barred from pursuing degrees in the state's community colleges, a recommendation that the president of the community college system chose to follow. The issue generated much discussion across the state based on the news media's regular attention to it. A writer's decision to argue in response to this issue would require choosing the kind of argument practical to the arguer's goals with a specific target audience.

The following paragraphs describe how different kinds of arguments might be applied to the issue of barring children of illegal immigrants from attending the state's community colleges. These paragraphs provide an overview of four kinds of arguments (see Figure 1.6). Think about how these approaches to argument can fit with issues you plan to address in argument.

Toulmin-Based Argument

Using a Toulmin-based approach, a writer would focus closely on his audience—in this case, the State Board of Community Colleges—and what it values. He knows that individuals on this board are committed to workforce training, economic development, and service to local communities. With this in mind, the writer can develop convincing support by using many examples of children of illegal immigrants succeeding in community colleges and going on to hold good jobs and contribute to their communities. Examples can include statistics, scholars analyzing the community college as a resource for the children of illegal immigrants, and firsthand student accounts. This varied support will honor values held by the board. Additionally, the writer can elaborate on why training, business, and service are important to the state's quality of life. And because the board is charged with carrying out the policies of the state's community colleges, the writer could craft a problem-based claim and ask that the board permit children of illegal immigrants to pursue degrees. Rebuttals brought to the argument would focus on the opposition's concerns with legality and citizenship. Central statements in the argument, such as the claim and reasons, would include qualifiers that keep writers away from making absolute, and unrealistic, points.

Middle Ground Argument

A middle ground argument on this issue would view the "for" and "against" positions as extreme and argue instead for a practical position in the middle.

Each extreme position would be analyzed in terms of why it fails to offer a practical perspective. Based on the reasons listed previously, those who favor barring children of illegal immigrants from seeking degrees could be analyzed as extreme because this position fails to note the many contributions immigrants make to their communities, the taxes they pay, the contributions they make to the workforce, and the long delays they endure with regard to immigrant legislation. Those on the other side of this issue could be considered impractical because they lump all immigrants together and thus do not take into account the very different experiences of the various immigrant groups living in the United States. For example, the immigrant group getting the most attention today is from Mexico, and its experience in American culture is in some ways quite different from that of groups from various Asian, Caribbean, and Latin American countries. Over-generalizing about diverse groups plays to a limited understanding of the varying immigrant experiences in the United States, and arguments built on such over-generalization can be considered impractical for this reason.

Several middle-ground positions are possible with this issue, and each has been argued over the course of the debate. One such position argues that the "for" and "against" reasoning described previously ignores the reason that many immigrants move to the United States—jobs—and that until local businesses enter the debate (because of their practice of hiring illegal workers), nothing will change. Another position argues that this issue should be moved into the courts and that in the meantime community colleges should remain open-door institutions, admitting all who apply regardless of citizenship status. While those holding these positions may consider them moderate and middle ground, each position must be proven to be a practical and logical choice between two extreme positions.

Rogerian Argument

In a Rogerian argument, the writer would aim to create a space for positive back-and-forth discussion between his view and one or more different views. To do this, the writer would need to present other views with respect and accuracy, emphasizing the values embedded in these views. Having established this respectful tone, the writer is now in a position to introduce his view by looking for areas where values on all sides overlap. This is the common ground that makes Rogerian argument a practical choice when parties are far apart on an issue.

If the writer opposes barring immigrant students from attending community college, he would pay close attention to the opposition and focus on its values and reasons for supporting the regulation. The writer notices strong emphasis on values of citizenship, employment, education, and rights. While the writer may differ in how these values can be extended to the children of illegal immigrants, he shares with the opposition a deep commitment to these values and their importance in community life. This is the common ground that the writer would hope to create. On the surface, the views are far apart, but underneath the sides share strongly held values. There is of course no guarantee that the writer of this argument and his opposition will now or in the future see eye to eye on this controversial issue, but the writer has made the effort to listen to and honor the opposition. Because an audience may acknowledge his objectivity and sense of fair play, he is in a position to earn some measure of credibility, a necessary condition to the success of any argument that seeks to create common ground.

Argument Based on a Microhistory

An argument based on a microhistory can be a practical approach to this issue because an arguer could provide specific history relevant to the recommendation to bar children of illegal immigrants from community colleges and then offer a claim. This kind of argument could be used to look closely at one feature of this issue—for example, the reaction of a student, parent, teacher, or concerned citizen. Studying the response of a prospective community-college student affected by the recommendation could bring in from the margins of this issue a voice that media and the general public do not hear, an aim of the microhistory. Primary materials needed to prepare such a microhistory could include interviews with the prospective student or something the student has written. The center of the microhistory would be the ways in which the student's life will be affected by having the opportunity to attend college withdrawn and how this student's experience reveals something about our culture and what it values. Additionally, the arguer will need to provide context for the student's experience, and this must include an overview of this issue in the state, region, and country. Having provided extensive information about the student and the history of the issue, the arguer is then in a position to offer a claim that an audience may view as credible based on the arguer's extensive research. Arguments based on microhistory focus an argument in the commonplace and everyday, perspectives that many mainstream and conventional approaches to history often neglect.

Reflect and Apply

Directions: The following questions ask you to step back and reflect on the concepts delivered in this chapter. You should think about the questions that conclude each chapter and apply them to your own writing. We encourage you to think about how the various pieces of an argument fit together and why they're all necessary.

1. In your own words describe what an effective argument does. Include in your description how you think about argument now contrasted with how you thought about argument before reading this chapter.

2. Early sections of this chapter encourage you to use skills associated with argument both inside and outside the classroom. Explain how these skills would be of value in everyday life.

3. Clarify why a target audience is essential to a good argument. Include in your response what an argument would look like with a vague or unspecified audience.

4. Define the term *context*. Describe its place in an argument in terms of your credibility as arguer.

5. Identify the reasons why arguments break down. Which of these reasons will you need to pay close attention to so that your arguments don't break down?

CHAPTER 2

Explore an Issue
That Matters to You

Seven weeks into the semester, you're between worried and anxious about next week's midterm exam in your online "Early American Literature" class. At a coffee shop on campus, you run into a pal you met in a class last year, and the two of you begin talking. A minute into your conversation, you confess your anxiety about the exam and suddenly realize that you're both in the same class and that your friend is also worried about the exam. You share the concern that the instructor does not participate regularly on the discussion board, takes too long to answer email messages, and sometimes does not respond to messages at all. He has made it clear from the beginning that he'll respond to messages "time permitting." The first two units in the course include much tough reading, and there have been times when you wanted honest and prompt feedback, especially as to your comprehension of the challenging readings. The instructor has informed the class that the exam will include a section on analyzing passages, and this makes you even more anxious. The two of you gather yourselves and decide to meet for a study session over the weekend.

All Illustrations by iStockphoto.com/A-digit

TOPIC: Life in the Online Classroom

ISSUE: Teacher–Student Interaction

AUDIENCE: Director of Distance Learning

CLAIM: Clear standards for teachers' commitment to interacting regularly with students should be stated in the introductions to online English courses.

An argument is a practical response to a pressing question, problem, or concern that generates differing points of view, such as the issue described above. An argument works best when you are invested in an issue, like online instructor response time, and when you feel that what you want to achieve is being hampered. For example, if you feel you're being paid unfairly at work in comparison with other workers of similar experience and seniority, you have an arguable issue. Or, if you feel strongly about stem cell research, about credit card marketing campaigns targeted at you and other college students, about accusations of racial profiling by local law enforcement, about the quality of food at your child's school, or about red light cameras at traffic intersections in your community, you can construct an effective argument that fully represents your point of view, your claim, on such an issue. But first you must assess current issues in your life and determine those that genuinely matter to you. This is the vital first step in the argument process. This chapter guides you through the process of choosing issues for argument.

In Chapter 2 you will develop a research plan to:

- Recognize yourself as a member of many communities.
- Identify topics associated with each community.
- Respond to issues within topics that you feel strongly about and may want to argue on.
- Aim your argument at a specific audience.
- Deliver your argument at a time when it is most likely to be taken seriously.
- Troubleshoot your issue by responding to practical prompts as a way to get started with an argument.

Determine What Matters to You and Why

All of us belong to many different communities—school, workplace, family neighborhood, social–cultural, consumer, and concerned citizen—and our individual worlds are defined, at least in part, by the issues we encounter in each of our communities. Some of these issues are the results of external forces acting on our lives (a directive from a supervisor at work, a public ordinance that permits one kind of gathering but not another, an assignment from a teacher) while other kinds of issues are of our own choosing (who we vote for in an election, our decision to become active in response to a community or national issue, decisions we make about parenting). And the issues you choose to write about, whether you argue for something to change or simply want your audience to reflect on your point of view, should originate with what is most important to you. Your arguments become compelling to readers when you write in an informed way about something that deeply concerns you. So, while you will learn how to build arguments in structured, logical ways, *what* you argue on should begin with issues that stir your emotions and that motivate you to speak out, as in the case of the mother speaking in Figure 2.1. Consider the communities you belong to and some, but not all, of the topics that can affect each community.

A **community** is a group of individuals that share common experiences, interests, needs, and expectations. Students in your classes, the general college community, people you work with, your neighbors, and citizens with a stake in local politics are examples of communities. Review the following communities and some of the issues associated with each community.

School/Academic

As a member of your academic community, what issues affect your goals of acquiring knowledge, learning new skills, and earning a degree so that you can move on to the next phase of your life? Consider below some of the topics that affect your life as a student.

AP Photo/The Laramie Boomerang, Barbara J. Perenic

Figure 2.1 Compelling arguments become possible when individuals argue about what matters most to them. In this photo, a mother speaks to a group of University of Wyoming students about her son, and seven other students, who were killed in a car crash caused by a drunk driver, the man to her right in the yellow shirt.

Costs

Degree requirements

Life in the real-time classroom

Teacher attitudes

Time management

Free speech

Diversity and tolerance

Student services

Curriculum design

Life in the online classroom

Issues in your field of study

Personal responsibility

Academic integrity

Privacy and surveillance

Campus safety

Transportation

Tuition

Blogging

Fairness

Plagiarism

Grade inflation

Extra credit

Workplace

At many points during our working lives, we face conditions that affect our motivation, engagement, and sense of fair play. Other times the workplace offers opportunities that are welcome challenges. What are your conditions at work? By what are you challenged? Consider the following list of topics as a way to identify issues that most matter to you.

Job expectations

Balancing work and life

Bureaucracy and red tape

Pay scale

Benefits

Commuting and telecommuting

Cubicle culture

Organizing and negotiation

Dispute resolution

Training

Bullying and harassment

Corporate social responsibility

Daily conditions

Stress

Downsizing and layoffs

Unions

Privacy and surveillance

Advancement

Discrimination

Leadership

Favoritism

Job security

Rankism

Team building

Office politics

Family/Household

This community refers both to a traditional family unit—parents (or parent) and children—and to any group of individuals sharing a home and its responsibilities. Issues can spring from relationships within and across generations, from economic and purchasing concerns, and from household maintenance arrangements, among many others.

Toy safety

Financial planning

Landscaping and grounds maintenance

Children and online safety

Home buying and mortgages

Home owners associations

Food safety

Diet/food consumption

Health care planning

Home improvement

Furniture and appliances

Product safety

Neighbors

Parenting

Same-sex marriage

Pet care

Senior care

Wills and trusts

Neighborhood

Neighborhoods are distinct geographical areas. Some neighborhoods comprise a three- or four-block square within a city or urban area. Other neighborhoods comprise only a single block or even a single complex of dwellings. People living in a neighborhood frequently are affected by residential and commercial development, by local government decisions, and by activities such as local parades or events, school closings, or rezoning.

Street improvement	Storm drains	Property alterations
Rezoning ordinances	Sidewalks	and additions
Graffiti	Economic development	Safety
Erosion	and housing	Gangs
Yard maintenance	Water and sewage	Noise
Neighbors with special	Waste collection	Traffic
needs	Parking	Crime
The digital divide		

Social/Cultural

Some communities link us to people we'll never meet, yet we share with them features that are central to our self-concept. Based on your religious, sexual, and political preferences, are there issues before you? And based on the racial or ethnic group you identify with, the virtual environments you spend time in, or the friendships and loyalties you keep, are there concerns that might motivate you to argue?

Profiling and	Relationships	Friendship
stereotyping	Local government and	Loyalty
Sex and sexuality	the individual	Gender
Public space	Racial and ethnic	Education
Political preference	identity	Economics
Virtual environments	Training and	Religion
Class status	opportunity	

Consumer

We live in a consumer-oriented society, one in which advertisements from competing companies and producers rain down on us every day. We regularly make decisions about what we eat and wear, how we transport ourselves, how we stay warm, what we purchase for our children, and how we entertain ourselves. Are there issues important to you as a consumer that fall under these and other topics?

Prescription drugs	Electronics and	Utilities/energy
Local lending	communication	Food consumption
practices	Consumer fraud	Insurance
Identity theft	Shopping at home	Investing
Telemarketing	Landlord/tenant	Credit
Home repairs	relations	Advertising
Transportation	Demographic profiling	

Concerned Citizen

While much of our focus concerns the local and the personal, many of us—as concerned citizens living in a democratic culture—naturally pay attention to politics, economic trends, and social concerns that extend beyond our communities; in other words, we pay attention to what we can term the *glocal* environment. Arguments deriving from some of the topics below, and many more, are vital to our commitment to democratic life, because democracy means speaking up about what matters to us; if we don't speak up about our issues, we may be left out of the conversation completely. What issues come to mind when you investigate some of the broad topics below?

Environment	Electronic voting	Animal research
Agricultural practices	Private corporations	Alternative energy
National security and	and the public	Individual rights and
surveillance	interest	counterterrorism
Substances and	Public schools	Scarcity and abundance
regulation	Immigration reform	Globalization
Prisons	Science/technology	Ballot access
Health care reform	and ethics	Military action
Class division	High school graduation	Digital access/privacy
Phone culture	rates	Homelessness
Genetically modified	Information	Air and water quality
foods	distribution	Climate change
Professional behavior	Criminal justice	Censorship

☞ tip 2a

Listen to Your Emotions
As you note issues in your life, pay close attention to your emotional responses. Are there some issues that make your heart beat faster? This is often where good arguments are born. While this guide will steer you through logical approaches to practical arguments, it is often these emotional and intuitive moments that signal the beginning of a strong argument.

Communities and topics listed above should get you thinking about what matters to you at this point in your life. These lists are not intended to be comprehensive; rather, they are intended to help you identify issues in the various communities to which you belong, especially issues that motivate you to argue.

your turn 2a ➤ **GET STARTED Focus on Communities**

For each community above, identify two or three topics that concern you, and then answer the following questions.

1. What issues within these broad topics most concern you?
2. Overall, what two or three issues matter to you most? Why?

Choose an Issue within a Topic

The categories listed previously help you identify the communities to which you belong and the important issues in your life—not that you necessarily need reminders of what's most pressing for you. Nevertheless, completing the "Your Turn 2a" exercise should get you thinking about what motivates you to argue, and it will likely affirm your sense that life is quite complex and varied these days. This section asks you to begin the argument process by narrowing your focus to a single, arguable issue.

An argument will fail if its focus is too broad. For this reason, it is essential that you distinguish between a topic and an issue. A **topic** is a category—such as local politics, transportation, neighborhood security, race relations, or family planning—that contains numerous issues. Topics are places from which issues and arguments are derived. In contrast, an issue is a specific problem or dispute that remains unsettled and requires a point of view and sometimes a decision. It always occurs within a larger topic and within a precise context, or set of conditions.

Monashee Frantz/Jupiterimages

Figure 2.2 This writer is gathering information from a print source for a single issue. Narrowing your focus to a specific issue, rather than writing generally about a topic, lets you write about a precise set of conditions and thus appeal to an audience more directly.

A good argument results from a process of narrowing from a broad topic to a specific, arguable issue. For example, as a concerned citizen, if you state that you want to argue about America's military presence in the Middle East, you'd be taking on a big topic, one that might require book-length treatment with chapters devoted to separate issues. This topic actually includes dozens of issues, and your job as arguer would be to narrow your focus and choose one specific issue. Instead of spreading out and writing generally about America's military presence in this region, choose a single issue and write very specifically about it. Any argument you build will be more effective when you focus on a single issue. This will give your argument depth and precision, features difficult to include when writing about a big topic in a relatively short argument.

The topic of our military presence in Middle Eastern countries includes, among many others, the following specific issues: the cost of wars; the wars' effects on economic growth; the spike in oil prices, the wars' effects on ethnic populations in Iraq, Afghanistan, and other countries; the decision to begin a preemptive war; concerns about weapons of mass destruction, diplomacy, reconstruction and humanitarian efforts; democracy and governance in these

 tip 2b

Narrow to a Single Issue

To make sure you are focused on an issue and not a topic, make a list of the reasons you intend to use to support your argument. Do some reasons seem substantial enough to become full arguments in themselves? If yes, consider refocusing on one of these issues.

Immigration Reform	Office Politics
• Border security • Citizenship • U.S. Intervention • Local business • Guest worker programs • Worker verification systems • Effects on citizen workforce • Workplace enforcement • Green cards	• Communication • Honesty • Taking credit • Rankism • Relationships • Trust • Dispute resolution • Fair treatment

Diet/Food Consumption	Life in the Classroom
• Who grows it? • Working conditions • Pay scale • Transportation and greenhouse gases • Processing and packaging • Genetically engineered food • USDA standards • Obesity and advertising • Advertising and customer perception • Environmental impact, biodiversity loss, and excessive pesticide use • Global trends and local effects • Regulating imports	• Disruptions and tardiness • Plagiarism • Assignments • Teacher performance • Course organization • Teacher availability • Relevance of course • Attendance policy

countries; the U.S. Constitution and the War Powers Resolution; returning veterans and their treatment; and the duration of the wars. Choosing one of these issues will make building your argument more manageable and more realistic.

The following section provides four topics, each from a different community, along with some of the many issues found within each topic. As outlined, immigration reform, office politics, diet/food consumption, and life in the classroom are broad topics containing many issues; if you're compelled to write within one of these categories, narrowing your focus to a single issue can result in a powerful, focused argument. Again, the issues identified for each topic are but a small sampling of the many issues related to each.

The work you do at this point—narrowing your focus to a single, arguable issue—can be the most important effort you make as you pull together an argument. Focus on a community, narrow your broad topic down to a single issue, probe the issue fully, and then determine where you stand and what you want to accomplish.

Pre-Think about Your Issue

Whether your topic has been assigned or self-selected, your argument will be much more successful if you are able to find an approach that is grounded in your own interests. It often happens that a topic is assigned and may not be one you wish to argue. As you work on your argument, at any stage before and after collecting your research, you should take some time to pre-think. Pre-thinking is a low-stakes process of thinking and writing about your issue. There is no right or wrong way to go about pre-thinking; its function is to give you time to reflect on your argument as it comes together. All pre-thinking methods do not work for all people. Some writers find freewriting provides them with the most ideas; some look at a blank page and freeze. Some love lists; others hate outlines. Find a process or method that works for you, but do spend time pre-thinking. During this process you may find an angle to your argument you had not expected, or you may be able to anticipate potential problems to avoid. The purpose of reflective thinking/writing at different points along the argument process is to allow you to see what you know so far versus what you still need to know, to question your assumptions, and to better explore your understanding of the audience.

There are some standard methods of pre-thinking that may already be familiar to you: brainstorming, mapping (or clustering), and freewriting. These are covered in this section, along with a more nontraditional method, "moving from boring to interesting."

Brainstorming

Brainstorming is one of the easiest prewriting techniques to use. Although you can brainstorm by yourself, it works best with several people. By yourself, you list as many topics that you can think of that relate to your topic, not bothering with connections, continuity, or practicality. The increased effectiveness of this technique when used with a group is apparent. As one person thinks of an idea, it prompts another person to think of another one, and a true storm of ideas can occur. Here is an example of a brainstorming session about an argument on wastewater assigned in an Urban Studies course.

• gray water	• chemicals	• cooking
• pollution	• household cleaners	• doll-making
• groundwater runoff	• white water rafting	• gardening

As you can tell, some terms likely inspired others (chemicals—household cleaners) and others are less obviously connected (pollution). Once a list is generated, you can begin seeing if there are any individual terms that may be a starting point for more brainstorming or a more focused argument topic. You may also find that there are terms that can be grouped together to make for a focused topic.

Freewriting

Freewriting is a technique made popular by Peter Elbow in his 1973 *Writing Without Teachers*. This technique shuts off the inner censor and frees you to write down all of your thoughts about a topic—random or focused. What do you know about your topic so far? What do you find interesting or boring about the topic? Can you find a personal connection to the topic? Some people time themselves or set a page limit, which forces them to produce material. When you have reached your time or page goal, you will no longer be faced with a blank page, and you may even have some ideas among the free-wheeling thoughts that could help you get started. An example passage of freewriting (on the same topic used for the brainstorm above) may look like this:

What can I say about wastewater? I don't think I have ever even thought about where the water from my toilet or sink goes. I have heard that some people use the water from their showers in their gardens. Is this even safe in a vegetable garden? But how safe is our water anyway? In a history course I learned that water from factories used to be directed into the rivers that people drank from. And people fuss about fluoride in their drinking water?

As the writer looks over the passage, she may find the idea of gray water a good starting point. Maybe the safety issue could lead to another round of freewriting to think more about those ideas.

Mapping

Mapping, also known as *clustering*, is a more focused form of brainstorming in which the writer consciously attempts to make connections between terms. In Figure 2.3, the term to be mapped is in the center circle, and the circles radiating from the center follow subterms.

Move from Boring to Interesting

One of America's best-loved authors, Ray Bradbury, loved to write and enjoyed his writing career immensely. The author of dozens of science fiction stories, Bradbury talked about the worst essay he ever wrote—a piece magazine editors asked him to write about life on other planets. Although he loved science fiction, he wasn't really interested in the assignment. Bradbury forged ahead and tinkered endlessly with the piece. He researched the topic to death and wound up producing a dead piece of writing. It took several editors to bring the article back to life. Bradbury, best known for his science fiction stories about life on other planets, was embarrassed. Bradbury's advice, and ours, is to write about what you are interested in, a topic that means something to you.

Angry at your city council for refusing to do anything about the graffiti problem near your child's school? Write a letter. See a problem at work? Send a memo. Have an assignment that seems boring? Find your own angle into the topic. Become engaged, and your writing will be engaging as well.

Writing about real-life situations rarely leads to boring arguments, but trying to write about an instructor-assigned topic can. How can you take a boring topic and find an interesting way to write about it? We call our method for addressing this problem "moving from boring to interesting."

This method can be applied to any topic. Let's say that in your Urban Studies course, you are assigned the topic of wastewater treatment plants, perhaps not the most exciting of topics. Can you really find something interesting to say about treating wastewater? Try this: list all the things you are interested in; it doesn't matter if they appear to have nothing to do with clean water.

Now try to make a connection between each of these topics and the one assigned: wastewater treatment plants.

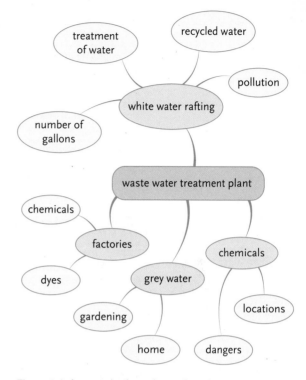

Figure 2.3 An example of mapping or clustering

- Where does the water come from for the new artificial white water rafting course in town? How is it treated?
- Cooking grease going down the drains—how does it get cleaned out of the water?
- How did the old process of draining dyes from nineteenth-century fabric manufacturers into rivers change the way water is treated today?
- Can gray water be used safely for gardens?

GET STARTED Use Boring to Interesting Strategies

For each of the following topics, make a connection to a topic that is of interest to you:

- Circadian rhythms
- The fall of the Roman Empire
- *Moby Dick*
- Rural health care

internet activity 2a Exploring

Based on the issues of concern you identified in "Your Turn 2a," conduct an informal Internet search for each issue. Use the academic databases your college provides, the online sites your teacher recommends, and the recommended websites described in Chapter 3, "Develop a Research Plan."

Define and Target Your Audience

A **target audience** is the group or individual at whom your argument is aimed; you want them to accept or at least acknowledge your position on an issue. Your audience initially may be opposed to your position, undecided about it, or lean toward accepting it. You may want audience members to take immediate action, to reflect on your argument, or to rethink their own points of view.

Aristotle, a founding father of what we know today as argument, encouraged his students to know their audiences before delivering arguments. As you choose issues on which to argue, make sure you know the people you plan to address. Are they inclined at first to accept or reject your claim? What are the ages and occupations of your audience? Are most people in your audience wealthy,

Jetta Productions/Iconica/Getty Images

Figure 2.4 When you make an argument, choose your audience carefully and work to understand that audience as fully as possible.

struggling financially, male, female? Use the following exercise to understand your audience. The work you do to understand your audience and its values will make it easier to craft a practical claim and find the best support to produce a solid, persuasive argument.

your turn 2c ▶ GET STARTED **Define Your Audience**

Your argument must be aimed at a specific target audience. To ensure that you're focused on a specific audience, answer the following questions about an issue and its relationship to your audience. Remember that you will argue before an audience that is as invested as you are in the issue at hand.

1. Who is the group or individual you want to persuade? List the reasons you want to target this audience. Be careful to avoid arguing to a general or neutral audience. Remember that you are writing to individuals with whom you may share certain values, goals, and expectations.
2. What are the physical characteristics, or demographics, of your audience? Consider these criteria as you make this determination: occupation, family size, age, gender, marital status, political leaning, religion, race or ethnicity, education, income, and geographic location.
3. Does your audience already have a position on your issue? Is your audience undecided about your issue? Is it likely to accept or reject your claim? Or does your audience occupy an extreme position? Explain.
4. What are the biases and limitations of your audience?

your turn 2d ▶ GET STARTED **Reach Your Audience**

Answer the following questions to identify the most practical ways to build an argument that is effective for your audience.

1. What sources will you use to establish full context for your issue? How will you research your issue so that you have a sense of how important the issue is to your audience? See Chapter 3, "Develop a Research Plan," for a guide to researching issues.
2. What kind of language makes your audience comfortable? Is it formal and academic, is it the language of political debate, is it the language of mainstream media, or is it informal language? Whatever language makes your audience comfortable, plan to use it in your argument.
3. How will you demonstrate respect for your audience?
4. Can you find common ground with your audience based on what audience members' values, experiences, loyalties, and likely emotional responses are? Explain.

5. Because establishing credibility with an audience is so important, what values and beliefs do you share with your audience?

6. What precisely do you want to accomplish with your audience? Do you want your audience members to question your issue, to learn more about it, to convert to your point of view, or simply to examine their current thinking on the issue?

7. To what extent will you need to inform your audience so that it can accept your argument? Based on what you know about your audience members, what can you assume they already know versus what they need to know in order to accept, but not necessarily agree with, your claim?

8. What will your audience permit you to claim; that is, what are the practical limits of your ability to persuade this particular audience? What is the range of perspectives audience members will accept regarding your issue? To determine the answers to these questions, you will need to know, at least generally, the beliefs and attitudes your audience holds on your issue. Guard against assuming that others share your views and values to keep you from "preaching to the choir," that is, addressing those who feel as you do about an issue.

Stake, Defend, and Justify Your Claim

Fully supporting your claim—your point of view on an issue—is vital to building a successful argument. And before you bring in specific information to defend your claim, it's essential that you use reasons in support of a claim. Many body paragraphs in effective arguments begin with reasons and then bring in specific support. Qualifiers, as noted in the second example below, make your claims and reasons more realistic and more practical.

Develop a Claim, Reasons, and Qualifiers

A claim is the most important part of your argument. Claims use precise language to let your audience know your point of view. For example, writing on the issue of bullying at your child's school requires orienting the reader right away to your point of view. Your claim organizes and centers an argument. Choose the kind of claim you want to use as the basis for your argument.

Working with Claims, Reasons, and Qualifiers: Three Examples

Each of the following three examples contains a sample claim and an explanation of that claim. Attention is also paid to the necessary elements of reasons and qualifiers, which are used to support the claim.

Claim: "Bullying at my child's school continues because school administrators refuse to thoroughly respond to this problem."

Discussion: The arguer has centered her argument in a clear claim that indicates cause and effect. The rest of the argument will be devoted to proving the accuracy of this claim. She'll need to be sure that readers understand the nature of school bullying and its effects, by defining the term *bullying* in specific language. The writer will also need to provide reasons that directly support her claim, and this will mean digging into the reasons administrators are failing to address the problem.

Figure 2.5 Defending a claim thoroughly with reasons and support is essential to a successful argument, especially when you have the attention of an audience. In this photo, the arguer is defending his claim to others who are also concerned about the issue.

Claim: "Most people in our state favor giving tax breaks to new companies able to produce alternative energies, but many of our elected representatives seem to be working against this kind of incentive."

Discussion: The arguer can use this claim of fact to articulate the priorities that separate voters and representatives based on the factual information he brings in. He must prove that his claim is factual by bringing in support—examples, studies, testimony from experts, and so forth. Staying with this issue but centering his position around a claim of value, the claim might look like this: "It is unfair that the representatives we voted for are working against our calls to produce more alternative energy in the state." The word "unfair" makes this claim one of value; he has judged his representatives for overlooking popular interest. In the rest of the argument, the writer must prove precisely how the situation is unfair. Note the qualifiers "most," "many," and "seem" in the writer's claim. While the writer believes that numerous representatives have differing agendas on this issue, he avoids claiming that *all* representatives differ from *most* people. Qualifiers make claims more believable.

Claim: "Start times for local high schools should be moved back one hour."

Discussion: A few years ago, a parent made a compelling argument about the issue of start times for local high school students. Reasons were something like this: The parent was motivated because her kids had to get up early and were not at their best during the school day, and early start times and rescheduling transportation caused problems at home for everyone. She used a problem-based claim because she wanted something to change.

Choose the kind of claim that works best for what you want to accomplish in your argument. Choose the kind of claim that will put you in the best position to persuade your audience. Chapter 10, "Build Arguments," discusses claims and how they can serve your purpose in an argument.

Argue with a Purpose

Make the claim in your argument match the intensity of your purpose by asking yourself what, exactly, you want to accomplish. When you land on an issue that matters to you, you're in a position to argue with a purpose and strength. From there, you must ensure that everything you bring to your argument relates to your purpose.

Do you want readers to understand your issue more clearly and in terms that differ from its mainstream representation? Do you want to argue that something should change? Do you want to redefine a term or terms that in your view need clarification? Do you want to argue what causes an issue? Or do you want to respond to an issue through the lens of your own strong values or beliefs? Answering these questions will let you narrow your focus and choose the kind of claim that matches your purpose, thus letting you argue more persuasively. The kinds of claims described in Chapter 10, "Build Arguments"— fact, definition, evaluation, cause, and problem-based—give you the chance to build an argument around the kind of claim that best matches your purpose.

If extra-educational problems at school (for example, lack of parking, financial aid services, or academic advisors) interfere with the deeply held belief that your education will afford you opportunities for future success, then you have a purpose and a center to an argument. The reasons, varied support, and attention to the opposition you bring to such an argument will anchor your purpose and provide readers the concrete evidence needed to defend your claim.

your turn 2e ▶ GET STARTED Identify Your Purpose

Focus on two current issues in your life, one academic and one personal, and answer the following questions.

1. What would be your purpose in building an argument for each issue?
2. What is the claim you want to make for each issue?
3. What reasons come to mind as you reflect on each issue?
4. Can you bring to your argument personal experience with each issue? Explain.

Vary the Types of Support You Bring to an Argument

Our understanding of how support functions in an argument begins with the work of Aristotle, a Greek philosopher who used the terms *logos, ethos,* and *pathos* to categorize the ways in which an audience can be persuaded to accept a claim. Aristotle knew that the impression the arguer makes on an audience often can determine whether an argument will be taken to heart; he theorized that a conscientious audience wants to be assured that you appeal to it in three essential ways—through practical evidence grounded in reason (*logos*), through your good character (*ethos*), and through emotional appeals that touch the audience's values (*pathos*). While a sound argument is typically a blend of these appeals, good writers often devote 60 to 70 percent of their support to rational appeals. Use all three kinds of appeals in order to build the credibility of your argument and make it more believable. Following is an overview of these three kinds of support, all of which are covered in more depth in Chapter 3, "Develop a Research Plan."

Support Based on Fact

Factual support, or *logos*, includes verifiable information gathered from your research and experience. Arguing before your local school board for or against end-of-grade testing, for example, you'll want to do much of your persuading with facts, statistics, a range of documents, and other kinds of rational evidence. Documented reports from other school districts, for instance, are a kind of rational appeal. They can be studied and evaluated as part of the problem you're attempting to solve.

Support Based on Your Character

This kind of support, which Aristotle termed *ethos*, establishes your credibility. It is your job to present yourself as knowledgeable and, just as important, honest and fair-minded. Doing this thoroughly can build trust with your audience, essential to a successful argument. On the other hand, if your audience senses that you have an unstated motive or that you're not representing other views fairly, then trust is usually impossible. To earn credibility with your audience, be informed, make smart use of your own

Gary Conner/PhotoEdit

Figure 2.6 This arguer is building a research base for an argument by drawing on the work of experts. By presenting his research in a fair, open-minded way, he can build trust with an audience, vital to any competent argument.

experience, bring in the testimony of experts, respect readers by making your language accessible, and reveal your motives. Bring in your child's experience with end-of-grade testing, for example, to provide an insider's perspective on testing issues. Balance your personal viewpoint by bringing in the findings of bipartisan and independent professionals who have studied your issue.

Support Based on the Emotions of an Audience

Using emotional appeals, or *pathos*, is effective when you know what your audience members value and the emotions that may sway them to accept your claim. Examples from your life or from the lives of others in your community are especially useful. When you let readers identify with an emotionally engaging example, you create a positive connection. If your neighbor believes that end-of-grade testing narrows what's taught and does not encourage intellectual curiosity, you can bring that perspective into your argument as a way to touch other parents who agree with the neighbor's perspective. This kind of appeal can also build a sense of community between you and your readers, adding to the momentum of an argument.

your turn 2f ▶ PRACTICE Vary Your Support

Practice working with support for a claim by answering the following questions, based on an issue you are considering for argument:

1. What kinds of facts can you offer?
2. How can you establish your credibility on the issue so that your audience will trust you?
3. Identify emotional connections you can create between your audience members and yourself that will allow readers to identify with your issue.

Working with a Target Audience: Two Examples

When you are motivated to argue on an issue, aim your argument at an audience willing to listen, rethink the issue, and perhaps act on your claim. Targeting the right audience can determine the success or failure of an argument. Review the following sample issues and arguers' efforts to target appropriate audiences.

EXAMPLE 1

Develop a Claim and Target an Audience

The explanations in this first example walk you through the process of determining a practical claim and audience for the issue of teacher workload. As you can see, there are important choices an arguer must make before the drafting process can begin.

TOPIC: Working Conditions

ISSUE: Workload

AUDIENCE: Readers of local newspaper

CLAIM: Current teacher workloads at our college limit the quality of education that students receive.

COMMUNITY:	Workplace
TOPIC:	Working conditions
ISSUES:	Salary
	Job description
	Interview and hiring protocol
	Benefits
	Workload
	Professional development opportunities
	Union representation
	Equal opportunity employment
	Dispute resolution policies
AUDIENCE:	State community college system officials
	College board of trustees
	State legislature
	College president
	Student body
	Coworkers
	Local government
	Readers of local newspaper
CLAIM:	Current teacher workloads at our college limit the quality of education that students receive.

Much thought has gone into this claim. Because it reveals an important issue in the lives of the arguers and because their purpose is to persuade, careful planning is needed when determining an appropriate audience. Review the following planning process regarding claim and audience for this "workload" issue.

Why this issue?

The workplace, a community nearly all of us belong to, is full of arguable issues. For example, we are authors of this text on purposeful argument, and we are workers in a labor force. As teachers we have issues, among them a deep concern about the number of classes we are required to teach each term. We feel that this issue of workload affects our job performance, our professionalism, and importantly, our ability to serve students. We plan to aim our argument at a specific audience and to prove our claim with specific kinds of support.

Why this audience?

This argument will target readers of our local newspaper and thus will appear both in print and online formats. We chose this audience because its members' tax dollars in part support our publicly funded college, because members of our community expect quality services, because individual readers of the argument (and perhaps their family members) have attended our college, and because the integrity of the local workforce is dependent on the graduates of our college and their training. We feel that other audiences may view our issue from different perspectives and may be less likely to be swayed by our claim.

Why this claim?

We will work with a claim of cause because our intention is to inform readers how teacher workload compromises our ability to meet students' expectations, the mission of the college, and the school's service to the community. We are not calling for immediate action; rather, the purpose of the argument is to let readers know in specific terms about the issue and to suggest that they reflect on it. As a first step in acting on this issue, we hope to generate interest and awareness. A follow-up argument would be aimed at a different audience, one with decision-making power, and may require a problem-based claim in which we argue for a reduced workload. But for now our goal is to raise awareness of this workload issue. (For descriptions of kinds of claims, see Chapter 8, "Consider Toulmin-Based Argument," and Chapter 9, "Consider Middle Ground and Rogerian Argument, and Argument Based on Microhistory.")

We assume that many of our audience members know the services our college provides, but that many may not be aware of teacher workload and how it affects delivery of the expected services. Accordingly, the support we bring to the argument, especially specific examples drawn from our experiences, will be vital to fully informing our audience. Because the college has served the community for many years, we can expect some immediate "permission" from our audience to argue our claim, but based on our research, we also know that there has been some persistent grumbling in the past two election cycles over bond proposals that, if passed, would earmark money to the college, and we will need to fully acknowledge and respond to this concern in one of our rebuttals.

EXAMPLE 2

Map an Argument for a Target Audience

TOPIC: The Online Classroom

ISSUE: Teacher–student interaction

AUDIENCE: Director of Distance Learning

CLAIM: Clear standards for teachers' regular interaction with students should be stated in the introductions to online English courses.

When you settle on a claim and a target audience, it can be helpful to rough out most of an argument. This example presents a preview of a Toulmin-based argument, typically the most common kind of argument used in academic writing. (Toulmin-based and other kinds of arguments are discussed in Chapter 8, "Consider Toulmin-Based Argument," and Chapter 9, "Consider Middle Ground and Rogerian Argument, and Argument Based on Microhistory.") The example picks up on the issue that opens this chapter. This will give you a sense of how the parts of an argument work together. All parts of an argument are fully discussed in chapters that follow.

COMMUNITY:	School/Academic
TOPIC:	The online classroom
ISSUES:	Course navigation
	Clarity of course objectives and expectations
	Online courses and ADA requirements
	Teacher–student interaction
	Grading policies

	Teacher feedback
	Accessibility of course materials
	Course technologies
	Student support services
AUDIENCE:	Teacher
	Department chair
	Other online students
	College dean
	Readers of your local newspaper
	Director of distance learning
	College president
CLAIM:	Clear standards for teachers' regular interaction with students should be stated in the introductions to online English courses.

Why this issue?

Of the many issues that fall under the topic of the online classroom, teacher–student interaction is the most compelling in the online course experience of this writer. Writing about distance learning in general is much too broad, and a writer is sensible to choose a single issue that can be argued in depth. Other issues listed may be of concern, but for this writer they are not as pressing as the need for clear guidelines regarding the interaction with and availability of instructors of online courses.

Why this audience?

The writer plans to aim this argument at her college's director of distance learning in the form of a substantial letter. While there are other possible targets for this argument, the director of distance learning may be the most practical choice because the director is invested in the integrity of the college's distance learning program and capable of acting on the writer's concern for regular interaction with her online teachers. Other audience choices are not as directly tied to online course concerns. Additional practical reasons to target this audience may include the director's ability to suggest options that address the writer's concern, such as disseminating to teachers online course templates that model effective student interaction; designing workshops for teachers; and producing comprehensive student opinion surveys where students' concerns about contact with teachers can be documented.

Because the director is the most important person associated with online instruction at this school, the writer can assume the director knows the importance of student–teacher interaction in online environments. Additionally, the director likely has training in current theoretical approaches to distance learning and thus is in a position to hear the arguer's concern. Writing to a department chair, dean, or college president would add another administrative layer and probably would require considerable explanation of the claim.

As the audience for this argument likely shares the writer's goal of supporting student success in online courses, the director of distance learning may find reasonable a claim for establishing clear standards; in addition, these changes are well within the director's decision-making limits. This kind of "permission" from an audience is essential.

Research

The writer would be wise to research the goals of the college's distance learning program and its commitment to students. This information should be available on the college's website and in the print catalog. However, a quick review of several institutions that offer online programs shows that the schools' websites offer little information about teacher–student interaction standards for online courses. The University of Illinois's online catalog, for example, describes the kinds of lectures that may be offered by its online faculty but suggests that students contact faculty for specifics about how the courses will be managed. And many community colleges in the state offer no information about expectations for student–teacher interaction in online courses.

Why this claim?

The writer is clear in her claim that she wants her audience to respond to this argument by way of direct action. In this case, the writer strongly implies that she wants the director to respond to her point of view and take action that will result in improved interaction with her online teachers. This kind of claim, where a writer is arguing for something to change, is a problem-based claim.

Other possible claims

The five kinds of claims available to a writer arguing on a particular issue are discussed in Chapter 10, "Build Arguments." The following types of claims represent those a writer might consider specifically when arguing the issue of student–teacher interaction in the online classroom.

- Teaching effectively in the online classroom includes interacting regularly with students. (This is a **claim of definition**, where the writer will center an argument by defining a key word or term and then provide reasons for the definition. In this example, the writer would define the phrase "teaching effectively in the online classroom.")

- Regular interaction with teachers is essential for success in online courses. (In this example, the writer would use a **claim of fact** and prove in the argument that it is a fact that succeeding in online courses requires regular interaction with teachers.)
- The absence of clear standards regarding student–teacher interaction in online classes is unfair to students. (A **claim of evaluation** involves the writer making a judgment or evaluation. In this example, the writer will be responsible for proving that it is unfair to students when they enroll in online courses that are missing clear standards for student–teacher interaction.)
- Regular student–teacher interaction in online courses will often result in better grades and better understanding of course content. (A **claim of cause** argues that one thing causes another. In this example the writer would argue that regular interaction in the online classroom can lead to better student grades and a better grasp of course content.)

When you are fully motivated to argue a point of view on an issue important to you and are realistic in the audience you target, you can begin building your argument. Continuing with the issue of student–teacher interaction in the online classroom, this is how the writer might outline the remainder of her argument before beginning work on a first draft.

Warrant/Justification   This term is discussed fully in Chapter 8, "Consider Toulmin-Based Argument," and refers to a deeply held value, belief, or principle you share with your audience. To make a successful argument, your audience must, in a sense, grant you permission to make your argument based on a shared value, such as the belief that students should succeed in online courses. In this argument, a successful warrant might be: "Student success in online classes means that students will complete their educations and the college will fulfill its mission to educate students."

Reasons   Reasons, similar to topic sentences, are used to support your claim. They are followed by more specific kinds of support. Here are reasons this writer might use in building her argument:

- Specific turnaround times for responses to email messages and graded assignments will guarantee feedback for my questions and performance on my assignments.
- Regular teacher participation on the class discussion board means that all members of a class benefit from the teacher guiding us through challenging parts of the course.
- Trust and teamwork in a class are more likely to develop when the teacher is prompt with feedback.
- Teachers can and should model practical ways to interact online.

Support   Specific kinds of support the writer can bring to these reasons fall into logical, ethical, and emotional categories (discussed in more depth in Chapter 11, "Support an Argument with Fact (Logos), Credibility (Ethos), and

Emotion (Pathos)." This writer certainly can rely on personal experiences in online classes, refer to experts in the field of distance learning and the experience of other students, and use examples that will appeal to readers' emotions.

Backing and Reservations   Backing is the support you bring for your warrant. In this argument, examples of student success will provide effective backing that, overall, the college does fulfill its mission. A reservation is a statement that cautions readers that the warrant does not apply in certain circumstances. For example, a reservation in this argument might be: "But if online students do not have the chance to evaluate teachers' abilities to interact with students during a course, then standards may not be effective."

Rebuttals and Differing Views   A writer brings rebuttals and differing views to an argument to acknowledge and respond to other points of view on an issue. Some objections to this writer's claim might include the following: online courses are more time consuming than real-time courses for teachers and thus there is limited time to interact with students; many online teachers feel that students should use online resources instead of depending on teacher feedback; and teacher–student interaction in online courses is not part of a teacher's annual review and therefore is not considered, by many teachers, to be important. The writer must answer, or counter, each rebuttal. Differing views on this issue may not argue directly against this writer's claim but may approach the issue from different perspectives. The writer may choose to build on and extend these views or to demonstrate their shortcomings.

Qualifiers   Qualifiers make an argument more practical because they involve words and terms like "in most cases" or "often" that replace words like "only" and "always." For example, would the second reason given above— "Regular teacher participation on the class discussion board means that all members of a class benefit from teacher guidance through challenging parts of the course"—be more believable if a qualifier were added and read, "Regular teacher participation on the class discussion board means that *many* members of a class would benefit from teacher guidance through challenging parts of the course"? Qualifiers should be used throughout an argument and are discussed in Chapter 10, "Build Arguments."

your turn 2g ▸ PRACTICE Map an Argument

Based on the overview of the argument process this chapter provides, identify a pressing issue in your life and perform the following tasks:

1. Write a first draft of a claim.
2. Identify the values you share with your audience.
3. Draft reasons and outline support for your claim.
4. Establish backing to address audience reservations.
5. Identify opposing viewpoints and rebuttals.
6. Use qualifiers to make your claim and reasons practical.

Argue at the Right Moment

The essential work you must do in planning an argument—determine an issue important to you, identify a practical target audience for your argument, and map your argument—requires another vital consideration: arguing at the right time. This means delivering an argument at a time when it is most likely to be heard and responded to. As a perceptive arguer, take advantage of current local and intellectual interest in an issue to energetically deliver an argument, something the individuals in Figure 2.7 are prepared to do.

An argument can be effective when you deliver it at the right time, what in classical rhetoric is known as *kairos*, or timeliness. This means having a strong understanding of your audience and how ready it is for your claim. It also means having a sense of the issue's urgency. For example, if your audience is your colleagues—your fellow students—when might be the best time to argue about the issue of increased campus parking fees? You may decide that early in the semester is best—a time when registration, textbook fees, and parking fees are fresh in the minds of other students *and* a time before projects are due or major exams are looming.

If, on the other hand, your aim is to inform readers of your local newspaper (via a substantial letter to the editor) that home foreclosure rates are increasing in your community due to predatory lending practices, you may determine that the best time to make your argument is when local media are reporting on this issue and when community interest is high. Likewise, an argument on the issue of air quality will have more currency during the run-up to an important policy decision on toxic emissions than after such a decision.

When you sense that the time is right to deliver an argument, take full advantage of the momentum surrounding your issue. This is good timing. Delivering an argument before an audience is ready for it or when an issue's urgency has passed can render the argument, and your efforts, ineffective. So how can you determine the right time to make your argument? Determine how an issue is affecting an audience. For example, if you're concerned about how wounded troops returning from Iraq and Afghanistan are being treated, and you know that local and national news media are reporting on this issue, you may decide to target your state's U.S. senators as your audience and let them know that legislation should be proposed based on this current problem. You can also keep your focus closer to home and target veterans' groups and area veterans' affairs hospitals. Deliver your argument when public exposure and interest in an issue

Figure 2.7 Deliver an argument to an audience when there is genuine and immediate interest in an issue. In this political rally, individuals are responding with genuine interest to the issue of health care reform.

Gerry Boughan/Shutterstock.com

have created an opening for change so as to ensure that your argument has currency and that your voice will be part of the conversation.

What might be the best times to argue the sample issues discussed previously? The writer who claims the need for clear standards of interaction with her online teachers may choose to deliver the argument toward the end of the academic term, a time when she will have established her credibility with her audience as a serious student wanting more from her online course and also a time when the director of distance learning may take seriously the need to implement new policies for the next term. Concerning our goal of raising local awareness of the workload issue at our college, we plan to deliver the argument to our local newspaper in October, approximately a month before voters decide on a bond proposal that would direct money to our school. We also note local and national media reporting on the trend of more students electing to complete their first two years of study at two-year and community colleges, as tuition cost in those institutions is substantially lower than at four-year colleges. With both issues, arguing at appropriate times will be crucial to attracting the immediate interest of an audience.

> **your turn 2h** ▸ **GET STARTED Argue at the Right Moment**
>
> Answer the following questions about your claim or one of your claims. Is it a good time to argue your claim with this particular audience? If not, how can you either adjust your claim so that it is timely or target a different audience that you determine is the right one to hear your claim right now?
>
> 1. Are you arguing at a time when your audience is aware of and invested in your issue? Explain.
> 2. Are you confident in your claim and prepared to defend it? Explain.
> 3. Describe the ways your audience can benefit from reflecting on or acting on your claim.
> 4. Are conditions such that your audience is willing to tolerate differing views on your issue? If yes, describe how you will take advantage of this time in an informed way in your argument.

Getting Started

After you decide on an issue, target an audience, map your argument, and decide on the right time to deliver your argument, use the following prompts to get started. These prompts are designed to move you deeper into your feelings about an issue and help you determine whom you want to persuade, what you want to change, and how accepting your claim can benefit the audience you're targeting. Answering these prompts can give you insight into the direction an argument should take.

 tip 2c

Read the Signs!
To determine if an argument will carry weight with an audience, make a list of the indications, or signs, that the time is right to craft and deliver your argument. This list can include conversations you participate in and overhear, articles in the local media, and references to the issue that you find in blogs, magazines, and websites.

your turn 2i ▶ GET STARTED **With an Argument**

Complete the following sentences as a way of getting started with an argument.

1. What topics *not* included in the earlier section "Determine What Matters to You and Why" might you be interested in addressing?
2. Thinking in terms of both your personal life and your academic life, what issues concern you the most?
3. What are the two or three most pressing issues for you both inside and outside the classroom?
4. What is the single issue on which you are most motivated to argue? Explain.
5. In response to question 4, what makes you sure that you are taking on a manageable issue and not a broad topic?
6. In addition to your own position on this single issue, briefly describe other points of view.

your turn 2j ▶ GET STARTED **Target the Right Audience**

With regard to the issue you have identified as motivating for you, describe your target audience by answering the following questions.

1. What are the two or three most practical target audiences for this argument?
2. How do you want your audience to respond after taking in your argument?
3. Based on how you want your audience to respond, what is the most practical target audience for your argument?
4. What is it about the demographics of your target audience that suggests it is a practical choice?
5. What are the values and beliefs you share with your target audience?
6. In practical, everyday terms, why do you want to persuade this target audience?

your turn 2k ▶ GET STARTED **Draft the Right Claim**

Respond to the following questions as a way to determine whether a claim is appropriate for your argument.

1. By accepting your claim, how will your target audience benefit?
2. Of the five kinds of claims described under "Example #2: Map an Argument for a Target Audience," what kind of claim is most appropriate for your audience? Explain.

Use Search Engines to Find Internet Sources on the Surface Web and on the Deep Web

Armed with a better understanding of the history of electronic privacy, Hal prepares to conduct an Internet search. This process will take place many times throughout the research and writing process, as new information is needed or new ideas elicit new searches. Many people content themselves with visiting their favorite search engine and using whatever sources appear on the first page of hits. This may be fine if you are looking for football scores (though there are better ways to find even that information), but if you are looking for sources suitable for academic writing, you'll need to dig further.

Not all search engines produce the same search results. Most people are familiar with Google, Ask.com, and Yahoo!, but there are many more search engines available that do different things. Even if you are happy with Google, you are probably not using all of the powerful research tools it has to offer. We will learn some of its features throughout this chapter.

Search the Surface Web

You are likely already familiar with **search engines,** vehicles for finding material on the World Wide Web. What you may not know is that search engines are not all the same. Type in the same query at each of the engines listed below, for example, and you will get different results from each. The way they each search, collect, and rank hits is different.

Some consistently useful search engines include:

- Google   http://www.google.com
- Yahoo!   http://search.yahoo.com
- Ask.com   http://www.ask.com
- Bing   http://www.bing.com

A considerable list of search engines is also available through Mohawk Valley Community College at http://mvcc.libguides.com.

Hal used the same search term ("electronic privacy" + work) in four different search engines: Ask.com, Bing, Yahoo!, and Google (see Figure 3.1). You can see that the search results and their organization are very different from one site to the next. In addition, three search engines offer additional search terms to use and one doesn't. Find a search engine that retrieves results in a method that makes sense to you.

Hal began a new search on Google using the phrase "workplace privacy" (see Figure 3.2). The sites highlighted in purple are the ones Hal visited. Notice that the ending of the URL (the website's address) for these three sites is ".org." This indicates that the site is maintained by an organization, although the rules for determining "organizational" status seem to be flexible. By visiting the Privacy Rights Clearinghouse, the Electronic Privacy Information Center, and the American Civil Liberties Union, Hal was able to come away with several views of the issue of workplace privacy.

Figure 3.1 The same keyword search conducted with different search engines

Figure 3.2 Google search screen

Other than .org domains, a URL can end with the following extensions:

- .com   a commercial site
- .edu   an educational site, such as a school or university
- .gov   a government site, for example the Library of Congress or the White House
- .int   not so common, but refers to an international site
- .mil   extension used by U.S. military organizations such as the Army or Navy
- .net   used as a generic extension for many types of sites
- .org   used by an organization

internet activity 3b Compare Search Engines

Select several search engines and conduct a quick basic search to see what hits are returned and how they are organized. Which search engine appeals the most to you based on page layout, number of hits, and organization?

Search the Deep Web

The search engines listed above will search the surface web, but did you know that there is more to the Internet than what Google and Yahoo! can find? There are thousands of sources that cannot be easily accessed by general-purpose search engines. This information is called the "deep web," or sometimes the "invisible web." Some studies indicate that what we can generally access on the Web is only 1/500th of what is out there. Some of this information is password or firewall protected, but much of it is just in formats that do not make it easy for the search engines to find. Many databases housing scholarly or scientific information are available in the deep web, and there are search engines and database sites developed to access much of it.

- LibrarySpot.com (http://libraryspot.com): Particularly useful are the site's link to scholarly journals that can be accessed online and its link to museum sites. The World Digital Library, for example, offers thousands of images from many countries.
- Infomine (http://infomine.ucr.edu): This site indexes scholarly Internet resource collections arranged by subject.
- Academic Info (http://www.academicinfo.net/subject-guides): This site has a wonderful directory of subject guides that offer links to resources. The link to Afghanistan News and Media, for example, offers links to Afghan newspapers, documentaries, and materials from the State Department.

- Scirus (http://scirus.com): According to the Scirus home page, the search engine finds "not only journal content but also scientists' homepages, courseware, pre-print server material, patents and institutional repository and website information."

- Librarians' Internet Index (http://www.ipl.org): This search site is organized by subject. The government subject link has 34 additional subtopics that can be browsed. It is a real gold mine for finding quality material. The Internet Public Library (IPL) has recently merged with the Librarian's Internet Index (LII) resulting in IPL2.

- Find Articles (http://findarticles.com): This site contains articles from many journals, but not all of the articles are free. You can always retrieve abstracts of the articles, however, which can help you determine if the article is one you may want to request through your library's interlibrary loan service.

- Intute (http://intute.ac.uk): According to the website, "Intute is a free online service providing access to the very best web resources for education and research." Sources are organized into four broad categories: science and technology, arts and humanities, social sciences, and life and health sciences.

Other search engines to use are Complete Planet, http://completeplanet.com and Surfwax, http://surfwax.com. Try them all to see what you can find on your issue. As you can probably tell, research is not a one-stop activity. The broader you cast your net, the more likely you will find sources that are reputable and pertinent to your issue.

Keep this template (and all the other publication information templates typed in red in this chapter) available as you collect sources. Not all information will be available on every website; record what is available. You may want to be careful about sites that do not have authors that you can find out more about.

☛ **tip 3b**

Using a Bibliography File

Always collect publication information for an electronic source. If you do not have this information when you write your report, you will not be able to use the source. And trying to relocate an Internet source can be exceedingly frustrating and time consuming.

A bibliography file is a great way to keep your sources organized. You may not have a use for a particular article once you've completed your assessment, but you may change your thesis at a later date, and a previously useless article may now be useful.

Source Information: Template

Author, if one is listed: _____

Title of the specific web page: _____

Website that hosts the page: _____

Date it was posted: _____

Date you accessed it: _____

Note that if you find a source that is actually an article from an online periodical, you will need to gather the complete periodical publication information in addition to the site information.

internet activity 3c **Explore the Deep Web**

The deep web is a great place to explore. Take your time playing with the search engines and databases, and mark the ones that include material on your issue for future searches.

Perform Keyword Queries

Now that you are familiar with some of the available search engines and database sites that will look for information on the Web, you should read the following instructions on basing keyword queries on the vocabulary lists you created during your basic fact and encyclopedia reading so that your searches will be more effective and efficient. Remember when Hal typed in the query "electronic privacy" + work? He was using a **search string** to tell the search tool what he was looking for. You can use Boolean search operators (*not, and,* and *or*) between your search terms to tell the search engine exactly what to look for. Boolean logic can be tweaked endlessly, whereas using + and – signs will only add or subtract terms from your search. The following chart lists the basic kinds of search strings you can use and what they mean.

Search String	What You Are Asking For
electronic privacy	Pages that have both the words *electronic* AND *privacy* somewhere on the page
"electronic privacy"	Pages that have both words next to each other
"electronic privacy" AND work	Pages that have both words next to each other AND include the word *work* somewhere on the page
"electronic privacy" + work	Same as above
"electronic privacy" NOT surveillance	Pages that have both words next to each other and do NOT include the word *surveillance*
"electronic privacy" – work	Same as above
"electronic privacy" 2010...2014	Pages that have both words next to each other AND only pages that have material between the date range of 2010 and 2014
site: .edu	Pages from educational websites only

You will need to gather the following publication information for articles found on the databases. Record all available information—not every site will have all the elements listed.

Source Information: Article from Website (Basic)

Author of article: _____

Title of article: _____

Title of periodical: _____

Publication information of periodical: _____

And then,

Author(s) of web page: _____

Title of web page: _____

Title of website: _____

Date originally posted: _____

Date you accessed the site: _____

MLA no longer requires the URL, but recording it is helpful in finding the site again.

internet activity 3d Perform Internet and Internet Database Searches

Using one of the search engines or database sites listed previously, find three Internet sources pertaining to your topic. Use the advanced search feature for your search engine, or use the search strings above to limit your results to .edu domains for the past three months only.

Find News Sites and Use RSS Feeds to Receive Updates

Hal also decides to take advantage of the archives that newspapers and other news sources provide. Although the issue of privacy in the workplace is a longstanding one, the constant development of communication technology makes this issue particularly current. News search engines are a good place to search for information about current issues. The following is a good beginning list:

- CNN   http://www.cnn.com
- CBS News   http://www.cbsnews.com
- ABC News   http://abcnews.go.com
- Google News   http://news.google.com
- Reuters   http://www.reuters.com

- BBC News   http://news.bbc.co.uk
- The Associated Press   http://www.ap.org
- *The Wall Street Journal*   http://online.wsj.com/home-page
- *The New York Times*   http://nytimes.com
- National Public Radio   http://www.npr.org
- *Slate Magazine*   http://www.slate.com
- Topix   http://www.topix.net (news aggregator that can bundle the news for your ZIP code)
- Yahoo! and Google also search for news and have searchable news archives

Play with the various sites to learn how the news is organized on each site and to use their search functions. When you find a news article you like, collect the following publication information for later use:

> ### Source Information: Article from News Site
>
> Author(s) of article: _____
>
> Title of article: _____
>
> Title of journal, newspaper, magazine, or web page: _____
>
> Original publication date: _____
>
> Title of website: _____
>
> Date you accessed the site: _____

MLA no longer requires the URL, but recording it is helpful in finding the site again.

internet activity 3e Perform a News Search

Visit two of the news search sites listed previously and find information on the same stories. How is the material treated differently by the different news sites? Which appeals the most to you based on design and organization? Which seem to have the most links to your issue?

If you find sites that consistently provide you with information you find useful on your issue, subscribe to the RSS feed at that site and you can receive updates on your issue as news becomes available. Many websites now offer RSS feeds to their readers. You will often find one of the two icons shown in Figure 3.3 on a site, which you can click on to subscribe to a feed. Sometimes you will see the RSS in a box.

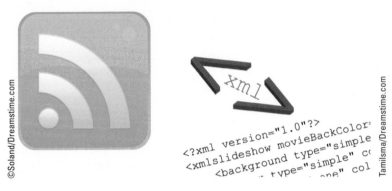

©Soland/Dreamstime.com

Tamilsma/Dreamstime.com

Figure 3.3 Look for one of these two icons to subscribe to a feed.

Subscribing to a feed can be a big time saver if you are following a changing story or if you are tracking several sites and don't want to have to keep visiting over and over to see if new information has been posted.

An **RSS feed** delivers updates on your issue to you, either through a reader that you can access online, to your email account as alerts, or to a mobile unit, such as your phone. These feeds are free to subscribe to, and so are most **newsreaders,** also known as "aggregators," which are needed to read the feeds as they come to you. Different newsreaders work differently, so you'll have to play around to see which may work best for you. Yahoo! offers links to many of the most popular newsreaders on its directory.

With newsreaders, you can control how often you receive updates: hourly, as they happen, or weekly. With a good search query, you can sit back and let the computer do some of the leg work for you.

 tip 3c

Use RSS Feeds

Other sources you can use to gather information about your topic are RSS feeds to newsgroups, discussion boards, and blogs.

Find and Use Databases in Libraries

Databases that you access through your library (EBSCOhost, MasterFILE Premier, ERIC, etc.) are collections of articles from various publications gathered in one place to make research easier. Instead of subscribing to hundreds of journals for which they have little physical space, libraries now subscribe to databases so that journals can be searched electronically. Some databases are field specific. For example, ERIC is a clearinghouse of education sources. There are databases specifically for newspaper articles, for business sources, for medical articles, and so on. Most of the time, though, a general database like EBSCOhost will work for you.

Searching a database is not so different from searching the Internet. You have choices such as date ranges, publications, and document type that can make your searching more efficient. Most libraries offer connections to their databases that you can reach from your home computer. Hal accessed EBSCOhost through his library's remote connection. When you use databases on the deep web, some of the search screens will look a lot like the ones described here;

GALE OPPOSING VIEWPOINTS IN **CONTEXT.**

All   Viewpoints   Academic Journals   Primary Sources   M

A

| Home | Browse Issues | Maps | Resources |

Advanced Search

Find

Search for workplace privacy   in Keyword ▾

And ▾   in Document Title ▾

And ▾   in Publication Title ▾

◆ Add row   ━ Delete row

[Search]

Limit To

☑ Full Text Documents
☐ Peer Reviewed Journals

Limit By

Publication Date

From January ▾ 1 ▾ 2010 ▾ To December ▾ 21 ▾ 2012 ▾

Document Type

A B C D E F G H I J K L M N O P Q R S T U V W X Y Z

Abstract   Article
Advertisement

Cengage Learning

Figure 3.4 Opposing Viewpoints advanced search screen.

others, though, will have their own idiosyncrasies for searching. Most database sites have tutorials that will walk you through the search process, and the results will be worth it—lots of articles you can use in academic writing.

Hal narrowed his date range to two years and selected the Full Text check box so that the results generated by his search would include available full-length articles only (see Figure 3.4). This step is necessary unless you have time to request through interlibrary loan articles that are not available in the database. Most professors will not allow you to cite from article abstracts alone; you must have access to the full-text article.

Documents accessed through a computer database such as EBSCOhost will appear in one of two formats: PDF or HTML. A **PDF document** requires that you have Adobe Acrobat Reader on your computer. If you do not, you can download Adobe Acrobat Reader free from the Adobe website.

An article in PDF format is simply a photocopy of the original article—page breaks, images, and so forth are maintained, and reading the article is no different than it would be if you were turning pages in a print journal. The publication information is usually found at the top or bottom of the journal pages (see Figure 3.6). When you cite from an article you accessed in PDF format, you can refer to specific page numbers as they appear, just as you normally would with a print document.

An **HTML document** appears as a continuous page, generally with no page breaks or images. The publication information you will need appears

tip 3d

Verify Citations

Before you end your database search session, verify that you have all of the article's publication information. Some databases will also help you generate a complete citation (see arrow in Figure 3.7).

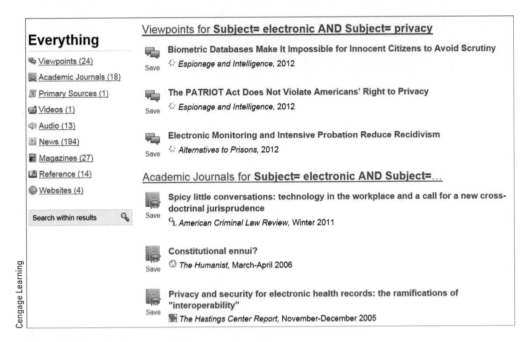

Figure 3.5 Opposing Viewpoints Database search results

MARKET SEGMENTATION

Because all customers do not have the same needs, expectations, and financial resources, managers can improve their pricing strategies by segmenting markets. Successful segmentation comes about when managers determine what motivates particular markets and what differences exist in the market when taken as a whole. For example, some customers may be motivated largely by price, while others are motivated by functionality and utility. The idea behind segmentation is to divide a large group into a set of smaller groups that share significant characteristics such as age, income, geographic location, lifestyle, and so on. By dividing a market into two or more segments, a company can devise a pricing scheme that will appeal to the motivations of each of the different market segments or it can decide to target only particular segments of the market that best correspond to its products or services and their prices.

Managers can use market segmentation strategically to price products or services in order to attain company objectives. Companies can set prices differently for different segments based on factors such as location, time of sale, quantity of sale, product design, and a number of others, depending on the way companies divide up the

PRIVACY, PRIVACY LAWS, AND WORKPLACE PRIVACY

Privacy, privacy laws, and workplace privacy are issues of major concern to individuals and organizations in the modern world. Privacy violation and encroachment have become a norm as a result of the surveillance capabilities of the new and emerging electronic gadgets and information technology (IT) systems. This trend has prompted many countries to pass laws that govern the handling and collection of personal information of individuals and organizations with the use of electronic instruments.

WHAT IS PRIVACY?

What constitutes an encroachment to an individual's or an organization's rights to privacy? In legal terms, privacy simply refers to the accepted standards of related rights that safeguard human dignity. Definitions of privacy vary according to the environment, the participating interests, and the contextual limits. In many countries, the concept of data protection is included in the definition of privacy to achieve an interpretation that views privacy in terms of boundaries to an individual's personal information or an organization's data.

Figure 3.6 Page from a journal article in PDF format

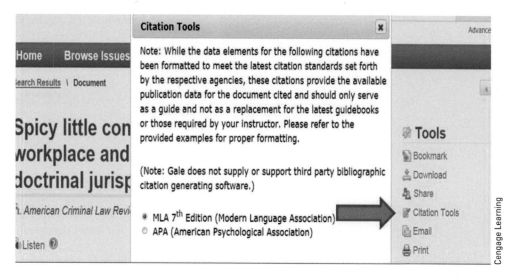

Cengage Learning

Figure 3.7 Some databases help you generate a complete citation

either at the beginning of the article or at the very end of the article. You cannot refer your readers to specific page numbers when you cite from an article in HTML format, as HTML documents do not contain page numbers. A reader would, however, be able to easily perform a search of the original article for cited material.

The publication information you need to gather for a journal, a magazine, or a newspaper article is as follows:

Journal	**Magazine**	**Newspaper**
Author(s)	Author(s)	Author(s)
Title of article	Title of article	Title of article
Title of journal	Title of magazine	Title of newspaper
Volume and issue numbers	Publication date (month/week + date/year)	Publication date (day, month, and year)
Year of publication (sometimes includes season—e.g., Fall)	Page numbers of article (if available)	Page numbers of article (if available)
Page numbers of article (if available)	Title of database	Title of database
Title of database	Date database accessed	Date database accessed
Date database accessed		

You can print an article, save it to a flash drive, send your selected articles to your email account (if you are on campus), or save them to your personal computer (if you are working from a remote location). Because Hal has the option of saving any articles that look interesting and reviewing them more closely later, he doesn't read them as he finds them. When he is ready, though, he will skim the articles looking for certain information, deciding at that point which articles he wants to read more closely and which he can delete from his research folder.

your turn 3a   **GET STARTED** Use Library Databases

Access your campus or public library's journal databases and conduct a search for your topic. Find two articles that have been published within the past two years. Copy all information that you would need to find the article again, including the database in which you found the article.

Find and Use Primary Sources

Using primary sources can help you get closer to the heart of an issue. Whether your argument is concerned with historical issues or current ones, whether you are arguing in the classroom or in the community, asking questions that can be answered by interviews, surveys, court transcripts, letters, photographs, raw statistics, or congressional hearings will put you in closer contact with the real people behind the issue. It is easy to fall into the trap of looking for the "truth" of an issue, looking only for hard facts to support your rational argument, when, in fact, there is rarely only one truth involved in any issue. People are rarely factual, nor do they usually operate on strictly rational lines of thought. Real people are motivated by a variety of reasons, which are not always based on the relevant facts of an issue. Determining the facts that are relevant to your issue is without a doubt extremely important. However, it is how these facts are interpreted by the stakeholders, the real people involved in your issue, that will determine how successful your argument ultimately will be.

We've already covered some of the many sources to choose from when you are researching your issue. Will newspaper or journal articles answer your research questions, or do you need to conduct interviews or gather statistics? **Secondary sources** are those that analyze or explain some aspect of your topic. A magazine article evaluating the dangers of factory emissions would be a secondary source. **Primary sources** are original documents or information gathered from firsthand research—yours or someone else's. An interview with a resident of a neighborhood affected by factory emissions would be a primary source.

Primary Sources
- Historical newspapers
- Public records
- Government documents

- Interviews
- Surveys
- Statistics
- Historical documents
- Diaries
- Letters
- Advertisements
- Maps
- Documentaries
- Archives

Secondary Sources
- Most articles from current newspapers
- Articles from magazines and scholarly journals
- Books

There are several excellent websites that offer tips and strategies for conducting primary research and for evaluating the sources once you have found them. One of the most useful sites is Patrick Rael's *Reading, Writing, and Researching for History: A Guide for College Students* at Bowdoin College (http://www.bowdoin.edu/writing-guides). Some of the general issues in evaluating primary sources are determining the purpose of a document, evaluating its validity or accuracy, and determining what was important to the author of the source, especially in the case of diaries or letters.

The U.S. Library of Congress has an amazing website that offers links to hundreds of sites housing primary sources in every area from literature to history to sociology (http://www.loc.gov/index.html). Here you can explore photographs, diaries, videos, links to statistics, interviews, maps, and so on.

Here are more sites that may help in your search for primary sources:

- U.S. Census Bureau—Data tables and maps presenting census data, plus materials to help use census information (http://www.census.gov).
- Survey Research—The Writing Center at Colorado State University presents this guide to conducting survey research and reporting on results (http://writing.colostate.edu/guides/research/survey/index.cfm).
- Public Agenda Online—Polling data on a wide array of topics and issues (http://www.publicagenda.org).
- National Criminal Justice Reference Service—Data, reports, and links from the Department of Justice on topics related to criminology and corrections (http://www.ncjrs.gov).
- National Opinion Research Center—This center at the University of Chicago indexes studies on a wide variety of topics from aging to energy consumption to substance abuse (http://www.norc.uchicago.edu).

- Pew Global Attitudes Project—This ambitious project from the Pew Research Center presents the results of more than 90,000 interviews in 50 countries (http://pewglobal.org).
- Population Reference Bureau—Articles, datasheets, and lesson plans on topics related to the study of population (http://www.prb.org).
- FedStats—A single point of access for statistics maintained by U.S. government agencies (http://www.fedstats.gov).
- First Measured Century—This companion website to a three-hour PBS special with Ben Wattenberg presents information on social trends in the twentieth century (http://www.pbs.org/fmc/index.htm).
- Institute for Social Research—Results of research studies done at this center at the University of Michigan. Topics range from attitudes toward cell phones, to why some women don't enter careers in math and science, to how wealth influences people's experiences in their last year of life (http://www.isr.umich.edu).
- U.S. Vital Record Information—Allows you to access certain public records (http://www.vitalrec.com).

Your college or university library may also have special collections of primary sources, particularly those related to the school, its surroundings, and famous people in the area.

☞ tip 3e

Primary Source Citations

There so many types of primary sources that it is often difficult to determine what publication information you need to gather. Part VI, "MLA and APA Documentation Systems," of this text covers quite a few primary sources you are mostly likely to come across in your research.

internet activity 3f Find Primary Sources

Visit a number of the sites for primary sources listed previously, and play with the search features to find sources relating to your issue. What kinds of material do your selected sites search? Historical? Literary? Legal? Business? Medical? What sites best meet your needs for your issue?

Hal decides to use several primary documents in his research project: (1) laws governing employees' rights to privacy; (2) a survey of employers completed by the American Management Association; and (3) interviews with both employees and supervisors at his company. He found several transcripts of court cases at the Electronic Frontier Foundation and one at Find Law, which covered the 2003 ruling against a Nationwide Insurance employee's complaint about invasion of his workplace privacy.

Find and Use Government Sources

These days it is very easy to find government-printed brochures and guides, copies of Senate and House reports, and bills. Don't be intimidated by the format of these documents. Most are searchable for keywords even though they can be tricky to cite. You can search for particular documents by title on any search engine, but visit the following sites to browse and conduct deeper searches.

- USA Government (http://www.usa.gov) is the U.S. Government's official website with access to consumer brochures, information on taxes, family care, and Internet security, among dozens of other categories. You can also find historical documents, statistics, maps, and links to various government agency libraries, including the Pentagon's.

- At the Library of Congress, Thomas (http://thomas.loc.gov) offers links to bills, the Congressional Record, treaties, and other government research.

- The Catalog of U.S. Government Publications (http://catalog.gpo.gov) provides access to and information about government publications. Many of the documents are online, but the search features are not easy to use. You'll need to follow its search tips for the best results.

- The White House website (http://www.whitehouse.gov) offers links to many primary sources as well.

- The U.S. National Archives website (http://www.archives.gov) houses 70 years worth of government documents including naturalization and war records.

Gathering publication information for government publications can be difficult. These documents are often written without a clear indication of author, title, publisher, or copyright date. Look for available clues, and give as much information as possible, including the URL and date accessed. In general, cite what you can find, in the order listed here. Not all government sources will have all of these items.

Source Information: Government Document

Name of government: _____

Name of agency: _____

Document title (underlined or italicized): _____

If applicable, number and session of Congress; type and number of publication: _____

Title of publication: _____

Name of editor or compiler of publication (first, middle initial, last):

_____

City of publication, publisher, date of publication: _____

Pertinent page numbers (if available): _____

Title of online collection (underlined or italicized): _____

Date of posting or most recent update (if available): _____

Name of project or reference database (underlined or italicized): _____

Name of sponsoring institution (e.g., Lib. of Congress): _____

Date of access and electronic address: _____

internet activity 3g Find Government Sources

Using the sites given above, perform keyword searches for government sources relating to your issue.

Find and Use Multimedia Sources

From audio transcripts of Barack Obama's inauguration speech, to videos of protestors in Iran, to podcast lectures of a professor at Stanford, to blogs of newspaper columnists, to the latest images of Mars craters, there is a host of valuable resources online that goes beyond print. Millions of viewers use YouTube to find serious lectures, music, and film clips, along with silly videos and instructional videos. Websites such as NPR and PBS have archives of video, and as of this printing, PBS is offering full-length episodes of some of its programs. Many libraries also subscribe to full-series PBS programs. The Library of Congress's (LOC) American Memory Project (http://memory. loc.gov/ammem/index.html) houses audio and video interviews with former slaves, documentary footage of Thomas Edison at work, and many other marvels of early film and recording technology.

The U.S. National Archives (http://www.archives.gov) just launched its own YouTube channel. Movies Found Online (http://www.makeuseof.com/dir/moviesfoundonline) offers access to free public-domain documentaries as does Truveo (http://www.truveo.com). Of course, news services such as BBC and CNN have live news feeds featuring breaking news around the world. FreeDocumentaries.org offers full viewing documentaries.

You will need to gather the following publication information for videos found on the Internet covering topics from slavery to animal activism.

Source Information: Video Clip

Author's last name, first name OR corporate/institutional author name, if available: _____

Title of document or file: _____

Document date OR date of last revision: _____

Medium (e.g., online video clip): _____

Title of larger website in which clip is located: _____

Name of hosting library or agency (if appropriate): _____

Access date: _____

URL: _____

In Chapter 12, "Enhance Your Argument with Visuals and Humor," you will learn about the power that visual images can add to your argument.

There are many repositories of photographs, drawings, artwork, and maps on the Internet. Be sure to document your images properly (see the discussion in Chapter 12 and Appendices A and B). Some wonderful sources of images are:

- Digital History (http://www.digitalhistory.uh.edu). A link to images is provided.
- Image searches at Google (http://images.google.com) and Yahoo! (http://images.search.yahoo.com). Try them both as they offer different advanced search options based on color, size, date, and so on.
- The Smithsonian Institute (http://photo2.si.edu).
- National Geographic Photography (http://photography.nationalgeographic .com).
- The New York Public Library Digital Gallery (http://digitalgallery.nypl. org/nypldigital/index.cfm).
- Pulitzer Prize winners for photography (http://www.pulitzer.org/bycat).

You will need to gather the following publication information for an image:

Source Information: Image

Artist name: _____

Title of the work: _____

Date it was created: _____

For artworks, include

Dimensions of the work: _____

Repository, museum, or owner: _____

City or country of origin: _____

Podcasts of all sorts are gaining space on the Internet. Podcast Alley (http://www.podcastalley.com) and the Podcast Bunker (http://www. podcastbunker.com) can help you find podcasts on dozens of topics from the arts, to politics, to the news, which you can download to your iPod or listen to on your computer. Some of the most reputable podcasts are those that come from syndicated shows such as *Face the Nation* and the news sites. You can subscribe to many podcast feeds as well. You can also perform a keyword search with your search engine as follows: inurl:podcast "your keyword." Hal tried this search with the keywords "workplace privacy" and found several podcasts covering the workplace privacy debates in California.

You will need to gather the following publication information for a podcast:

> ### Source Information: Podcast
> Name of author, host, or producer (if available): _____
> Title of podcast: _____
> Date of podcast: _____
> Podcast series: _____
> Title of podcast show (if different from title of podcast): _____
> Title of larger site (if available): _____
> Date of download: _____

Blogs are online journals that focus on any topic imaginable. Many news columnists have blogs affiliated with their news sites. For example, the *New York Times* has blogs covering Afghanistan, Pakistan, and Iraq reportage; the arts scene; business mergers and acquisitions; medical science; the latest technological trends; and photographic, visual, and multimedia reporting (http://www.nytimes.com/interactive/blogs/directory.html).

Although many blogs are useful and entertaining, you will need to be careful about what blog information you use in your argument. Do you care what the man on the street in Anchorage thinks about the cost of college tuition? You might, but whether you want to cite information from his blog will be determined by the scope of your argument.

You will need to gather the following publication information for a blog entry:

> ### Source Information: Blog Entry
> Author: _____
> Title of the entry: _____
> Title of the blog: _____
> Name of the blog host: _____
> Date: _____

internet activity 3h Find Multimedia Sources

Find images that will support your issue. Find audio and video links of speeches, press conferences, or breaking news. Finally, find a blog that discusses your issue. How reputable do these sources feel?

In Chapter 4, "Evaluate and Engage with Your Sources," you will learn how to evaluate Web content, but for now, base your response on how the host site is organized, how neutral the coverage of events are, how the words are or the speech is presented, or how the tone of the blog feels. Would you use these sources in your argument? Why or why not?

Find Books

It may seem odd that books are listed last in this chapter. It's not that we don't think books are important; it's just that, for most issues, your readers are looking for the most current, up-to-date information. It can take years from conception to printing to make a book available. An issue can change a lot in a few years. For very current issues, books may not be the way to go. For issues that have a history or that will always be on the table (child care, human and animal rights, some environmental issues, etc.), older books can still be useful in establishing a context or background for the reader. In this section, we will cover how to find books in brick-and-mortar libraries and in virtual libraries.

Find Books in Libraries

Most libraries have similar catalogs. You can search for books by title, author, or subject. Hal's next step is to look for books in his school's library. He will perform the same search in his local public library as well. Hal is looking for books that are fairly current.

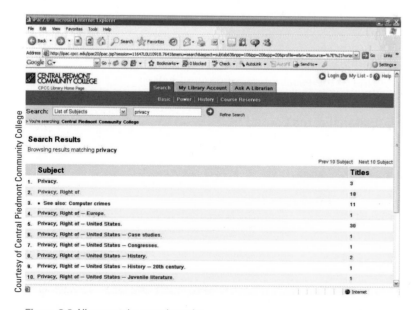

Figure 3.8 Library catalog search results

Hal decides to search by subject and types his search term "workplace pri-vacy" into the library catalogue. This term doesn't yield any results, so he tries the more general term "privacy" (see Figure 3.8). His library has 18 titles on the subject of the right of privacy, not so many that he needs to narrow his search further. He clicks on the subject "Privacy, Right of" and scans the titles for books that meet his criteria of being predominantly about privacy in the workplace and specifically about emails and Internet usage.

Hal finds a couple of sources, and depending on how much material he feels is useful in each one, he either photocopies the useful pages or checks out the book to review later.

You will need to gather the following publication information for books:

Source Information: Book

Author(s) or editor(s): _____

Title of the book (in italics): _____

City of publication: _____

Name of publisher: _____

Year published: _____

If you are using an essay from a book, collect the following publication information:

Source Information: Essay from Book

Author(s) of the essay: _____

Title of the essay (in quotation marks): _____

Title of the book (in italics): _____

Editor(s) of the book: _____

City of publication: _____

Name of publisher: _____

Year published: _____

Page numbers of essay: _____

---

your turn 3b ▶ **GET STARTED** Find Books in Libraries

Find two books on your topic. Make sure that they have been published within the past five years. Copy all information that you would need to find the book again, including the call number, which indicates where on the shelves to find the book.

Find Books on the Internet

Even large colleges may have limited library space. Students can find ebooks in the library catalog and have access to many databases with more current information that is frequently updated. The number of books available electronically is growing rapidly, which is great for libraries with space limitations. Library resources such as the Opposing Viewpoints Database allow readers to access chapters and essays from hundreds of titles covering every issue imaginable.

The Opposing Viewpoints Database houses a collection of articles, book chapters, and other types of documents organized by subject. The title is a bit misleading: The articles are wide ranging, not just pro-subject and con-subject. Your professors are not looking for you to find material supporting only your side and the opposing side; this structure implies that there are only two sides to each issue, which, of course, is nowhere near reality for most argumentative issues.

your turn 3c ▶ **GET STARTED** Find Books in the Opposing Viewpoints Database

Access your library's Opposing Viewpoints Database or any other database available to you to find books or book essays on your issue. Find as many viewpoints as possible.

Most libraries require a library card to access their **ebooks.** Ebooks are just like print books, except they can be searched and read online. Many times, you cannot copy from them, though, and must take notes manually.

Books can also be found on the Internet, the majority of these titles being out of copyright. Project Gutenberg (http://www.gutenberg.org/wiki/Main_Page) and ManyBooks.net (http://manybooks.net) offer thousands of books that can be downloaded or read online. The Internet Sacred Text Archive (http://www.sacred-texts.com) houses full-text books on every religion imaginable. For more recent scholarship, though, you can read significant chunks of some current titles at Google Books.

Research can seem daunting. There are so many resources available to us that this wealth of riches can seem more of a curse, and it is tempting to rely on Google and the first few hits that match our search terms. But take the extra time to go beyond the first page of search engine hits or Wikipedia entries. By searching for types of sources that you may not normally consider, such as blogs, documentaries, or news feeds, you will open your research up to paths that will provide you with many rewards.

Reflect and Apply

1. In what ways can you use encyclopedias and basic reference sources to help orient you to your issue and its parameters, vocabulary, and viewpoints?

2. Much of Chapter 3 is devoted to finding sources through Internet searches. How are you using primary sources to gain insight into different facets of your issue? What sources are you using to find secondary material that is academically acceptable?

3. How are you using your school's research databases? Are there databases that seem to be consistently useful in researching your issue?

4. How will you manage your materials as you find them? What organizational system are you using to efficiently track your notes from print sources?

5. How are you keeping track of bibliographic information as you find it? How are you managing image, video, and audio sources along with their publication information so you can access it all readily?

KEEPING IT LOCAL

Playing a game of solitaire on your computer during work?
Surfing the Net while answering voicemail?
Sending personal emails from your office?

ALL OF THESE activities can be monitored by your boss and can get you fired. Whether you work in a small local company or a sprawling national or even global firm, you need to know your rights as an employee. Not asking can get you in trouble. But performing better on your job requires work on your part as well, work that includes knowing where to look for answers. Knowing how to develop a research plan and how to find the sources you need to answer questions about your privacy rights and anything else that pertains to your employment is crucial to your job success. Books, journals, Internet sites, and libraries all have valuable information, if you know where and how to look for it.

● – – – – – – – – – – – ●

Research is at the heart of your argument. Your credibility and support rest on the thoroughness of your research strategies. Unlike some college skills, research is one skill that you will use in every part of your life: at school, at work, and even while addressing the needs of your community. What research sources will work for your needs? Can you use multimedia sources to help you address a problem at work? Will newspapers provide the support you need to solve a neighborhood dispute?

CHAPTER 4

Evaluate and Engage with Your Sources

This morning you sat down to read the newspaper while you ate breakfast. An article in the financial section about employees' rights caught your attention. The author of the article made some claims that didn't seem accurate to you. Later in the day, you tried to find sources that supported the author's claim but couldn't find anything. One database search uncovered several studies that seemed promising. As you began reading, however, you realized that one study used so much jargon that you couldn't understand it at all. Another report was 50 pages long. Although the title looked promising, you just didn't have time to read the entire report. Frustrated, you gave up.

COMMUNITY

School-Academic

Workplace

Family-Household

Neighborhood

Social-Cultural

Consumer

Concerned Citizen

TOPIC: Computer Usage

ISSUE: Privacy and Computer Use

AUDIENCE: Business Ethics Professor

CLAIM: Workplace electronic monitoring practices should be revealed to employees through company policies.

Chapter 3, "Develop a Research Plan," focused on introducing the various types of resources available to you and on how to find them. Chapter 4 will focus on how to evaluate and read the various types of resources. You will also learn how to incorporate information from those sources into your writing and how to cite them appropriately. For full information on creating a works cited page for your researched report or essay in MLA and APA formats, see Part VI, "MLA and APA Documentation Systems."

As you find materials, you will need to evaluate their accuracy and their usefulness for your argument.

In Chapter 4 you will learn to:

- Take notes, read critically, and evaluate Internet sites, articles, and books critically.
- Take notes and evaluate primary sources.
- Introduce sources and engage with them.
- Quote and cite quotations.
- Summarize and cite summaries.
- Paraphrase and cite paraphrases.
- Avoid plagiarism.

Take Notes, Read Critically, and Evaluate Internet Sites

In Chapter 3, "Develop a Research Plan," we followed Hal's research strategies as he found a wealth of information on electronic privacy in the workplace on the Internet. Finding material, though, is only the beginning. Now he must evaluate the sources and determine what he needs to use in his argument. Internet sources are easy to find but not always as easy to evaluate as print sources.

Hal's method of note-taking for Internet sources is a good one. He pastes the information he finds useful into a document he saves as "Workplace Privacy Notes." Hal is careful to keep track of information he copies verbatim so that he does not accidentally plagiarize it. His favorite method is to leave all verbatim sources in a different font color so that he does not forget that the material is not his original wording. He will keep all of the research he gathers from electronic sources in a folder he saves on his computer. He will also keep a folder for print sources that he photocopies and for newspaper clippings, brochures, and so on.

There are also online services that allow you to save links to web pages. Some of these tools even allow you to clip, highlight, and write comments on your clippings, gathering them all in one spot. There are many online organizational tools that can help you keep track of your research, for example, Zotero.org.

Figure 4.1 Critically reading content on the Internet is the first step you can take when determining credibility.

Seriousguy/Dreamstime.com

As he gathers electronic sources, Hal makes sure to comment on *why* he saved this material and *how* he thinks he may use it. Of course, how and why may change over the course of his research, but always determining the reason for keeping a source will keep him from gathering material that will not be of any use. Hal also remembers to copy any publication information that he will need later to document the sources he uses in his paper. As of the 7th edition, MLA documentation no longer requires the inclusion of a URL in a citation, but you should keep this information so that you can find the site again if necessary.

Critically Read Material on the Internet

Narrowing his search still left Hal with thousands of results, but the first one he looked at, "E-Mail Privacy in the Workplace," seemed promising. Now he had to decide not only if the information provided on the site was useful but also if it was **credible**. We all know that, along with the wonderfully useful information on the Web, there is also a lot of garbage. Reading critically will help you sort through it all. The first step Hal took when he accessed the site was to determine its credibility.

Hal asked himself a few questions about the article "E-Mail Privacy in the Workplace." The first step Hal took was to determine who sponsored the web page. By clicking on the "About" link, he found that the authors of the site are concerned with providing accurate information to those working in the security industry. They provide only articles that are well-researched so that decisions based on their material would meet current security laws. Hal felt that this site, although not geared toward employees of companies, had solid, trustworthy information about employees' rights to email privacy, so he marked the site for further reference.

When you are accessing unfamiliar websites, it is best to evaluate them using a series of questions like the ones below. Taking this precaution will ensure that you have credible material to use in your argument.

Evaluate Internet Sites

The following checklist provides some important questions you should ask about Internet sources before you use them.

Internet Evaluation Checklist

☐ **Author of Page/Site**

Who is the author of the page or source? Can you contact them or is there an "About Us" tab with author details? Is the author credible? Have they published other material on the topic or are they considered experts in their field?

☐ **Extreme Bias**

Chapter 5, "Read Critically and Avoid Fallacies," will discuss bias further, but ask if the bias exhibited in the web source exceeds what you feel comfortable with. In other words, is there evidence of racism, sexism, or extreme political or religious views?

☐ **Up to Date**

When was the site or source last updated? Are there links to the latest publications or sites?

☐ **Navigation**

Do all links to other sites work? Do images and files open quickly? Are there any dead links or dead ends in the site itself?

internet activity 4a **Evaluate Internet Sites**

Using the Internet Evaluation Checklist, evaluate one of the sources you found for Internet Activity 3d. Is it a credible source? Why or why not?

Take Notes, Read Critically, and Evaluate Articles

The Computer Age has made research worlds easier than it was even 20 years ago. Along with the advantages of researching and writing with computers are some disadvantages that can cause headaches. There are still many sources, particularly older ones, that are not accessible either through library databases or on the Internet. Let's address journal articles that you have accessed in print (paper) journals on the library shelves that you cannot find online or in your library's databases.

The better way to take notes is to photocopy the article you want, making sure that all the needed publication information is printed somewhere on the photocopied pages, and to write your notes directly on the article itself. Highlight those passages that you think are useful, writing notes in the margins about how to use this material or making note of questions you need to ask, words to look up, or other sources to gather. Keep these photocopies in a folder so that they will be available when you are ready to write the report.

So that's easy enough. You'd think, then, that taking notes on articles you have downloaded to your own computer would be even easier. After all, there is no retyping to do—you can use your computer's cut-and-paste function to copy material from the original article to your own document.

But there are several errors that writers can make during this process, some of them costly. To avoid errors while taking notes on computer documents, follow the steps in the following Careful Note-Taking Checklist.

◗ Careful Note-Taking Checklist

☐ Have you made sure to differentiate your own ideas from the ideas you have borrowed? When pasting material from the original source, remember to highlight this material in some way to indicate to yourself later that this material is not based on your own ideas or words. Some people, like Hal, type all their original ideas in a different color or font to separate them from the information borrowed from an article. Forgetting to give credit to borrowed material, whether intentionally or accidentally, will be viewed as **plagiarism**, cheating by using the work of others as your own. (See the tips for avoiding plagiarism at the end of this chapter.)

☐ Have you commented on your sources? Writers frequently paste information into their own document and then later have no idea what this information means or why they saved it. Always make comments on the copied material, discussing what its function will be in the argument and why it is important. For example, will it support your own claims or provide an illustration of an opposing viewpoint?

☐ Have you included documentation for all sources? Another costly error is neglecting to include documentation for where you retrieved the material. A simple note in parentheses as to the origin of the source will save you time tracking down a source later, and sometimes saves you from having to leave out a source because you cannot document it.

Read Articles Critically

Articles, whether accessed through an online database or elsewhere, are originally published in academic journals, magazines, or newspapers. Understanding the differences between the sources can help you better understand the articles they contain. Although magazines and journals share similarities, a journal differs from a magazine in several ways. Both types of periodicals can be directed toward a particular audience. For example, the 2012 issue of *IUP Journal of Chemistry* includes the article "Arsenic Removal from Potable Water Using Copolymer Resin-III Derived From P-Cresol." The article's abstract offers the following:

Copolymer was synthesized by condensation of p-Cresol (p-C) and Adipamide (A) with Formaldehyde (F) in the presence of 2M HCl as catalyst with 4:1:5 molar ratios of reacting monomers. Water is the most important constituent of our body. Thus, its quality should be good and perfect because it directly affects our health. Water pollution due to arsenic leaching is one of the biggest problems all over the world. Ion-exchange studies of this purified copolymer resin were carried out for As^{3+} ions. 'A' proved to be a selective chelating ion-exchange copolymer for certain metals. Chelating ion exchange properties of this copolymer were studied for As^{3+} ions. Batch equilibrium method was employed to study the selectivity of metal ion uptake involving the measurements of the distribution of a given metal ion between the polymer sample and a solution containing the metal ion. The study was carried out over a wide pH range and in media of various ionic strengths. The copolymer showed a higher selectivity for As^{3+} ions.

Compare the language from the technical journal to that used in a magazine aimed at the general reader in the article about arsenic in the drinking water, "Textile Dyeing Industry an Environmental Hazard," in the magazine *Natural Science*.

Color is the main attraction of any fabric. No matter how excellent its constitution, if unsuitably colored it is bound to be a failure as a commercial fabric. Manufacture and use of synthetic dyes for fabric dyeing has therefore become a massive industry today [. . .] Synthetic dyes have provided a wide range of colorfast, bright hues. However their toxic nature has become a cause of grave concern to environmentalists. Use of synthetic dyes has an adverse effect on all forms of life.

Rita Kant. "Textile Dyeing Industry an Environmental Hazard," Natural Science, Vol. 4, No. 1, 22–26 (2012).

You can easily see the difference—the *IUP Journal of Chemistry* article is more technical, using **jargon**, language that is used in a specific field and may be unfamiliar to those outside the field. Besides the language difference, journal articles are written by scholars or industry experts. The journals themselves are often peer reviewed, which means the articles are reviewed by other experts in the field before they are printed. Journals are also usually sponsored by a university or organization.

Magazines, on the other hand, are written for the everyday reader. Even someone with little familiarity with the topic of drinking water contamination would be able to read and understand the magazine article published in *Natural Science.* Less technical in nature, magazine articles are often written by freelance writers with little experience in the area about which they are writing. Your project may include information from both journal and magazine articles, depending on the assignment's requirements.

Finally, newspapers are usually produced daily. Those with online versions often provide updates during the day. They feature articles on crime and politics, along with human interest stories. Editorials and opinion pieces express the views of individuals, whereas the news stories themselves are mainly reportage of events.

None of these three types of periodicals are free of bias. **Bias** refers to the particular viewpoint or slant that an author or a publication leans toward. Bias is neither good nor bad, as readers can choose to read a publication or not depending on their own interests, beliefs, and values. A good researcher/writer understands that biases exist and is careful to select sources that are not bigoted, misleading, or downright false.

Reading Strategies for Longer Articles

A few reading strategies will make your time spent reading longer articles both more efficient and successful. At this stage, you are trying to quickly determine if an article is useful to you. Use the following questions to aid you in making that determination.

Initial Assessment Checklist

☐ Is there an **abstract**? An abstract is a brief overview of the author's argument, usually outlining the article's thesis and main points of support. Reading the abstract is no substitute for reading the full article, but the abstract will tell you at a glance if the article fits your needs.

☐ If no abstract exists, can you determine what the author's argument is? Although critical articles are longer than essays you may write, there still should be a clear beginning (with a thesis statement within the first one to three paragraphs), a body with supporting ideas, and a conclusion. Read the introduction and the conclusion for the main idea—in a critical article, the author's argument should be in one if not both places.

- [ ] Scan the article subheadings and any graphics (tables, charts, etc.). Being aware of how the author has organized the material into sections can help you both navigate and understand the article more easily. Tables and other graphic organizers can also help you understand the article's material.

- [ ] Is there a bibliography or footnotes? Although you should not necessarily reject an article that does not have a works cited page or a bibliography of further reading, the appearance of one is a bonus, as it gives additional avenues of research.

- [ ] Look up all words that keep you from understanding the article. Most journals are trade or field specific. They are not written for the general reader but for those already in the field; the vocabulary, therefore, can be a stumbling block. The language and vocabulary of a scholarly article may be unfamiliar to you, but the writing should not be so dense that you cannot read it at all. If you cannot comfortably read *most* of an article, then reject it in favor of an article that is easier to comprehend.

That may look like a lot of steps to take before you actually read an article, but following them will save you a great deal of time. After assessing your article, you will be able to determine if it is right for your purposes instead of reading 20 pages only to come to the same conclusion.

Using the Initial Assessment Checklist, the first step Hal takes when he is ready to review his journal articles is to look for an abstract. The article on email privacy does not have an abstract, so Hal continues to the second step and reads the introductory paragraphs and conclusion. At the end of the second paragraph, he finds the article's claim: "This article examines the employer/employee workplace privacy relationship, identifies the existing federal and state law governing workplace privacy, and discusses the rapidly developing monitoring software market."

Hal's next step is to scan the article subheadings and any graphics (tables, charts, etc.). At the end of the article is a list of references and a brief biography of the author, including contact information. The inclusion of references and author contact information is reassuring to Hal as is the easy-to-read format and language of the article. This one is a keeper. Hal decides that this article is worth reading and adds its publication information to his bibliography file.

But where do you find the elements to help you assess a journal article? Pages 87–88 include examples of these elements—Abstract, Key Words, Conclusion, and Works Cited—from an article in a humanities journal. The annotations in the margins identify key parts.

The Carnivalesque in Nathaniel Hawthorne's *The Scarlet Letter*

by Hossein Pirnajmuddin and Omid Amani

ABSTRACT: This study sets to examine the applicability of Bakhtin's theory of the carnivalesque to Nathaniel Hawthorne's *The Scarlet Letter*.

Abstracts are useful for identifying the central claim of the author's argument and often provide an explanation of how the claim is going to be supported. They can also set the context for the claim.

Along with the abstract, some journals require a list of keywords. Pay attention to these keywords as they not only help you grasp the scope of the article, but can help you when you are performing your own searches.

The conclusion of most arguments in the humanities often restates the initial claim.

The canonical novel of the American literature published in the middle of the nineteenth century portrays the genesis of the American Puritan culture, while the polyphonic nature of the novel, it is argued, exposes the rifts of and the grotesqueness of this culture.

Key Words: Nathaniel Hawthorne, *The Scarlet Letter*, Bakhtin, Carnivalesque, Polyphony, Heteroglossia, Grotesque

Conclusion

Nathaniel Hawthorne's *The Scarlet Letter* deftly addresses the Puritan culture of the seventeenth-century America as, to use Bakhtin's terms, a "monological culture." Hawthorne's novel is, among other things, the fact that laughter and the spirit of carnival cannot be totally repressed even in the most ideological and monological cultures. Although the writer apparently creates a Romantic grotesque, that is, one of dark, gloomy monstrosities, to intimate the distorted nature of the society he portrays, the implication is that the Bakhtinian conception of the grotesque, one associated with "light" (Bakhtin, *Rabelais and His World* 41), with the carnivalesque, capable of subverting the rule of 'darkness,' 'decrowning' it, is in the background too.

A works cited, references, or bibliography can provide additional sources, and depending on the format of the source, even links to other materials that can help you write your argument.

Works Cited

Adamson, Joseph. "Guardian of the 'Inmost Me': Hawthorne and Shame." *Scenes of Shame: Psychoanalysis, Shame, and Writing.* Eds. Joseph Adamson and Hilary Clark. New York: State U of New York P, 1999. 53–82.

Arac, Jonathan. "Hawthorne and the Aesthetics of American Romance." *The Cambridge History of The American Novel.* Eds. Leonard Cassuto and Clare Virginia Eby and Benjamin Reiss. Cambridge: Cambridge UP, 2011. 135–150.

your turn 4a   ## Conduct an Initial Assessment of Your Articles

Using the Initial Assessment checklist, find a source and determine if it is right for your argument. Which of the steps helped you make a decision?

The next set of questions will help you make sense of articles you have determined will be useful. You need to be able to find the author's main argument(s) and the examples being used to support the argument(s). You should also be able to determine the article's strengths and weaknesses. Use these steps to find the main ideas and examples.

Reading Checklist

☐ Look for the main idea. If the thesis cannot be found on the first page, write the main idea at the top of your photocopied or saved article for easy reference. (If you do find the thesis on the first page, simply highlight it.)

☐ What evidence is the author offering to support his or her argument(s)? If an article is very long, there may be subsections, titled or not, that indicate movement from one example (or argument, if the author has more than one) to another. Look for these. Skim quickly, reading only the first and last sentences of each paragraph as you look for ideas and arguments. When you find something particularly useful, read the entire paragraph to make sure you are not reading anything out of context.

☐ Make notes throughout. Highlighting a passage is great, but if there are no comments made next to the passage, chances are good that, when you are ready to write your paper, you may not remember what struck you as important when you highlighted it.

☐ What are the article's strengths and weaknesses? Skim through several articles, reading the bibliographies and noting which sources are mentioned frequently. These are the sources you should definitely read. They will serve as touchstones by which to gauge the arguments of the articles you've selected. This is not to say that all of your articles need to agree with your touchstone articles. However, the touchstone articles will give you some idea of the general trends of thought concerning a topic, and they will allow you to judge if your selected article is too far off base to be reasonably considered.

☐ Come to a conclusion about the author's arguments. Do you agree or disagree? Do you see how the article can be used in any part of your own essay? Do you agree wholeheartedly and therefore can use the article as support for your own thesis? Do you disagree and want to use the article as an argument you wish to rebut (destroy)? Is the author's idea useful but limited? Maybe the author doesn't take an idea as far as you would like to take it?

your turn 4b ▶ **Read the Articles You've Selected**

Using the Reading Checklist, skim quickly through the article you evaluated from Your Turn 4a, or if that article did not work, select a new one. What is the author's claim? What support is provided by the article? What are the article's strengths and weaknesses? What is your final opinion of the article? Is it one you can use effectively in your argument? Why or why not?

Evaluate Articles

Before you add information from that article to your argument, make sure that you have determined that it is credible. Is your source actually an essay from a college student? A graduate student may have written a solid researched argument on homelessness, but your professor is undoubtedly looking for material that is more expert in scope. Research the author of the article, whether it is in a magazine, a website, or a scholarly journal. Answer the following questions before using any article:

◗ Article Credibility Checklist

- ☐ Who is the author? Conduct a quick Internet search to determine if the author has published anything else on the topic. With whom is the author affiliated (an academic institution, or an industrial or business institution, for example)? Is there any scandal surrounding the author's integrity that may throw suspicion on his or her work?
- ☐ What is the reputation of the venue (periodical or site) in which the article is published?
- ☐ How current or reputable is the information cited in the article? A bibliography is not always necessary, particularly if original research is being conducted, but it helps to see what sources the author uses to support his or her argument.

Take Notes and Read Books Critically

So now, like Hal, you've completed your review of the library's catalog and you've got a long list of books you think may be useful in your research project. You gather them and set them all out on a table in front of you. Now what? Well, what you shouldn't do is take them all home with you. Do a cursory inspection of their tables of contents and their indexes; read a bit of the authors' prefaces or introductions. Make sure that you are not aggravating your tennis elbow unnecessarily by lugging 15 pounds of books to your car. Select books that seem promising. Are there any chapters or essays specifically on your topic, or at least near enough? Do your search terms appear in the index? Is the book's age appropriate? For some projects, older books may be fine, but for others more current material is preferable. Once you've made your selection, save yourself a great deal of time by using the FLOI method, discussed next.

The **FLOI method** will help you investigate books in a consistent manner and will save you time.

First: Read the author's introduction or preface. Read the first chapter looking for a thesis or a main argument.

Last: Read the final chapter to find out the author's conclusion and to make sure it is summarizing what you thought was going to be proven.

Outside: Look at those materials that are outside the text. The table of contents and the index will direct you to supporting examples and illustrations of the book's thesis. The dust jacket can be very helpful, providing a brief overview of the author's intent. Skim through any maps, appendices, glossaries, tables, or charts.

Inside: At this point, you can take one of two steps. If you have plenty of time, or the book appears to warrant it, you can read the entire book. Most of the time, however, it will suffice for you to skim the text carefully, looking for words and phrases that pop out—you'll notice that the things that catch your attention are the good examples, things that are interesting to you that you can use in your report.

your turn 4c **GET STARTED Use the FLOI Method to Skim a Book**

Use one of the books you found for Your Turn 3b, and skim it using the FLOI method.

1. First: Skim the preface and any other introductory material, and record the author's claim or main point.
2. Last: Read the last chapter. How does the author conclude the argument? Are you surprised by the conclusion? Is it what you thought it would be based on the preface?
3. Outside: Skim through the table of contents and the index. List any of your search terms or additional topics of interest that are covered. Flip through the book looking for graphs, charts, or illustrations. Are they clear and easy to understand? Do they offer any insights into your topic?
4. Inside: Does the book warrant your time reading it, will skimming suffice, or is the book not a good match for your subject?

Take Notes and Evaluate Primary Sources

Hal gathered a large number of primary sources, including interviews, documentaries, acts, and laws. Before he uses any of them, he asks himself a series of questions to determine who produced the source, why, for what audience, and under what circumstances.

▶ **Primary Sources Checklist**

- ☐ Who created the source and why? Was it created through a spur-of-the-moment act, a routine transaction, or a thoughtful, deliberate process?
- ☐ Did the recorder have firsthand knowledge of the event? Or did the recorder report what others saw and heard?
- ☐ Was the recorder a neutral party, or did the creator have opinions or interests that might have influenced what was recorded?
- ☐ Did the recorder produce the source for personal use, for one or more individuals, or for a large audience?
- ☐ Was the source meant to be public or private?
- ☐ Did the recorder wish to inform or persuade others? (Check the words in the source. The words may tell you whether the recorder was trying to be objective or persuasive.)
- ☐ Did the recorder have reasons to be honest or dishonest?
- ☐ Was the information recorded during the event, immediately after the event, or after some lapse of time? How large a lapse of time?

Source: Questions for Analyzing Primary Sources, Library of Congress http://lcweb2.loc.gov/learn/lessons/psources/studqsts.html

internet activity 4b Evaluate Primary Sources

Select one primary source you gathered in Internet Activity 3f. Answer the eight questions above about your source to determine its credibility.

Introduce and Comment on Sources

One of the more difficult aspects of writing any sort of research report is smoothly incorporating your own ideas on a subject with ideas you've gathered from other sources, such as newspaper articles, books, a television documentary, or a web page. It's very important to be clear about what material in your report is yours and what comes from an outside source. You must make sure that any ideas you use, whether you are quoting a source verbatim or paraphrasing, are attributed to their original author.

Three steps should be followed when using source material, either quoted or paraphrased:

1. Introduce the source, also known as *source attribution*.
2. Provide the source.
3. Cite the source.

It is often best to introduce the author of your source material, especially if you are paraphrasing and likely to confuse source material with your own original ideas. The phrases used to introduce sources are called **attributive phrases or statements**. An attributive statement tells the reader who is being cited. It may indicate the author's name and credentials, the title of the source, and/or any helpful background information. Here are some examples of attributive words:

accepts	considers	explains	rejects	acknowledges
affirms	argues	asserts	contradicts	adds
contrasts	criticizes	declares	interprets	shows
defends	lists	states	believes	denies
maintains	stresses	cautions	describes	outlines
suggests	claims	disagrees	points out	supports
compares	discusses	praises	concludes	emphasizes
proposes	verifies	confirms	enumerates	confutes

The first time you introduce a source, you should provide the first and last name of the author you are citing. It is also helpful to give the author's credentials.

> David Solomon, the leading critic of Ira Levin's novels, argues . . .

> In *Rosemary's Offspring*, David Solomon's recent book of essays on Levin's novels, he explains . . .

In subsequent references to the author, you may just use the last name.

> Solomon defends . . .

If there is no author, you should introduce the source by a title.

> According to the USDA website, nutrition . .

> The article in the *New York Times*, "Fowl Play on Chicken Farms," states . . .

Never include website addresses within the text of the paper; these will appear in the works cited page.

your turn 4d ▸ PRACTICE Introduce Sources

Select three passages from this excerpt from "Notification, an Important Safeguard against the Improper Use of Surveillance" by F. Boehm and P. de Hert. Introduce the sources properly, using the list of attributive words or other words or phrases.

1. Introduction

The surveillance of individuals and the resulting collection of information are regarded by the security community as an effective tool to locate terrorists and other criminals. In addition to the establishment of crime-fighting databases, the travel behaviour of citizens is recorded, and telecommunication and internet data are required to be retained for possible use in investigations. Databases and information systems containing such data exist at both national and EU levels. Personal data are increasingly collected, analyzed and interlinked. This article examines the importance of the right of citizens to be informed that their data has been collected, or that they have been the subject of surveillance, by reference to current laws. It first provides a brief overview of the increasing surveillance measures at EU level, then analyzes the current notification requirements existing in the EU, and discusses the right of notification in the framework of the Council of Europe and the case-law of the ECtHR. With the proposed changes to EU data protection law in mind, an overview of potential future regulation in this field is then essayed.

2. Increased surveillance at EU level

Before discussing existing and potential notification rules, a brief impression of the current databases and systems of surveillance within the EU is instructive. Post 9/11 policy concepts, such as proposed in the Hague and the Stockholm programme led to an increase of systems developed to control various parts of our daily life. Surveillance thereby takes place at different levels: On the initiative of the EU, Member States implement the data retention directive to reinforce their police and secret service activities. At EU-level, so called anti-terrorism measures are increasingly often initiated: travellers are comprehensively checked when they enter EU territory and EU databases and information systems serving multiple purposes are installed to collect and analyze information (see further, Boehm 2012). In addition to databases serving police purposes (the Europol Information System) (EIS), the Schengen Information System (SIS) and the Customs Information System (CIS), databases initially installed to facilitate border control such as the Visa Information System (VIS) and Eurodac are increasingly used for surveillance purposes. In fact, almost all existing databases have multiple functionalities. The SIS for instance is a database in the framework of law enforcement and immigration control and collects data of third state and EU nationals. The CIS serves customs control purposes but also contains personal data of individuals suspected of illicit trafficking activities. The VIS serves the purpose of the exchange of visa data and entails information of third state nationals who apply for a visa to enter the EU. Plans to give law enforcement access to the VIS are under consideration. Eurodac stores fingerprint data of asylum seekers and should prevent that asylum seekers make multiple asylum applications in different Member States of the EU. The EIS and Eurojust's database entail data of criminals, but also of suspects, victims and witnesses. Frontex is the EU's border agency and collects data of third state nationals trying to pass the external borders.

The rise of techniques and databases developed in recent years touches therefore on different aspects of the daily life of citizens. Not only traditional criminals are targeted by such measurers, but also individuals not suspected of having committed a crime. A shift towards the preventive entry of citizens in databases serving police but also other purposes can be observed. The rights of individuals affected by such measures do not always keep up with this fast developing field of different surveillance techniques (Van Brakel & De Hert 2011).

Source: Boehm, F., and P. de Hert. "Notification, an Important Safeguard against the Improper Use of Surveillance - Finally Recognized in Case Law and EU Law." *European Journal of Law and Technology* 3.3 (2012).

Quote and Cite Quotations

When you use an author's exact words in your own writing, you are **quoting**. There are certain rules to follow to properly introduce, quote, and cite the material you take directly from a source.

First, you want to use direct quotes very sparingly—it is almost always better to put original material into your own words (see paraphrasing below). Occasionally, though, a quote is the way to go. Save quotations for those times when there is no better way to say things, or for when you are citing laws, definitions, or comments that are best quoted in full to avoid confusion or misrepresentation.

Let's use the following excerpt from an Internet source as an example. The highlighted text is what Hal wants to use in his paper on privacy in the workplace.

Employee Monitoring: Is There Privacy in the Workplace?

Employers want to be sure their employees are doing a good job, but employees don't want their every sneeze or trip to the water cooler logged. That's the essential conflict of workplace monitoring.

A 2007 survey by the American Management Association and the ePolicy Institute found that two-thirds of employers monitor their employees' web site visits in order to prevent inappropriate surfing. And 65% use software to block connections to web sites deemed off limits for employees. This is a 27% increase since 2001 when the survey was first conducted.

Source: "Fact Sheet 7: Workplace Privacy." Privacy Rights Clearinghouse. January 2013. Retrieved February 25, 2013, from http://www.privacyrights.org/fs/fs7-work.htm

The paragraph that includes the desired material has survey results for employer monitoring. Hal wants to use just the first item and decides to quote it directly. Here is that highlighted information included in a paragraph as a direct quote.

DIRECT QUOTE[1]

In 2007, the American Management Association and the ePolicy Institute conducted a survey on the use of monitoring practices of employers. The survey found that "two-thirds of employers monitor their employees' web site visits in order to prevent inappropriate surfing" ("Fact Sheet 7"). These results seem extremely high and indicate the widespread use of monitoring software used in the workplace.

Hal does not have an author to introduce. Notice how he instead introduces the quote by indicating that a survey was conducted by the American Management Association and the ePolicy Institute. He leads into the quote with the attributive "the survey found." Then he begins his quote with the words "two-thirds" and ends where the original sentence ends. Note that the quotation marks only surround the quoted material, not the citation information in parentheses (highlighted).

After the quote, Hal comments on the information, helping the reader to understand the importance of the quoted material to his argument. Never just drop a quote into a paragraph without any explanation. Provide commentary that explains the cited material. Does it provide an illustration of a point you've made? Does the quote represent confirmation of or disagreement with a point you've made?

When you use an outside source, either as a direct quotation or as a paraphrase, you need to provide readers with information that tells them the origin of that source. This is done both internally and in a reference list at the end of the paper. This reference list is usually called a **works cited page** and includes only those sources you have actually used in your report. To cite the quote Hal used from the Internet source above, he will have to put in parentheses at the end of the quoted material where that information can be found. This information should be the same as it appears on the works cited page. A longer title may be abbreviated as Hal has done here. See the following sample works cited page; the source in question is highlighted.

---

[1] These examples are in MLA format; both an MLA and an APA formatting guide is found in Part VI, "MLA and APA Documentation Systems," of this text.

Works Cited

18 USC Chapter 119—Wire and Electronic Communications Interception and Interception of Oral Communications. Legal Information Institute. 2013. Web. 25 Feb. 2013.

"Fact Sheet 7: Workplace Privacy." Privacy Rights Clearinghouse. January 2013. Web. 25 Feb. 2013.

Lazar, Wendi S., and Lauren E. Schwartzreich. "Limitations to Workplace Privacy: Electronic Investigations and Monitoring." *Computer & Internet Lawyer* 29.1 (2012): 1–16. *Business Source Complete.* Web. 26 Feb. 2013.

Taylor, Raymond E. "A Cross-Cultural View Towards the Ethical Dimensions of Electronic Monitoring of Employees: Does Gender Make a Difference?" *International Business & Economics Research Journal* 11.5 (2012): 529–534. *Business Source Complete.* Web. 26 Feb. 2013.

In the citation, then, Hal should include as much information as the reader needs to be directed to the source on the works cited page:

> The survey found that "two-thirds of employers monitor their employees' web site visits in order to prevent inappropriate surfing" ("Fact Sheet 7").

Because this source does not have an author, it is alphabetized on the works cited page by the first word of its title: Fact. When you provide article titles in parentheses, as done here, you may shorten lengthy titles to the first few words.

There is no page number included in our example because the source is from a website. If there are page numbers (from a book, print copy of a periodical, or from a document in PDF format), then the page number(s) from which the cited material comes is included; for example, (Lazar and Schwartzreich 9).

Notice that the quotation mark ends after the last word in the quote. The citation is considered part of the sentence, and the period comes after the parentheses.

The excerpt in Figure 4.2 is from the third item on Hal's works cited page (the Lazar and Schwartzreich article) and includes page numbers.

If authors are introduced in the attribution, their names do not need to be repeated in the parenthetical citation; only the page numbers are necessary, if there are any.

> In a study of workplace privacy conducted by Wendi S. Lazar and Lauren E. Schwartzreich, the authors found that the courts must be able to "balance a business's need to protect data and proprietary information against individual rights and freedoms" (9).

Hal introduced the authors in the preceding example, so he only included the page number of the quoted material in the parenthetical citation. Notice, too, that the authors' first and last names in the body of the paragraph are in the normal order—reverse the order of the first author's name only in the works cited page for alphabetization purposes.

Privacy

false light invasion of privacy (*e.g.*, for online misrepresentations about employees, such as statements made by managers on social networking sites like LinkedIn),[115] intrusion of seclusion,[116] or tort claims arising out of workplace cyberstalking.[117] It may also be possible to bring a tortious interference with contract claim against an employer that requires an employee to authorize employer access to a social networking site profile by claiming that this act violates a service agreement or that doing so violates public policy concerns.[118]

International Trends in Workplace Privacy Protections

Unlike the United States, many countries have had strong privacy policies in place since World War II, in both the public and private workplace. In fact, in many countries such as Chile, France, and Mexico, the right to privacy in regard to emails in the workplace is an unwaivable right.[119] In most European Union (EU) countries this was a direct reaction to the holocaust and widespread civilian collusion with the Nazi regime.[120] In certain Asian countries and in parts of South America, data privacy and other individual privacy rights in the workplace are protected by statute and in some countries they are constitutional rights.[121] In the global workplace, however, all of these countries, much like the United States, share an increased sense of urgency in dealing with the technological revolution in the workplace and its resulting lack of employee privacy.

Specifically, in many European countries, monitoring, gaining access to employees' computers, and video surveillance are void *ab initio* or circumscribed by statute.[122] In 2007, the European Court of Human Rights held, under Article 8 of the European Convention on Human Rights, that employee email messages are protected communications.[123] More recently, the EU released a plan to revise European data protection rules based on the Commission's position that an individual's ability to control his or her information, have access to the information, and modify or delete the information are "essential rights that have to be guaranteed in today's digital world."[124] Increasingly, individual EU nations are poised to enact more stringent privacy laws. For instance, Finland recently introduced a statute expanding employee privacy rights,[125] and Sweden is expected to follow suit.[126] Within the last year, Germany (a country that instituted strong data privacy and anti-monitoring laws after the holocaust) also approved a draft law amending its Federal Data Protection Act, which prohibits employers from disciplining employees for their private online activities, to provide even broader protections.[127]

Even outside the EU, other countries continue this trend toward protecting employee privacy rights. In the Middle East, the Israeli National Labour Court issued a decision in February 2011 that severely limits the extent to which employers can monitor their employees' emails. According to the opinion, employers must now create an understandable policy for employee use of communications systems at the workplace. This policy must be clearly communicated to all employees, and must be written into their contracts.[128]

Conclusion

The changing forms of technology and their vast access to information will undoubtedly continue to dictate operational realities and expectations of privacy in the workplace. The challenge for courts is that they must continuously monitor these changes and balance a business's need to protect data and proprietary information against individual rights and freedoms. In the wake of *City of Ontario v. Quon*, and facing the risk of sacrificing overbroad constitutional rights, courts may consider the societal role of the particular electronic communication at issue and refrain from issuing rulings based solely on the language of a standardized privacy policy. In *Quon*, the Supreme Court recognized the increasing importance of technology in workers' lives, noting that "[c]ell phone and text message communications are so pervasive that some persons may consider them to be essential means or necessary instruments for self-expression, even self identification."[129] As the Court explained, the more pervasive and essential or necessary an electronic tool becomes for an individual's self-expression or identification, the "[stronger] case for an expectation of privacy."[130] As new technologies become the norm of everyday life and employees' private lives intertwine with their work lives, the law will have to respond accordingly with safeguards that prevent employers from abusing and interfering with their employees' everyday communications and recognize that workplace privacy is a value worth protecting.

Notes

1. Social media sites are "a popular distribution outlet for users looking to share their experiences and interests on the Web," which "host substantial amounts of user-contributed materials (*e.g.*, photographs, videos, and textual content) for a wide variety of real-world events of different type and scale." Hila Becker, Mor Naaman, & Luis Gravano, "Learning Similarity Metrics for Event Identification in Social Media," Proceedings of the third ACM international conference on Web search and data mining, WSDM '10, 291–300. This umbrella term encompasses social networking sites such as Facebook, LinkedIn and MySpace, and microblogging information networks, such as Twitter. *See* Lisa Thomas, Comment," Social Networking in

Figure 4.2 Source material from a PDF article including page number

> A study of workplace privacy found that the courts must be able to "balance a business's need to protect data and proprietary information against individual rights and freedoms" (Lazar and Schwartzreich 9).

In this second example, Hal needs to include the authors' names in the parenthetical citation because they do not appear in the introduction to the quote.

Quoting Material Quoted in the Original Source

Occasionally you will want to quote material that your source itself is quoting (see Figure 4.3).

In this excerpt from the Schatt article, an item is quoted from a source in which the author was quoting another source. To use quoted material, you do not need to track down the original source. (Note that in the parenthetical documentation in Figure 4.3 there is an author's last name, year, and page. The article's authors are using APA style, which is covered in full in Part

Motivation is the foundation for human achievement. A psychological construct, "motivation is considered both a catalyst for learning and an outcome of learning" (Hurley, 1993, p. 17). Without motivation little can be achieved, but with the appropriate inspiration, substantial growth may occur. A study by Cattel, Barton, and Dielman (1972) noted that nearly 25% of student achievement might be attributed to motivational elements. Asmus (1994) suggested that estimates of student achievement that were due to motivation ranged from 11 to 27 percent in the literature. Experienced educators may believe that this percentage is even higher yet.

"Achievement Motivation and the Adolescent Musician: A Synthesis of the Literature." Research & Issues in Music Education 9.1 (Sept 2011).

Figure 4.3 Quoted material in original source

VI. In MLA, you would use the author's last name and a page number, with no comma separating them.) You need only indicate that the material you are using is a quote from another source:

> There are several definitions of motivation that have to do with learn-ing and music: "Motivation is considered both a catalyst for learning and an outcome for learning" (Hurley qtd. in Schatt 4).

"Qtd." is the abbreviation for "quoted." The use of it here indicates to the reader that, although the quoted material appeared in the Schatt article, this author got that information from Hurley.

Alter Quoted Material

Here is an example of quoting a quote, where the original material was altered slightly to fit the sentence into which it is to be inserted.

> The court explained: "If [an employee] had left a key to his house on the front desk at [his workplace], one could not reasonably argue that he was giving consent to whoever found the key, to use it to enter his house and rummage through his belongings. ..."

In the original material that Lazar and Schwartzreich cited, the material in the brackets [ ] was in the plural form—"employees" and "their workplaces." The authors needed these terms to be in the singular form to fit the rest of their paragraph. It is acceptable to alter quoted material so that it fits grammatically with your sentence as long as you indicate changes by using the brackets. If you remove material, you would use an ellipsis where words are missing.

your turn 4e ▶ PRACTICE Quote a Source

Use the first page of Wendi Lazar and Lauren Schwartzreich's "Limitations to Workplace Privacy: Electronic Investigations and Monitoring" to write a paragraph on workplace privacy. Incorporate two quotations from the article in your paragraph, making sure (1) to introduce the quote, (2) to quote the original using quotation marks, and (3) to include a parentheti-cal citation. The passage below is from page 1 of the article.

As cell phones, the Internet, and social media continue to define personal and professional communication, federal and state laws are redefining and, in many ways, broadening the concept of workplace privacy. For years, employers in the private sector paid little attention to concerns over workplace privacy, as few laws prevented employers from monitoring employees and employees had greater control over their personal communications. As technology developed, however, employers quickly obtained resources to conduct sophisticated searches of employees' or prospective employees' backgrounds, to monitor employees in and outside the workplace, and to track and access employees' Internet usage. Most recently, employers have begun to demand access to employees' personal communications through third-party service providers, such as wireless cell phone providers and social networking sites.

Over the last decade, courts and legislatures have responded to these developments by applying existing laws in ways that protect employees' privacy rights and enacting new laws to provide a remedial effect. Nevertheless, private sector employees continue to face many challenges to their workplace privacy.

Source: Lazar, Wendi S., and Lauren E. Schwartzreich. "Limitations To Workplace Privacy: Electronic Investigations And Monitoring." *Computer & Internet Lawyer* 29.1 (2012): 1–16. *Business Source Complete.* Web. 26 Feb. 2013.

Summarize and Cite Summaries

Sometimes you will want to summarize the contents of an article, its main ideas or arguments. In summarizing, you do not need to explain secondary ideas, details, or tangents. It sounds easy, but it takes skill to summarize effectively. Follow these guidelines when you need to summarize the contents of a source.

Summary Checklist

- ☐ Provide the title of the source and the author, if available.
- ☐ In your own words, explain the source's thesis (i.e., claim or main idea) in one sentence.
- ☐ Make sure that you are not using any phrases from the original; if you decide to use a phrase, maybe a special term the author has created, put that phrase in quotation marks.
- ☐ Answer as many of these questions as are relevant: who, what, where, when, how, and why.

☐ Do not include any opinions or first-person commentary.

☐ Do not include details or examples.

You will introduce your summary as you would any other source, by author or title.

Paraphrase and Cite Paraphrases

It is tempting to use only quotations in your writing as it is easier to avoid plagiarizing. After all, you only have to put quotation marks around the borrowed material and put any additional information in the parenthetical citation and you're finished. But a collection of quotes does not make a research paper. You are being asked to incorporate your research with your own ideas, and this involves reading and digesting your sources and connecting ideas into a cohesive argument. This can best be accomplished with paraphrasing: putting source material into your own words. Let's look back at Hal's source on employee monitoring again.

Employee Monitoring: Is There Privacy in the Workplace?

Employers want to be sure their employees are doing a good job, but employees don't want their every sneeze or trip to the water cooler logged. That's the essential conflict of workplace monitoring.

A 2007 survey by the American Management Association and the ePolicy Institute found that two-thirds of employers monitor their employees' web site visits in order to prevent inappropriate surfing. And 65% use software to block connections to web sites deemed off limits for employees. This is a 27% increase since 2001 when the survey was first conducted. Employers are concerned about employees visiting adult sites with sexual content, as well as games, social networking, entertainment, shopping and auctions, sports, and external blogs. Of the 43% of companies that monitor e-mail, nearly three-fourths use technology to automatically monitor e-mail. And 28% of employers have fired workers for e-mail misuse.

Here was how Hal quoted material from that source:

In 2007, the American Management Association and the ePolicy Institute conducted a survey on the use of monitoring practices of employers. The survey found that "two-thirds of employers monitor their employees' web site visits in order to prevent inappropriate surfing" ("Fact Sheet 7"). These results seem extremely high and indicate the widespread use of monitoring software used in the workplace.

Taylor, Raymond E. "A Cross-Cultural View Towards the Ethical Dimensions of Electronic Monitoring of Employees: Does Gender Make a Difference?" *International Business & Economics Research Journal,* May 2012.

Hal also could have incorporated the same material by putting it into his own words, as shown in the following example.

> In 2007, a survey was conducted by the American Management Association on the use of monitoring practices of employers. The survey found that a large percentage of employers, 66%, keep a watch on how often and where employees go online ("Fact Sheet 7"). These results seem extremely high and indicate the widespread use of monitoring software used in the workplace.

This is called **paraphrasing**. As you can see, the paraphrase is very different from the wording of the original, yet it conveys the same meaning. You can still tell the difference between Hal's words and the words of the source. Even though Hal may put the survey information in his own words, the ideas have been borrowed from a source—they are not his—and he must provide a citation to that source material in the same way as if it were quoted.

Hal avoids plagiarism by carefully paraphrasing material from the article "A Cross-Cultural View Towards the Ethical Dimensions of Electronic Monitoring of Employees: Does Gender Make a Difference?" published in the May 2012 issue of *International Business & Economics Research Journal*. Hal's first task was to decide what parts of this article he could use as source material. He came up with three items he wanted to use:

1. A summary of the author's argument
2. A paraphrase of the criticisms of electronic monitoring
3. A quote from one of the author's research questions

After Hal reads "A Cross-Cultural View," he decides he wants to offer a summary of the main points of the article. For our purposes, a passage from the article's introduction is provided here, in which the author states the purpose of his article:

> *In developing partnerships between Chinese and foreign companies, it is important to be sensitive to the mindsets of both parties, especially when merging organizational policies. With this in mind, this article presents the results of a study examining the attitudes of Taiwanese and American study participants regarding the ethics of electronically monitoring employees. (page 529)*

Hal's summary of the article may appear in his paper in this way:

> "A Cross-Cultural View" offers a good overview of some of the issues involved in electronic monitoring in the workplace in Taiwan. Raymond E. Taylor feels that to establish sound partnerships with Taiwanese businesses, the different attitudes of the Taiwanese and Americans need to be examined. To understand ...

> Business executives have always monitored their employees' behavior. Electronic monitoring may be especially useful in training and improving productivity (Blylinsky, 1991, and Laabs, 1992). However, critics of electronic monitoring suggest that the more obtrusive forms of electronic monitoring can lead to elevated levels of stress, decreased job satisfaction and quality of work, decreased levels of customer service and poor quality (Kallman, 1993). Electronic monitoring, by imposing excess control over employees' behavior, can alienate employees and develop a feeling of working in a modern "sweatshop" (Kidwell and Bennett, 1994). Employers have the legal right to electronically monitor their employees (Kelly, 2001). The question is not whether or not employers can electronically monitor their employees, but rather "how should it be done?"

The Clute Institute

Figure 4.4 Passage from "A Cross-Cultural View"

Notice that Hal summarizes the article's main ideas, or at least those that are relevant to his essay (the ethics of electronic monitoring). Use only what you need from a source. Too often writers include information that is not needed, cluttering a paper and diluting its strength with unneeded material. Also note that Hal did not cite any page numbers. This is because he is not citing anything specific from the article; he is only summarizing the article's contents. He does, however, mention the authors' names and the title of the article.

Next, Hal is interested in the passage in Figure 4.4. The article offers many criticisms of electronic monitoring, and he is interested in discussing a few of these. In doing so, he must be careful to put the material in his own words and not to include any phrasing that too closely resembles the authors' words.

Original Source

Hal's first attempt at paraphrasing the passage did not go well:

> Electronic monitoring by imposing excess control over employees' behavior, can alienate employees and develop a feeling of working in a modern "sweatshop" (Kidwell and Bennett, 1994).

PARAPHRASE

> Kidwell and Bennett argue that imposing excess control as a means to monitor employees' behavior makes people feel they are working in a modern sweatshop (qtd. in Taylor 539).

You can see that many of the phrases of Hal's paragraph come directly from the passage. Even though Hal has indicated that the material came from an article and even cited the authors' names and page number, he is indicating that he has put all of the material into his own words when in fact he has not done so. This is an example of plagiarism.

Plagiarism is, of course, using materials produced by someone else as if they are yours. This includes a range of infractions extending from the accidental omission of a citation to passing off an entire essay as your own. In this case, Hal has used much of the authors' wording and indicates by his lack of quotation marks that the material is in his own words.

SECOND ATTEMPT AT PARAPHRASING

Kidwell and Bennett argue that the use of electronic monitoring is detrimental to employees' morale and creates an unhealthy environment where their every action is monitored to make sure they are constantly working (qtd. in Taylor 539).

The concept of the sweatshop, a place where employees are closely watched to make sure they meet their work quotas, is still there, but it is now in Hal's own words.

Sometimes it is just easier to quote, and as suggested earlier this is often the case when citing policies and laws: these materials usually need to be presented in their original form. The author of this article provides two research questions, and Hal wants to include one of them. A direct quote would be appropriate here as well.

ORIGINAL SOURCE

Does "giving notice" versus "secretly monitoring" make a significant difference in the ethical dimension of electronic monitoring?

Notice that in this example there are quotation marks around certain words. When Hal cites this research question, he needs to turn those double quotation marks into single quotation marks to indicate a quote within a quote.

HAL'S USE OF THE SOURCE

Taylor provides two research questions for his study. The first one, "Does 'giving notice' versus 'secretly monitoring' make a significant difference in the ethical dimension of electronic monitoring?" (530). The importance of determining the ethics of monitoring employees' computers and cell phones hinges on whether they know such monitoring is going on.

Hal does a few important things here.

1. He introduces his quote; it is not just dropped in via parachute to land where it will. He sets up the quote for the reader.
2. He begins and ends his quotation with quotation marks. The marks indicate that everything inside of them comes directly from an outside source. Note that the quotation marks end after the quote, not after the parenthetical citation.

3. Hal takes into account the fact that, in the original, the phrases *giving notice* and *secretly monitoring* were in quotation marks. Hal follows the rule for reducing the quotation marks to 'single' quotes and using "double" quotes around the entire quotation.

4. After Hal ends his quote, he comments on why the material is important.

Following these techniques when summarizing, paraphrasing, or quoting will save you a lot of grief and help you avoid charges of plagiarism.

Avoid Plagiarism

The definition of plagiarism is using the work of others as if it were your own without proper attribution. To most readers (instructors, bosses, etc.), there is no difference between accidentally forgetting to cite a passage and deliberately presenting outside material as your own. How to avoid a failing grade (or a job dismissal)? Avoid plagiarism by following these guidelines.

Avoiding Plagiarism Checklist

☐ Cite all outside material whether you have quoted it or paraphrased it.

☐ Introduce source material and comment on it afterward so the reader is clear which ideas are yours and which came from the source.

☐ When pasting material from a source into your paper, make sure to mark it in some way (e.g., by using boldface type, by using a different font color or size, by highlighting) so that you will remember that the words are not yours. Then go through your document thoroughly to make sure you have cited all the highlighted material correctly.

☐ Always include the source publication information in your bibliography file or on your photocopies. If you do not have author or publication information when you are ready to use the source, you cannot use it.

your turn 4f ▶ **PRACTICE Paraphrase Properly**

Read the following article on some of the costs of delaying comprehensive immigration reform legislation, an issue in 2008, when the essay was first published, and for today's U.S. Congress as well. Write a paragraph about immigration reform and include paraphrasing of two passages from the article by following the tips to avoid plagiarism and citing them correctly.

I'm Not Dangerous

By DANNY POSTEL

The past six months have seen three of the largest workplace immigration raids in U.S. history. In May [2008], the rural Iowa town of Postville was convulsed when 900 Immigration and Customs Enforcement (ICE) agents stormed a kosher meatpacking plant and arrested 389 workers. In August, ICE agents descended on an electrical equipment factory near Laurel, Mississippi, detaining nearly 600 workers. And in October, the scene was repeated in Greenville, South Carolina, where 330 workers were swept up at a chicken-processing plant.

The humanitarian costs of the raids, according to a statement issued by the U.S. Conference of Catholic Bishops Committee on Migration, were "immeasurable and unacceptable in a civilized society." Children were separated from their parents for days. Those arrested were not immediately afforded the rights of due process. And local communities were, in the words of John C. Wester, bishop of Salt Lake City and chairman of the Committee on Migration, "disrupted and dislocated." These raids, he said, "strike immigrant communities unexpectedly, leaving the affected immigrant families to cope in the aftermath. Husbands are separated from their wives, and children are separated from their parents. Many families never recover; others never reunite."

The bishop called on the Department of Homeland Security, of which ICE is an agency, on President George W. Bush, and on then-candidates John McCain and Barack Obama to "reexamine the use of worksite enforcement raids" as an immigration-enforcement tool. He noted that immigrants "who are working to survive and support their families should not be treated like criminals."

Having visited Laurel after the ICE crackdown, I must report that is exactly how the workers there have been treated and made to feel. The majority of the immigrant workers caught up in the raid were taken immediately to a holding facility in Louisiana. ICE released a number of women, some of them pregnant, on "humanitarian" grounds. But many of them were shackled with ankle bands equipped with electronic monitoring devices. Several expressed their humiliation and shame—not to speak of their physical discomfort—at having been branded this way. For days, one of them told me, she avoided going out in public or to the grocery store. "It makes me look like a criminal, like a dangerous person," she lamented. "I'm not dangerous."

This woman told me she had come to the United States out of sheer desperation. She said she was unable to feed her children in her home village in Mexico. Now, with deportation imminent and no means to pay her bills, she and her coworkers were facing a further harrowing fate.

Immigration raids, even large, media-covered ones, are selective and symbolic in nature. They are orchestrated to send a political message that the government is willing and able to enforce the law. But why penalize the least among us—hardworking people who earn very little and endure some of the harshest conditions in the American workplace? The Postville and Laurel plants both have long histories of taking advantage of their workers. Iowa's attorney general recently filed charges against the Postville meatpacking plant for more than nine thousand labor violations. In July, religious and labor leaders joined more than a thousand marchers in the town to show solidarity with those seized in the ICE raid.

Indeed, religious communities have been playing a pivotal role in the aftermath of these raids. Catholic parishes have been safe havens for families scrambling to feed their children amid the turmoil. Immaculate Conception Church in Laurel and Sacred Heart Catholic Church in Hattiesburg worked virtually round-the-clock to feed and provide for the affected families.

To remedy what the U.S. bishops call "the failure of a seriously flawed immigration system," they "urge our elected and appointed officials to turn away from enforcement-only methods and direct their energy toward the adoption of comprehensive immigration reform legislation." That is now up to the new administration and to Congress.

Documentation: Works Cited Page

One of the most tedious aspects of writing research reports of any type is the documentation. You must supply publication information for every source you use in your report. This information must appear in a standardized format or style sheet dictated by your company or instructor.

- In the humanities (fine arts, literature, and history), the most common format is MLA—the Modern Language Association.
- Fields such as sociology, anthropology, education, psychology, and business often require writers to document sources in APA—the American Psychological Association.
- The Council of Science Editors' manual (CSE) is used for the natural sciences, such as biology and geology.

All of these style guides are similar in *what* information you should provide for a source, but they vary in *how* that information is presented. For example, see how a book is cited for MLA, APA, and CSE side by side:

MLA	APA	CSE
Collins, Harry. *Basics of Welding.* New York: Anchor Books, 2005. Print.	Collins, H. (2005). *Basics of welding.* New York: Anchor Books.	1. Collins, Harry. (2005). *Basics of welding.* New York: Anchor Books; p. 532

The complete guides to MLA and APA can be found on the Internet at a variety of sources. If you do not have access to the manuals themselves, a very reliable Internet source for both is The Online Writing Lab at Purdue University:

(MLA) http://owl.english.purdue.edu/owl/resource/747/01/

(APA) http://owl.english.purdue.edu/owl/resource/560/01/

In Part VI, "MLA and APA Documentation Systems," we will cover how to cite sources in both MLA and APA format, how to use the hanging indent function, and the strengths and weaknesses of citation-generating software.

your turn 4g ▶ **Integrate a Source**

Once you have found the information you want to use, follow Hal's example and (1) introduce your sources. Explain to the reader why you have selected this source. Why this author? Then (2) paraphrase the source, putting it entirely in your own words. Your argument should not be a string of quotations. Quotations should be used sparingly. And finally (3), comment on the source. Do you agree with the author's points? Is this a source you disagree with? Do you have more to say on the subject or point the author raises?

Reflect and Apply

1. As you are collecting your sources, how are you evaluating them for unacceptable biases?

2. How are you maximizing your time as you determine which sources are the most useful for you? As you read through your sources, how are you taking notes that pull from material at the beginning, middle, and ends of them in order to avoid using material out of context?

3. How are you determining the value of any primary sources you are finding on your issue?

4. When you use research material, in what ways are you making sure the reader knows why you are using that particular source at that particular time?

5. How are you guaranteeing that all source material in your argument is properly paraphrased and cited, eliminating accidental plagiarism?

KEEPING IT LOCAL

THE WORLD IS SHRINKING, or expanding, depending on how you view the changes in technology. We have access, even in small towns, to vast amounts of published research from all over the world. We can access blogs written by experts in every field imaginable. We can also access blogs written by anyone who wants to write one on any subject, whether they are an expert or not. We can read articles published by highly credible sources in distinguished journals. We can also learn that those same experts are guilty of plagiarism, making all their work suspect. It is important, now more than ever, to use the Internet wisely to learn as much as we can about the authors of any material we plan on using to support our arguments. Embrace all that the world of technology offers, but do so with great caution.

Approach the sources you have selected for your argument by assessing their usefulness. How many sources are still useful after your initial assessment? Do you need to find more sources that fit your argument better? Take the remaining sources and assess their credibility. Do you feel the articles are credible once you have assessed them? Finally, read the sources, making sure you have identified the authors' claims and all supporting and opposing views. Answer these questions: Who is the author? What is the claim? What are the supporting views? What are the opposing or alternate views addressed?

CHAPTER 5

Read Critically and Avoid Fallacies

Once again, you receive an email request from your boss to donate to a large national charity. Because of recent misappropriation of the charity's funds in particular and the downturn in the economy in general, the charity is receiving fewer donations. It's not that you have anything against the charitable organization, and you recognize that it does great work. You feel pressured, however, to give to an organization that you have not chosen. Your boss has sent several emails encouraging donation, emails that ask employees not to leave children without proper meals or winter clothing. You don't want to be the only bad guy, so you write a check.

Later, you are approached by a coworker to buy Christmas wrapping paper as a fundraiser for her son's fourth-grade fieldtrip. If enough money isn't raised, the children won't be able to go, and then they won't be able to compete for future opportunities with the kids at the more affluent schools because they won't have the same background experiences. Again, you reach for your checkbook.

All Illustrations by iStockphoto.com/A-digit

COMMUNITY

School–Academic

Workplace

Family–Household

Neighborhood

Social–Cultural

Consumer

Concerned Citizen

TOPIC: Workplace

ISSUE: Peer/Employee Pressure

AUDIENCE: Fellow Employees

CLAIM: Employees should be free from solicitations for donations or purchases in the workplace.

It is difficult to sort through the arguments that seem logical on the surface or that stir your emotions. Which arguments or causes are valid, and which are meant only to part you from your money? Which arguments contain fallacies to get you to do things you don't want to do? In Chapter 5 you will learn how to identify the four major categories of fallacies in the arguments of others and learn to eliminate each type of fallacy from your own arguments.

In Chapter 5 you will learn to:

- Define fallacies.
- Identify and avoid:
  - Fallacies of choice.
  - Fallacies of support.
  - Fallacies of emotion.
  - Fallacies of inconsistency.

Define Fallacies

Very often when we are listening to a speaker's argument or reading an argument in a magazine or newspaper, it is easy to get caught up in the speaker's excitement and overlook the fallacies in his argument. **Fallacies** are errors in an argument, whether accidental or deliberate, that serve to draw attention away from the problems in the argument's claim or support. They can be the result of a poor understanding of the subject, or they can be deliberate manipulations of the argument to misdirect readers. The difficulty with fallacies is that they are often hard to spot, in your own writing and in the writing of others.

ryccio/Getty Images

Figure 5.1 Information overload can make us feel that we are always a step behind.

Detecting fallacies in arguments is a component of reading well. How well do you know how to read? "I can read just fine," you say. But there is a type of reading that many struggle with—critical reading. **Critical reading** is a more active form of engaging with a text, be it a newspaper article, a politician's speech, or a note from your son's teacher. For example, what is really being said in that politician's speech? You are hearing her words, but are you really listening to what she is saying? The two actions are not the same thing. The best-sounding arguments can fall to pieces when examined closely by a reader who is actively responding to them, rather than passively receiving them.

We are bombarded daily with an overwhelming amount of information. We must sort through emails; phone messages; and newspapers and news programs, which now have 24-hour-a-day updates. You can even subscribe to sites so that updated news on certain topics can be emailed to your computer or sent to your phone. Then there are all of the other sources of information you encounter: reading for your courses; updates to the Operations and Procedures Manual at work; and the buzz about the latest movies, television shows, music, and fashion trends. Miss one day's information due to a cold, and you feel you have fallen behind a week. This anxious feeling is called **information overload**—the sense that you are always one step (if not more) behind.

Spotting fallacies can be difficult, but it is not impossible. The more tools you have at hand, the easier your job of cracking someone's argument will be. In Chapter 4, "Evaluate and Engage with Your Sources," you learned that there are some methods that will help you get to the heart of any argument, whether the argument is presented in print (such as a book, an article, or an Internet posting) or orally (such as a speech or an advertisement). In this chapter, you will learn to demand of authors that they convince you that their claims and support are valid. By learning to identify fallacies in the arguments of others, you will also learn how to avoid using them in your own arguments. Let's tackle the most common forms of fallacies.

Identify and Avoid Fallacies

Many arguments can sound good until you begin to follow them closely. All of a sudden, those high-flying words seem to be saying very little. You begin to suspect that the writer is trying to hoodwink you. And you may be right.

Dishonest arguers often use fallacies to direct the reader's attention away from the real issues or to hide their real purposes. Just as frequently, though, inexperienced writers use fallacies because they don't know any better. Fallacies are errors in a writer's argument—not errors in fact, but errors in reasoning.

In a recent class, a student writer argued, "I think we should stop spending so much money on the space program because people are starving here on Earth." Other students disagreed, but they were not sure what to say to counter the argument. One traditional way of arguing is to learn to recognize specific fallacies and then see if the argument you disagree with contains one of these errors in logic. Is this an *ad hominem* or an *ad misericordiam*? Is the argument a *post hoc* fallacy, a *com hoc* fallacy, or maybe a *tu quoque* fallacy? One thing is certain: if you take this route, you may be studying fallacies *ad nauseum*.

The good news is there is a far easier way. All fallacies boil down to four categories. There is overlap between types, and you could argue that a fallacy can fall into more than one category, but in general the four categories are as follows:

1. Fallacies of choice
2. Fallacies of support
3. Fallacies of emotion
4. Fallacies of inconsistency

In the argument against the space program, the fallacy happens to be a false choice, an either–or argument that tries to force you into supporting either feeding the hungry or exploring space. This is a smart move. Of those two choices, what ethical person would ever choose space exploration over feeding people who are starving? But there is also inconsistency. The arguer is assuming that there is only enough government money to do one of two things: (1) feed the hungry or (2) explore space. But, of course, that same arguer drives over roads paid for by government money, lives in a country defended by a military, and will someday retire and receive Social Security benefits from the government. In fact, there are lots of programs she doesn't propose to sacrifice in order to feed the hungry, so why should she pick on the space program? She is being inconsistent. The problem is that she is not directly articulating the inconsistency. Some fallacies are obvious, but most require you to dig a little deeper into the arguer's assumptions. Luckily, you don't need to know the name of each fallacy in order to find the inconsistency.

Keep in mind that even a fallacious argument can be right—just as a stopped clock is right twice a day. We shouldn't just accept fallacious arguments any more than we should tell time by a stopped clock. In each case, further investigation is warranted. How else might it be? Maybe the clock is working after all, and we just looked at it wrong. Or maybe we can fix it; it might just need a new battery. And maybe it's telling the right time, even though it won't be in just one minute from now. The goal is not understanding all of the types of fallacies but learning how to recognize when someone is being inconsistent. Every time you want to test the strength of an argument, look closely at what it is saying and what it assumes.

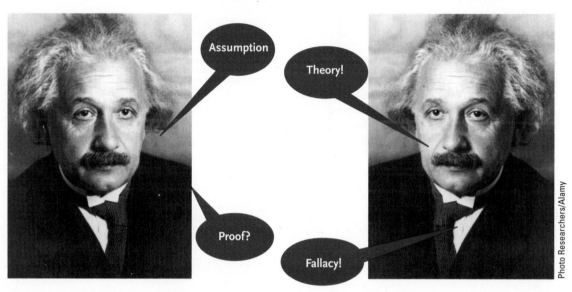

Figure 5.2 Albert Einstein

Before we go any further, let's discuss bias. Say you're writing a paper with the following claim: the study of extrasensory perception (ESP) deserves equal funding with stem cell research. One obvious assumption (warrant) the claim makes is that ESP is real. Another is that it is worth studying. It is impossible to write any argument without some fallacies, especially bias, since we are all biased. The very fact that we are making a certain claim and dismissing alternatives to that claim is evidence of our bias toward our own claim. We also tend to give short shrift to competing evidence and make leaps of logic that may not be warranted.

The heart of critical thinking is asking, "How else might it be?" Looking for fallacies involves a search for answers to that same question. If I use a blanket statement and say, "Everyone is born with paranormal powers," I am dismissing the possibility that some people are born without any extra-mental powers, that they can't read minds, tell the future, or move objects simply with the power of thought. The first category of fallacies involves making bad or unwarranted choices about what to believe.

Avoid Fallacies of Choice

Fallacies of choice ask you to make the wrong choice by limiting your view of what the future holds or what the choices are. They put things into simplistic terms that don't allow for positive alternatives. They tell you that only the choice they want is possible or worthwhile. You will see how this overlaps with scare tactics and other emotional fallacies.

Blanket Statement

Blanket statements use the language of absoluteness. They use words like *all, always, never, no, every,* and *none.* They are fallacies as soon as someone can think of an exception. If someone claims that all dogs have tails, you could go home and chase your dog around with a pair of scissors, trying to prove that person wrong. (See Figure 5.3.)

Some people take the sixth commandment to mean that a person should never kill. But, of course, people kill to live by eating plants and animals. And people kill to defend themselves, or to serve their country in times of war, or to mete out punish-

Yann Arthus-Bertrand/Documentary Value/Corbis

Figure 5.3 The Schipperke is a tailless dog

ment for murder. To say that we should never kill is a blanket statement. If you believe that killing is sometimes okay, then you have found an exception and turned the blanket statement into a fallacy. Some examples of blanket statements include:

- Cell phone use in the classroom is *always* inappropriate.
- The *only way* to understand the increasing high school dropout rate is to study the lack of student motivation.

Both of these claims use unqualified terms (*always, only way*) that can easily be rebutted. Of course there are times when it is appropriate to use a cell phone in the classroom—calling security, for example. Students drop out of school for many reasons, not just lack of motivation. Avoid absolutes. Blanket statements hinge on the following terms and terms like them. Be careful to qualify these **absolute terms** in your own writing. Also note that plural nouns can imply absolutism (for example, using the word *students,* implies "all students"). You can modify these terms using the qualifiers in Chapter 10, "Build Arguments."

Absolute Terms			
all	no	none	100 percent
every	always	never	must
has to	can't	won't	only

False Dilemma, Either–Or, and Misuse of Occam's Razor

False dilemma/either–or thinking suggests that only one thing can happen—either A or B. As in the sample claim that the space program can exist only at the expense of the poor, arguers who make this type of mistake state that there are only two choices in the argument.

> So much of the food I eat, the fuel I expend, and the clothing I wear work against the idea of sustainable living. Why should I even bother to try?

This student's claim suggests that there are only two choices available to the speaker. He can either (a) live a lifestyle that is completely geared to sustainable living, from food to fuel, or (b) not even try to make any efforts at sustainability. A critical reader will ask, "Does it have to be either–or?" This author has created a false choice, a dilemma that is not really there. A person may not be capable of living in a totally green way, but most people agree that anything done to help the planet is a good thing.

Occam's razor is a philosophical point of view that argues that the simplest solution is usually the correct one. If it walks like a duck, looks like a duck, and quacks like a duck, chances are very good it is a duck. Most of the time, using Occam's razor to cut through far-fetched and overly complex theories is the way to go. But this chase for simplicity can be misused.

The following story is an example of public officials finally breaking out of fallacious false choice/either–or thinking. For many years, suicidal people had been leaping to their deaths from the Golden Gate Bridge, yet nothing had been done to stop it. Partly the inaction was born from a desire to maintain the landmark beauty of the structure by not cluttering its profile with high fencing. Partly the inaction stemmed from the fallacy of thinking that any suicide prevented at the bridge would simply take place elsewhere. There were, the doubters argued, only two choices: either keep letting people kill themselves and leave the bridge unchanged, or force depressed people to kill themselves elsewhere by marring the beauty of the bridge with new barriers. In this view, nothing could be done about suicides, because anybody who wanted to kill themselves enough to jump off a bridge would simply find another way to do it. Either people wanted to keep living or they didn't, in which case there was nothing anyone could do to stop them. Because it was impossible to prevent all suicides, the decision was made to prevent none. Any other choice, such as the plan recently adopted, was considered impossible.

In fact, suicide is often preventable, and it's also an act of opportunity. No sane person would hand a suicidal individual a loaded gun. Why? Because it would be giving the person an opportunity. Because it could *change the person's behavior.* Therefore, it stands to reason that removing opportunities for suicide might also change behavior. At last, bridge officials decided to break free from their loop of fallacious thinking by adding nets below the bridge's surface. This solution prevents suicides at the bridge, while damaging the bridge's landmark profile very little. As a result of breaking through the either–or thinking, a solution that considered both sides of the argument was reached.

Slippery Slope

A **slippery slope (or staircase)** argument is one of the easiest fallacies to recognize. You will often hear people say that, if we let one thing happen, then that will cause some other thing to happen, which in turn will lead to something bad, which then will cause chaos. If we take that first step, then we will fall all the way down the slippery slope to chaos or evil, as illustrated by Figures 5.4 and 5.5.

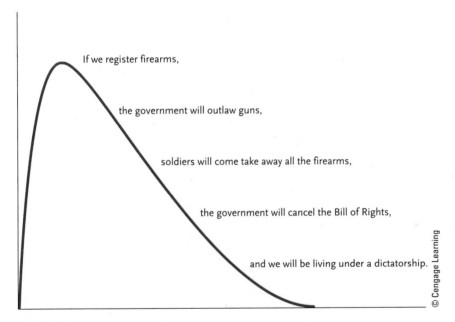

If we register firearms,

the government will outlaw guns,

soldiers will come take away all the firearms,

the government will cancel the Bill of Rights,

and we will be living under a dictatorship.

© Cengage Learning

Figure 5.4 A slippery slope argument

But events do not always follow the predicted slope. For example, in contrast with common gun-control arguments, some societies have taken away guns without becoming dictatorships, or they took them away for a while and ended up giving them back later on. A good history lesson often reveals that the "slippery slope" in an argument is actually an unlikely series of events. A better description for most such cause–effect chains might be a "staircase" because we usually can move up the slope and down the slope. Sometimes it is a slippery staircase, but it's rarely inevitable that if we take the first step, we will slide all the way down.

internet activity 5a

Use the Opposing Viewpoints database or another available database to find arguments about gun control. Read through these arguments and see if you can find slippery slope fallacies. What makes them fallacious? Where do they start, and where do they end?

Signs that you may be reading or writing fallacies of choice include:

☐ Support for extreme positions: we *must* do something (e.g., bomb, invade, kill, torture, outlaw, silence, close a factory, fire an employee, censor objectionable material).

☐ The language of certainty: all, every, 100 percent, never, none, each, always, everywhere, there is just no reason to go to Mars, I can't think of a single benefit of joining the military.

☐ Hard, even impossible choices: it's either this or that, my solution or your hellish problem, my way or the highway.

☐ Surprising conditionals: if we don't do X, we'll face Y; if we do A, the sky will fall; if we do A, we'll reach nirvana; if we do A, then B will happen, and B will naturally lead to C, which in turn . . .

☐ Support for a decision already made: that page was already written; we're going to do X, it's just a matter of how; one way or another we have to . . .

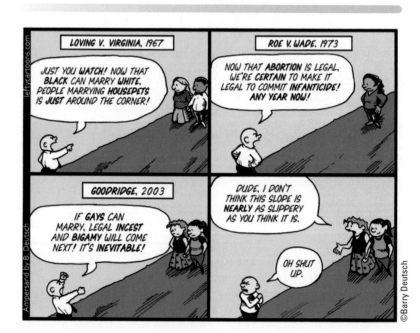

Figure 5.5 This cartoon uses the slippery slope fallacy to make its point

your turn 5a **PRACTICE** Identify Fallacies of Choice

Here is a paragraph from the paper on ESP. See if you can spot the types of fallacies. Match the numbered fallacies with the correct box below.

The study of extrasensory perception (ESP) deserves equal funding with stem cell research. ❶ We can recognize this fact, or we can continue to waste the opportunities such funding represents. ❷ No medical treatment comes without a price in terms of research funding. ❸ It's hard to think of treatments that didn't involve some government-funded research; therefore, it's safe to assume there aren't any. ❹ If we continue ignoring this potentially valuable source of knowledge, we can expect to begin ignoring other valuable types of innovation, and after that, what's next? Like any species, human beings survive and prosper by constantly learning and adapting to a changing environment. Without ESP funding, we may well face extinction.

Which numbered sentence in the paragraph best represents each type of fallacy? Fill in each box with a different number.

☐ Blanket Statement   ☐ False Dilemma/Either–Or

☐ Misuse of Occam's Razor   ☐ Slippery Slope

Avoid Fallacies of Support

Fallacies of support involve making connections and conclusions that aren't warranted. If Michelle had two ducks and someone gave her two more ducks, no one would suggest that she now had five ducks. Yet this often is exactly what people do with the logic of their arguments. They support their claim with their claim. They jump to conclusions based on very little evidence. They make superstitious connections between events, build arguments on falsehoods, and support their claims with facts that aren't even relevant.

Circular Argument

A **circular argument** is simply one that ends up relying on its own claim for support. In this way, it seems to chase its own tail. A person who doesn't agree will tend to see the arguer as trapped in her own logic. The arguer is caught in the circle of her own prior beliefs. For example, she may assume that God exists and is all-powerful. Anything less than God's full existence would violate her assumption of God's full existence. That's the circle. (See Figure 5.6.) Other arguers might believe in other, equally powerful beings. Do they all have to exist? Only to someone trapped in that particular circle of logic.

> We need to drill more for oil. Why? Because gas prices are high. Why? Because we need more oil than we have available to us. Why? Because we haven't drilled enough oil wells.

god is all powerful and a non-existent god would not be as powerful so therefore we know god exists because

Courtesy of the author

Figure 5.6 A circular argument that uses its claim as its support

This kind of argument ignores all other possibilities, such as conservation, alternative energy sources, or simply letting shortages raise prices to the point that we only use the oil that is absolutely necessary, a kind of conservation that would be enforced by the marketplace laws of supply and demand. The argument also ignores any balancing of costs and harm from more oil drilling and simply treats it as a good thing that we may or may not do, instead of a complex thing that may do as much harm as good, for example, by continuing global warming.

Hasty Generalization and Jumping to Conclusions

The fallacy of **hasty generalization** involves taking a single case and generalizing from it. Your friend takes a ride in a vintage automobile from the 1930s and the axle breaks, causing an accident that breaks your friend's leg. Now, you refuse to ride in anything older than last year's model. Or your grandmother smoked cigarettes and lived to be 90. Therefore, smoking must be harmless and all this talk about lung cancer and early deaths is just a scare tactic.

Faulty Causality: *Post Hoc, Ergo Propter Hoc*

Post hoc, ergo propter hoc: This Latin phrase sounds complicated, but it's really simple, and it represents a fundamental process in animal thought. The entire phrase can be translated as "After this, therefore because of this." When two events happen one after the other, we naturally tend to think the first event caused the other event. We kick the sleepy copy machine, it starts working, and we assume it was our kick that did the trick. In fact, maybe it had just then finished its warm-up cycle. This is how superstitions get started. A baseball player forgets to change his underwear, and he pitches a no-hitter. Well, no way is he changing that underwear. No, he's going to wear the same pair every time he pitches until the magic finally wears off.

> Parents should not have to vaccinate their children because vaccinations cause autism.

A classic case of *post hoc* fallacy presents itself in arguments that claim vaccinations cause autism. We don't yet know what causes autism, but we do know that it exists. A certain percentage of children will be diagnosed with autism at a young age. If virtually all young children are given, for example, the MMR (mumps, measles, and rubella) vaccine, it is certain that, soon after, some of those children will develop autism. If none of the children are vaccinated, it is equally certain that, soon after, some of those children will develop autism. After all, the MMR vaccine is given to children at 12 to 15 months of age. Autism is usually diagnosed around three years of age. Therefore, MMR almost always comes before a diagnosis of autism, making it is easy for parents to assume a causal connection, even if there isn't one.

The fallacy comes into play when parents assume that the vaccine caused the autism, even though they would never assume that the lack of a vaccine would cause autism, though the evidence is the same in both cases. That is the inconsistency at the heart of the *post hoc* fallacy: just because one thing happened after the other doesn't mean the first thing caused the second thing. The MMR vaccine comes before autism, but often so does potty training. Could potty training be the cause of autism? Could baby formula? The fact is, we don't know what causes autism. It might be a genetic disorder. It could be caused by hormones while the fetus is in the womb. It could be a result of exposure to common household materials or chemicals. The fact is, we don't know.

Many errors in arguments come from making mistakes in causality. You may believe that a chain of events exists where it doesn't. You may believe that one event is caused by another. You may believe that only one cause is responsible when there may be a combination of causes leading to an effect.

Fallacies in causality are not easy to spot. Keep your eyes open, and do some investigating on your own about claims of causality that seem too easy or are not well supported.

> Some people have claimed that the city council's decision to again postpone its discussion of homelessness is only increasing the number of homeless in our community.

Here, it cannot be proven that the city council's inaction has anything to do with the increase in homelessness. More research would need to be done.

Non Sequitur, Red Herring, and False Clue

Authors of murder mysteries are famous for planting false clues, otherwise known as red herrings. They force the detective and the reader to follow a scent that doesn't lead anywhere or leads to the wrong conclusion. A false clue in a murder mystery is simply one that doesn't support our attempt to identify the real killer. But false clues appear in all kinds of arguments. So do statements that don't follow what came before, that are out of order, or that might sound good but don't actually relate.

In Latin, *non sequitur* means "it does not follow." Often, an arguer will write or say something that doesn't seem to belong, that suddenly shifts the focus or the argument, or that makes a conclusion that doesn't seem justified from the evidence that has been presented.

Some of these *non sequiturs* are accidental. A writer might suddenly change the subject or make a point that comes from out of the blue. Or the writer might even force in a point that doesn't belong, simply because he likes it. This is known as "shoe-horning," after the old metal scoops that people used to use to guide their feet into tight leather shoes. Another term for a person's pet interest is a "hobby-horse," and a person with a pet argument "has an axe to grind."

If a writer's claim is that diet can help to prevent diabetes, discussion of issues not related to diet or diabetes may seem like *non sequiturs*. Discussion of illness prevention in general could be risky, in that it could seem like it's off topic. Or it might simply be an example of broadening out the claim to include other kinds of disease prevention besides diet or diabetes prevention. In the following passage, however, the writer goes way off the track.

> Diet can help prevent type 2 diabetes. A new study published in *Diabetes Care* compared the glycemic control (blood sugar levels) of patients on traditional American Diabetes Association diets with a low-fat vegan diet. Patients on the vegan diet did roughly twice as well in reducing their glycemic index. This goes to show that the Texas beef producers were wrong for suing Oprah Winfrey for her 1996 anti-beef comments. When it was pointed out that cows were being fed to other cows, Oprah said, "It has just stopped me cold from eating another burger!"

Sentence 4 came out of left field, didn't it? The writer shifted suddenly from discussion of diabetes prevention to a lawsuit concerning a statement by a celebrity.

Some *non sequiturs* represent conscious efforts on the part of the arguer. The intent might be to change an unpleasant subject. A politician who is unpopular for her handling of a state's economy might take a strong interest in creating harsher penalties for child molesters. A skeptic of global warming might bring up the subject of government conspiracies in hopes that an audience upset about the possibility of too much government control might forget all about potential harm from changes in the climate.

Straw Man Argument or Argument Built on a False Fact or Claim

Straw man arguments are those that are based on incorrect information, whether the intention is to deliberately misrepresent an opponent's claims or because the facts that are being used are plainly incorrect. For example, someone might claim "One piece of the solution to homelessness in our community is more affordable housing." You would be committing a straw man fallacy if you said "My opponent says that we can end homelessness just by building cheap apartments." The misrepresentation of that position makes it easy to dismiss.

Signs that you may be reading or writing fallacies of support include:

- ☐ Making the same point in two places in a chain of reasoning: the economy is bad because the housing market fell, which happened because wages were not rising fast enough for people to afford the higher prices, which resulted from a weakening economy.
- ☐ Support based on a single case, anecdotal evidence, or making too much out of a few cases: back in 1979 . . . , reports of similar occurrences indicate . . . , this incident shows that . . .
- ☐ The language of time or events happening after each other: then, after, when, preceded by, I'll never get a flu shot—my aunt and uncle got a flu vaccine and then they came right down with the flu.
- ☐ Sudden or unexplained shifts in topic.
- ☐ Unquestioned assumptions: everything hinges on . . . , the key is that . . .
- ☐ Statements that put words in someone else's mouth instead of quoting them in context.

your turn 5b ▶ PRACTICE Identify Fallacies of Support

Here is a paragraph from the paper on ESP. See if you can spot the types of fallacies. Match the numbered fallacies with the correct box below.

❶ Whenever researchers take ESP seriously, they document many more cases, which shows that the first step toward unlocking paranormal powers is simply to look for them. ❷ In one case, the paranormal researcher herself began reporting the ability to move objects without touching them, showing that if she, a trained, hardened scientist can do it, anyone can. ❸ According to that researcher, Dr. Ruth Bandylegs, ESP could even lead to an increase in religious faith and consequently better our world in that way too. ❹ However, paranormal powers are not taken seriously by most scientists, most likely due to their bias toward traditional science. In traditional science, the emphasis is placed on the known laws of physics, but ESP must work based on physical laws that are unknown. Otherwise, traditional science would have taken it seriously by now, and those laws would be recognized. ❺ Since paranormal research has been shown to increase both incidents of ESP and also its importance in religious faith, an increase in funding is definitely warranted.

Which numbered sentence in the paragraph best represents each type of fallacy? Fill in each box with a different number.

- ☐ Circular Argument

- ☐ Hasty Generalization/Jumping to Conclusions

- ☐ Straw Man Argument

- ☐ Faulty Causality/*Post Hoc*

- ☐ *Non Sequitur*/Red Herring

Avoid Fallacies of Emotion

Appeals based on emotion are those that evoke sentiment, fear, desire, and so on. But wait a minute, we said in earlier chapters that emotional appeals are a good thing. Can they also be fallacies? Well, not in theory, but in practice they can be. Whenever we rely too much on any one kind of support, we can run into trouble because we are giving it more weight than another kind of support and, therefore, being unbalanced. Many people would claim that in the end, everything we believe comes down to emotion. Perhaps this is true; even when an argument is based on scientific evidence, at some point we accept that evidence because we like it. In other words, we accept it not because it fits the definition of good scientific evidence, but because it's a definition that we like. Fallacies of emotion are a problem because they completely replace evidence with feelings. They play on the heart strings and the fears of the audience. They name-call, they poison your view of things, they make you feel left out, and they use famous people to vouch for things they know very little about.

Ad Hominem

Ad hominem simply means "to the person." It is the fallacy of arguing based on the arguer's personality or character, credibility, or authority. It's the opposite of shooting the messenger because you don't like the message. Here, you shoot the message because you don't like the messenger.

> We cannot believe she will follow through on her plans to funnel more money toward charities. Can we trust a former alcoholic?

The inconsistency of *ad hominem* fallacies is that we dismiss arguments from people we dislike but accept the same arguments from people we admire. Another way to say it is that, when we do like the arguer or when we do not have an emotional response one way or the other, we generally judge an argument as good or bad on its own merits. To be consistent then, when we don't like the arguer, we should still judge the argument on its own merits.

Testimonials and False Authority

The opinions of people with authority can provide valuable support to an argument, but only if the **testimonials** come from true experts in the relevant subject area. Otherwise, the arguer is guilty of using **false authority**.

Consider this the flip side of an *ad hominem* attack. Here, instead of attacking the messenger instead of the argument, we embrace the argument because we like the messenger. This often means giving someone unwarranted credibility. If Einstein said that whales should wear velvet waistcoats to hit home runs, should we believe it? We love Einstein, and he was a genius. But what did he know about baseball, or marine biology, or fashion design?

A well-known commercial for diabetes supplies presents Wilford Brimley as someone you can trust to give you good advice on buying these needed supplies. Wilford Brimley is a famous character actor, so what does he know about medicine or medical supplies? It turns out that he has diabetes, and so he is an expert in using the supplies. He is an expert consumer, someone who other consumers of diabetes supplies might want to listen to. A close look reveals that Brimley is not a false authority. Michael Jordan does commercials for men's underwear. Well, he is a man, so we can assume that he does wear men's underwear. Testimonials like these don't represent a fallacy. However, they still should be balanced against the bias that comes from the "expert" being paid to represent a product.

Vice President Al Gore and U.S. Senator James Inhofe are both famous for their views on global warming. Gore has spent decades calling for action, and he even won the Nobel Peace Prize for his work. Inhofe has long been a denier who has called global warming the "greatest hoax ever perpetrated on the American people." What are their grounds for authority? Senator Inhofe has a bachelor's degree in economics and has worked in business and insurance. Gore got a bachelor's degree in government and has also studied law, divinity, journalism, and English. Neither is a climate scientist. If they have any authority at all, it has come from studying the work of those scientists who do the actual research and who are the actual experts.

In some cases, the fact that a person is an anti-authority actually makes the case stronger. President Ronald Reagan famously opposed funding for AIDS research, thinking that AIDS patients were responsible for having the disease. After he left office, he made a television commercial pleading for Americans to give money for AIDS research. He said, "You see, sometimes old dogs can learn new tricks."

Sometimes, even a true authority can be used in a fallacious way. Email and the Internet are often used to spread stories or warnings on the basis of fraudulent information or testimony. In one such case, the Apollo moon landings were argued to be a hoax staged by NASA. One piece of "evidence" offered was a statement by Stephen Hawking that humans could not survive a trip through the Van Allen radiation belt. Stephen Hawking is a renowned physicist, so he could be trusted as an authority on this issue. The problem is he never made such a statement.

Bandwagon

A **bandwagon fallacy** means that since everybody believes it, I should too. This is the fallacy of following popular tastes, or accepting a claim simply because other people do.

There is a clichéd response to this fallacy that clearly shows the inconsistency: "If everyone jumped off a bridge, would you do it?" This type of fallacy involves people basing an argument on the popularity of the claim or proposal, rather than its merits. "Everybody is getting tattoos, so you should get a tattoo" is an example of a bandwagon argument. But if everyone says "Hey, I really like that Hitler—he really has some good ideas," is it then okay to jump on the Hitler bandwagon and accept those Nazi arguments? Of course not, because to be consistent, we need to consider every argument on its merits, rather than accepting the ones we like and denying the ones we don't.

> There must be something to that Kennedy assassination conspiracy, or why would so many people believe it?

There is power and peril in group thinking. The power is that we can rely on other people to get there ahead of us, to discover things we don't have time or resources to discover. Other people blaze the trail. We just follow along. That's also the peril. If the trail they blaze leads to a cliff, then we can find ourselves in big trouble, believing things that don't make sense, or that are even harmful. In the case of the John F. Kennedy assassination, so many different kinds of people have raised questions about the lone gunman theory that it feels like "Where there's smoke, there's fire." All those theories with all those points of evidence can't be wrong—can they? The fact that many people believe something is not, by itself, evidence.

Ad Misericordiam

Ad Misericordiam is an appeal to pity. Users of this fallacy are trying to win support for their argument by manipulating the audience's feelings of guilt or pity. As instructors, we are frequently on the receiving end of this type of fallacy: "Please let me take the exam. My dog died, I lost my job, and I think I have the flu. Please don't make me fail school as well!"

Governments often use gut emotions like fear, revenge, or pity to motivate their citizens in time of war. This poster from World War I show the extent to which our government used images portraying Germans as barbarians, animals, and rapists terrorizing innocent women and children. Did our government do the same after 9/11 in the war with Al Qaeda?

Scare Tactics

When all else fails, frighten your audience. Fear is a powerful emotion. Fear of homosexuality, fear of Islam, fear of MRSA, fear of other races: humans have a long history of acting poorly when they are afraid. Scare tactics capitalize on poor economies, war, and any other controversial issue to persuade their audiences to act or not act in a way that is beneficial to the arguer.

A common advertising technique is the use of scare tactics in order to sell products or encourage people to vote or act in a certain way. (See Figure 5.7.) Either the audience acts in the desired way, or it will suffer some terrible fate. Don't buy our brand of teeth whitener? Your dates will draw back in horror when they see your gray teeth. Use our competitor's vacuum cleaner? It actually manufactures toxic dust that will quickly fill your rooms to the depth of your ankles. Scare tactics always work to create this kind of either–or choice.

Sometimes, there is good reason to be scared. The stock market in 2008 lost almost 50 percent of its value. Investors are now gun shy, and it looks like the very worst time to invest in stocks. Even in this case, reacting purely out of fear represents fallacious thinking. Bad times can often bring opportunities. Many successful businesses are started in a down economy when everyone else is retrenching. Companies often cut their advertising budget when sales drop, but that's the most important time to advertise. The most successful companies—Dell, Coca Cola, McDonald's—advertise no matter what their sales look like. Success in business often means not letting fear influence decision making. Buying stocks when times are terrible might just mean getting a bargain. The opposite is also true. In 1996, Alan Greenspan,

RBC, The University of North Carolina

Figure 5.7 Posters from World War II encourage the viewer to feel a strong bond against the enemy

chairman of the Federal Reserve Board, referred to people's excitement over rising stock prices as "irrational exuberance." The lack of fear was sure to precede a crash. Just four years later, Internet and technology stocks crashed.

The best way to avoid being taken in by scare tactics is simply not to react. It's best to react when a bus is flying toward you down a hilly street. When there is no immediate danger and someone argues that there is, that's a good time to pause, and do nothing except examine the situation more closely.

Signs that you may be reading or writing fallacies of emotion include:

☐ Discussion of someone's background or life, or of aspects unrelated to their argument

☐ Reasoning based on what the crowd is doing: mention of high or increasing popularity; discussion of how new something is

☐ Off-topic testimonials: for example, a baseball player used as support for a type of plant fertilizer; celebrities touted for their opinion, not their expert judgment

☐ Emotionally charged language: worry, hope, fear, desire; that would be a disaster; such a thing should worry any sane person

> **your turn 5c** ➤ **PRACTICE Identify Fallacies of Emotion**

Here is a paragraph from the paper on ESP. See if you can spot the types of fallacies. Match the numbered fallacies with the correct box below.

> *If it led to breakthroughs in the practice of ESP, a full-fledged research program could help us tackle some of the world's biggest problems. ❶ Right now, countless children in the Third World are going to bed without their supper; millions of thinking, feeling animals are being mistreated in factory farms; and far too many women are suffering the torments of oppression and domestic abuse. ❷ In a world with so many problems, we simply can't afford to neglect any possible avenue for solutions, and we do so at our own peril. ❸ We also can't afford to miss the boat, as France, Belgium, and Botswana have each set up their own state-of-the-art government-funded research facilities. ❹ No less than the Royal Prince of England has called for similar efforts in his own country. ❺ It seems clear that anyone who would refuse to explore such promising opportunities for advancement just isn't thinking straight.*

Which numbered sentence in the paragraph best represents each type of fallacy? Fill in each box with a different number.

☐ *Ad hominem* or other inappropriate negative personal argument

☐ Testimonials, false authority, or other positive personal argument

☐ Bandwagon

☐ *Ad misericordiam*

☐ Scare tactics

Avoid Fallacies of Inconsistency

All fallacies boil down to an inconsistency, but some arguments are blatantly inconsistent. One obvious but all too common kind of inconsistency is a **double standard**. Someone might say, "I like Chairman Gripspike because he is vocal and really speaks out for what he believes, but Chairwoman Leadpocket sure got on my nerves; she was so pushy and opinionated." A common complaint women leaders make is that, when men assert themselves, they are considered strong and capable, but when women assert themselves, they are considered difficult to work with. Anyone with a strong enough bias will use this kind of inconsistency, often without realizing they are doing so. To a white racist, a white criminal is simply a bad egg, an exception, but a black criminal is one more bit of evidence to show that black people are thugs. A black racist might see a wealthy black business person as a hero to be admired and emulated, while seeing a wealthy white business person as a typical selfish oppressor who only looks out for himself.

Sometimes instead of treating similar things inconsistently, people will treat different things as if they are the same. This is a fallacy of false consistency, or false equivalence, treating things as the same when they really aren't the same.

Moral Equivalence

In this fallacy, two very unequal things are balanced against each other *morally,* as if they are equally bad or good. Your boss catches you leaving the office with a company pen on the same day she fired your coworker for embezzling thousands of dollars from the company advertising account. She confronts you and says you are just as guilty as your coworker and need to be fired. Technically, stealing is stealing, but are these two acts really morally equivalent?

Material Equivalence

Here, two very unequal things are equated, or balanced against each other as if they are *materially* equivalent. If an apple a day keeps the doctor away, does it matter if the apple is a red one or a green one? An apple is an apple, right? Well . . .

Sweet gum trees give off gases that, when mixed with automobile emissions, can contribute to ozone pollution. Trees also take in carbon dioxide and give off oxygen. Someone might say that these two things balance out, that the material effects of a tree cancel out so completely that cutting down trees will neither help nor harm the environment. President Reagan was famous for his statement that trees pollute more than cars, so we shouldn't complain or worry when they are cut down. In reality, trees suck in carbon dioxide, a principal greenhouse gas responsible for global warming, and they also give off oxygen. Until we actually weigh trees' beneficial effects against their harmful effects, we don't really know if the material evidence is equal. And it turns out, trees do far more good than harm, so we should not cut them down.

Definitional Equivalence

In *definitional* equivalence, two things are defined as being the same, whether they are or not. Often, before we can tell if two things are morally equivalent or have equivalent material effects, we first have to know what the things are. Do they even belong to the same category? The abortion debate centers around the definition of personhood. Is a fertilized egg a human life? Is a fetus a person? The U.S. Constitution defines a citizen as someone born or naturalized in the United States. What does science say? What do the courts say?

Life is so diverse that scientists can't agree on a single definition of what a species is, so more recently they have begun using a combination of definitions. These kinds of arguments sound pretty esoteric, but in fact they can matter in the real world. Suppose a population of foxes is threatened by a home builder's development activity. If it represents a separate species, it could be protected under the Endangered Species Act. If it is defined as simply a subgroup of a common fox species, it might be exempted from any protection. A developer could lose big money, and people might not be able to buy homes where they'd like, or a species might disappear from the earth. A definition, then, can seal the fate of an animal.

Inconsistent Treatment (from Dogmatism, Prejudice, and Bias)

Often this fallacy shows itself in the way an arguer supports a claim. Arguers look for facts to help their side of the argument but ignore facts that work against their side.

One infamous case of inconsistent treatment involved voting laws. Various poll taxes were levied and literacy tests adopted to make it harder for black Americans in Southern states to vote. Many black citizens in the early twentieth century were poor and so could not pay the tax, or they would have had trouble answering detailed written questions about the U.S. Constitution. They were effectively disenfranchised when they went to the polls to cast their vote. Poor and illiterate white citizens were often waved through or given easier questions to answer.

Even strictly equal treatment can be considered unequal when the audience is unwittingly biased and looks for treatment that favors their own point of view. The issue of media bias is a good example. During any election cycle, watch the letters to the editor. Democrats write to complain of bad pictures and negative stories about their Democratic candidates, while Republicans write to complain about similar treatment of the candidates they favor. Truly unbiased studies that could find true cases of bias are rarely done. When they are done, they are often attacked for using biased criteria to measure bias. For instance, next time there is an election, gather an equal number of friends from different political sides (say, Democrat, Republican, and Independent). Set some criteria that you can all agree are unbiased (number of minutes spent on a story about a candidate or issue, number of words, pictures with a smiling or frowning candidate), and start counting to see if your own impression of bias holds true.

Equivocation

Good thinking requires us to look at various sides of an issue and consider contradictory evidence. Or we might consider various sides because we are trying to explore a subject, or even come to a compromise. In that case, it would be okay to consider contradictions without resolving them.

In a traditional persuasive argument, however, it is considered a fallacy to make contradictory claims. People call it "arguing out of both sides of your mouth." A cliché line of attack in a courtroom is to catch a witness making two opposite statements and then to ask the witness, "So which is it, Mr. Knucklepump, were you lying then, or are you lying now?" Equivocation occurs in a context, and that context is crucial. For example, equivocation undercuts an argument because, if the arguer can't even agree with her own argument, why should we agree with her? But in a more exploratory situation, equivocation can actually help to build trust with an audience, to establish a spirit of going forward together in order to find enough evidence to form a conclusion.

Equivocation often happens because we keep arguing a claim we like, regardless of the support. If one reason fails, we try another, and so we set one reason against another. The war in Iraq could be considered representative of this type of equivocation. It was first presented as a means of defending the world against weapons of mass destruction. Later it was declared to be about fighting terrorism by Al Qaeda. When resistance by Saddam Hussein's armies collapsed, a banner was raised that said "Mission Accomplished." Later, the U.S. Government claimed that a premature end to the Iraq war would be disastrous. This example of equivocation shows how the seeds of doubt in an argument can be sown. That is why they are considered fallacious.

False Analogy

An analogy is a comparison between two things or a claim that two situations are similar. A good analogy can help people think about things in a new way by pointing out parallels. A **false analogy** occurs, however, if an arguer says the situations are comparable but they really aren't.

Arguers use many analogies to support a position, and often those analogies don't hold up because the situations are more different than they are alike. In other words, analogies do not always present fallacies; often an analogy does hold up, and the situations are alike in some essential way. The Bush administration argued that we could help a defeated Iraq become a democracy because after defeating Japan and Germany in World War II, the U.S. helped them become democracies. It is a judgment call whether or not that is a worthwhile or a false analogy. One strike against the argument may be that both Japan and Germany were homogenous societies, whereas Iraq is divided into several ethnic and religious groups, making a transition to a working democracy difficult if not impossible.

All fallacies boil down to an inconsistency of one kind or another. We're almost always inconsistent when we argue, because we have our own point of view. We have values and beliefs. We want to believe certain things, and we want to support those beliefs. Intentionally or unintentionally, these factors sometimes leads us to argue inconsistently, favoring our view of things.

Even though fallacies are to some extent inevitable, they are a matter of degree. We can be as fair as possible, including and weighing other views along with our own. We can be somewhat fair, acknowledging other claims, or we can purposely try to manipulate our audience by ignoring evidence that supports another side of things.

▸ Signs that you may be reading or writing fallacies of inconsistency include:

☐ Unbalanced discussions: 90 percent of the support falls on one side of an argument.

☐ Undeservedly balanced discussions: 50 percent of the support falls on each side of an argument (33 percent with three sides), with no real justification.

☐ Language of contradiction: but, however, on the other hand, still, while at the same time.

☐ Language of equivalence: this is like, just as, in the same way that, similarly.

☐ Comparisons that don't sound right: being a president is a lot like being a restaurant owner.

your turn 5d ▸ **PRACTICE Identify Fallacies of Inconsistency**

Here is a paragraph from the paper on ESP. See if you can spot the types of fallacies. Match the numbered fallacies with the correct box below.

❶ *Perhaps those who dismiss paranormal research are thinking straight; maybe they just don't know the facts.* ❷ *They might not realize that not funding ESP is essentially the same as using Jewish prisoners in dangerous medical experiments.* ❸ *It's just as unethical, too.* ❹ *Perhaps they don't know that, just as the hard sciences have their flagship institution, the Massachusetts Institute of Technology (MIT), paranormal research also has had its flagship in the Institute for Parapsychology at Duke University, an equally prestigious institution, albeit that the university broke ties with the Institute in 1965, when its founder retired.* ❺ *The advancements of the paranormal sciences should receive exactly the same funding as the natural sciences; nay, they should in fact receive more, to make up for the funding inequities of the past. If we do these things, we will likely ensure a better future for our children, and isn't that what it's all about?*

Which numbered sentence in the paragraph best represents each type of fallacy? Fill in each box with a different number.

☐ False analogy: Moral equivalence

☐ False analogy: Material equivalence

☐ False analogy: Definitional equivalence

☐ Equivocation

☐ Inconsistent treatment (from dogmatism, prejudice, or bias)

To be able to identify fallacious strategies in the arguments of others is a great asset to being a stronger reader and thinker. To be able to avoid these same fallacious strategies in your own arguments makes you a stronger writer.

your turn 5e ▶ PRACTICE Identify Four Types of Fallacies

In the following passage, try to spot the fallacies from all four groups:

- Fallacies of choice
- Fallacies of support
- Fallacies of emotion
- Fallacies of inconsistency

> We should get rid of our current male president and put a woman in the White House. Every bad thing that has happened in this country has happened under a male president. We had slavery, the Civil War, the Great Depression, Pearl Harbor, and the defeat in Vietnam all under male presidents. Therefore, a woman president could only do a better job. There is nowhere to go but up.
>
> Furthermore, little girls all over this country have grown up with no presidential role model. The damage of this injustice has been devastating to the psyche. We might as well have shackled these girls and tied them to a ball and chain. There is no doubt that this lack of inspiration has held women back.
>
> One perennial problem that traditionally faces this country has been budget deficits, yet this is an area a woman president is uniquely qualified to handle. For centuries, women have successfully managed home finances, keeping a budget, spending their limited incomes wisely to keep their families fed and clothed. A woman would bring that same kind of efficient money management to the White House.
>
> Women have run countries before. Margaret Thatcher was widely considered to be an excellent prime minister of the United Kingdom. That proves that women in general can lead and lead well. Men, on the other hand, are worthless as leaders. Consider recent history. We elected Richard Nixon, and we lost the Vietnam War. We elected Jimmy Carter, and we had an oil crisis. We elected Ronald Reagan, and the stock market crashed. We elected Bill Clinton, and the White House was used for sleazy activities. If we keep electing male presidents, the country will keep falling. If the country keeps sliding into corruption and moral decay, we may soon find ourselves a mini-power instead of a superpower. We could end up last among nations. And keep in mind that Hillary Clinton would have beaten John McCain in a head-to-head match-up.
>
> It may be true that the gender of a candidate has no bearing on how effective a leader he or she may be. On the other hand, the famous musician Gidget Snotbrackler has said that we need now more than ever to "Go pink." For the sake of our little girls, can we afford not to?

Reflect and Apply

1. As you read your sources, what steps are you taking to evaluate them for fallacious information?

2. As you write your argument, what are you doing to ensure that you are not including fallacies? Do you have a way to identify these fallacies as you review your argument?

3. If you are using emotional support, how are you preventing your images or anecdotes from becoming fallacies of emotion?

4. As you include material from multiple points of view in your argument, how are you avoiding fallacies of inconsistency?

5. What is the harm in selecting sources only because they support your own views, or because they espouse views that are easy to dismiss? Which type of fallacy is involved in doing so?

KEEPING IT LOCAL

You like your coworkers and want to get along with them all, but you don't like feeling pressured to participate in every fundraiser that comes along; you would like to be able to pick the fundraisers that seem to support the most important causes or that are selling products in which you are truly interested. The same holds true for donations. Many charitable causes are legitimate and do a lot of good work. But again, you don't want to have to donate to causes that you have not selected.

The biggest obstacle to taking a stand is that so many of the arguments your coworkers give seem so persuasive. "If we don't raise enough money, the Tigers bowling team will be disbanded and these children will never learn to work as a team." "How can you look at the faces of these poor hungry people and not contribute to hunger relief?" "Everyone else has already placed an order for doughnuts." These are fallacies—each and every one of them. Ask questions, dig deeper, and find out more before you pull out your wallet. Maybe you will be perceived as heartless, or maybe you will be seen as the department hero.

● – – – – – – – – – – – – ●

Detecting fallacies in the wide variety of sources you read, view, or listen to can be difficult. But actively asking questions about each source and each claim can keep you from passively accepting illogical or manipulative arguments. Look for fallacies of choice, of support, of emotion, and of inconsistency in the sources you are using in your argument. Secondarily, can you turn your critical focus on your own writing and detect any fallacies in your own writing? Doing so will make you a stronger reader, writer, and thinker.

CHAPTER 6

Work Fairly with the Opposition

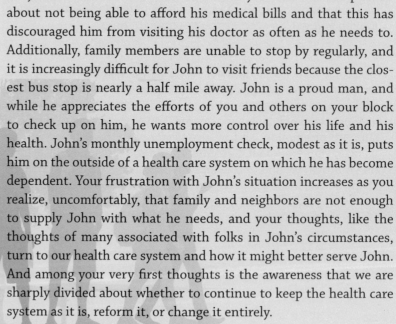

For the past few months, you have been aware of a neighbor whose health and well-being seem to be suffering. From others in the neighborhood, you learn that the neighbor, John, lost his job and health insurance earlier this year and has complained about not being able to afford his medical bills and that this has discouraged him from visiting his doctor as often as he needs to. Additionally, family members are unable to stop by regularly, and it is increasingly difficult for John to visit friends because the closest bus stop is nearly a half mile away. John is a proud man, and while he appreciates the efforts of you and others on your block to check up on him, he wants more control over his life and his health. John's monthly unemployment check, modest as it is, puts him on the outside of a health care system on which he has become dependent. Your frustration with John's situation increases as you realize, uncomfortably, that family and neighbors are not enough to supply John with what he needs, and your thoughts, like the thoughts of many associated with folks in John's circumstances, turn to our health care system and how it might better serve John. And among your very first thoughts is the awareness that we are sharply divided about whether to continue to keep the health care system as it is, reform it, or change it entirely.

TOPIC: Health Care

ISSUE: Universal Health Care

AUDIENCE: State and Federal Representatives

CLAIM: Universal health care should be a right guaranteed to all American citizens.

We build arguments to articulate positions on issues that matter to us, like the one described above, and knowing who disagrees with us and why is vital to the success of any argument. This chapter is devoted to strategies useful in responding to those who argue positions different from your own. When you conduct your research thoroughly and understand what motivates an opposing argument and how this argument is supported, you are in a position to interact with respect and fair-mindedness. This will earn you credibility with an audience.

When we plan and deliver an argument, we're nearly always in conversation with others. It's important to remember that those opposed to a claim we make are equally invested in the issue at hand—but from different perspectives. Treat the opposition respectfully and as fellow members of the community tied to your issue. Acknowledge the values that motivate an opponent. Send the message to your audience *and* your opponents that you can accurately identify and summarize positions other than your own. In an argument, it is your job to remain critical and fair-minded at the same time. This chapter offers guidelines for working with the **opposition**, guidelines that will be helpful when you construct various kinds of argument—Toulmin-based, Middle Ground, Rogerian, and the Microhistory—all of which are discussed in Chapter 8, "Consider Toulmin-Based Argument," and Chapter 9, "Consider Middle Ground, Rogerian Argument, and Argument based on Microhistory."

In this chapter, we discuss why the opposition matters in an argument; additionally, you will learn how to:

- Resist easy generalizations about an opponent.
- Listen to local and scholarly voices on an issue.
- Summarize other voices fairly.
- Avoid bias when you summarize.
- Find points of overlap.
- Respond to other views.

Why the Opposition Matters

Opposing points of view on an issue matter. Like you, your opponents are part of a conversation on an area of life important to them. In most cases, you'll learn more about an issue when you study the opposition. For example, based on how an opponent supports a position, you can:

- Acquire new context.
- Learn to see the issue from another perspective.
- Recognize the values that motivate an opponent.
- Familiarize yourself with a body of specific support different from yours.
- Recognize what you have in common with your opponents.

Suppose you plan to argue on free universal health care for Americans, both a national and a local issue. Based on your experience with your neighbor, you feel compelled to encourage your state's senators and representatives in Washington, D.C., to move beyond the Patient Protection and Affordable Care Act, commonly referred to as "Obamacare," and to support free universal health care. From your research, you know that the issue is complex in terms of its many well-supported positions. For example, various opponents claim that universal health care would undermine the insurance industry, that higher taxes would result, that the government bureaucracy would mean long delays for patients in need,

Figure 6.1 Paying close attention to points of view that differ from your own builds credibility with an audience.

that consumers would no longer be able to shop for their best health care values when government replaces free-market competition among providers, and that health care standards may erode with a single provider. These differing positions matter. If your view on free universal health care is to be taken seriously by your audience, you must negotiate your way through these different views. As you do so, you'll learn about the strengths and weaknesses of arguments competing for the attention of your audience. This can make all the difference to an audience—your willingness to study the opposition thoroughly and to present it in both fair and critical terms.

your turn 6a **GET STARTED** Size up the Opposition

Based on an issue you're working with, respond to the following questions and prompts:

1. On what issue do you plan to argue?
2. What motivates you to argue on this issue?
3. Based on your general awareness of this issue, identify two or three positions different from your position.

Resist Easy Generalizations

Oversimplifying an opponent's position weakens your argument. Different positions on an issue endure because they are built on solid foundations that appeal to people. Your task in an argument is to resist **easy generalizations** of other views and instead summarize them in dignified, respectful terms. This means reading the other position closely so that you can identify and put into your own words its claim, warrant, reasons, and support. This method will get you away from generalizing another position in just a sentence or two. Plan to devote a substantial paragraph to each differing view you bring to an argument.

In your background reading, you likely note a persistent opposing claim arguing against universal health care for Americans. Principal reasons supporting this claim include problems in other countries where universal health care is provided: long waits in doctors' offices, frequent cancellations of appointments, and the pain that patients often must endure while waiting for health care services. This opposing argument brings in effective support, including data that reveal the number of Canadians (Canada's universal health care system is often suggested as a model for an American system) who have died or suffered heart attacks while waiting for health care services. Other data suggest that an alarming number of Canadians perform their own medical and dental procedures instead of waiting. Additionally, examples of the suffering of some individuals make for compelling support. This view also holds that universal health care in Canada is unfair to many everyday people.

The argument is thoughtful and well structured. Your aim in working with this opposing view, or rebuttal, is to summarize it accurately. Doing so will set a respectful tone of fairness.

internet activity 6a **Exploring**

Conduct an informal Internet search, and identify two or three differing positions on your issue. For each opposing view that you might include in your argument, answer the following questions.

1. What, exactly, does each differing position claim?
2. What reasons support each differing claim?
3. What effective support—such as particularly compelling facts and data, personal examples, and research from experts—does each differing position use to support its claim?
4. What makes these other positions valid and arguable? Is your perspective on your issue getting broader based on familiarity with these other views? Explain.

Listen to Local Voices

Before beginning your formal research into scholarly sources on an issue, there are many ways to get a sense of why an issue is important to people in your community and your peers in the classroom. Conversations with colleagues, friends, and family are one way. Another is your local media. Many online sources, like news sites, information sites, and opinion blogs, can provide useful glosses of an issue. Your local and regional newspapers can also be helpful, and most online editions of newspapers contain a search feature that allows you to read past articles and thus get a sense of the history of an issue in your area. Refer to Chapter 4, "Evaluate and Engage with Your Sources," for specific information on gathering online sources.

Listen closely to **local voices**. This will allow you to craft an argument that becomes part of a local conversation on an issue that means something to you and your neighbors, coworkers, or classmates. Whether you take in differing perspectives on an issue over coffee with friends, in conversation with coworkers, during a class discussion, at the dinner table, from your local news, or by interacting on Facebook or a favorite blog, open yourself to the range of attitudes on an issue. Familiarizing yourself with this local knowledge will make your argument more focused and immediate; it will also let you appeal to your audience with specific information.

As we know, the issue of health care in our country can elicit strong points of view. If you happen to be in conversation with a health care professional—a nurse, doctor, or emergency medical technician—you may run across the view that a universal health care system might limit earning power, as government-assigned fees would be less than what market value is now and that this would in turn reduce the number of trained professionals entering the health care field. Additionally, many argue that burnout would occur when the government overloads doctors with patients. Another conversation might avail you of the financial hardships a family endures because of rising costs and that free health care is necessary. Still another conversation puts you in touch with the view that free health care would eliminate the advantages of a

Stan HONDA/AFP/GettyImages

Figure 6.2 Take advantage of informal, local moments as a first step in familiarizing yourself with the opposition.

competitive, free-market system, a system that many feel is responsible for innovation and efficiency in the medical field. Listening with an open mind and heart to these and other views can sensitize you to others and their investment in the issue. Your fair acknowledgement of their views in your argument will make positive impressions on your readers.

your turn 6b ▸ **GET STARTED Listen to Local Voices**

Answer the following questions as a way of acknowledging local views on an issue you plan to argue.

1. What individuals in my community are most deeply invested in this issue?
2. What, in their personal and professional lives, motivates them to speak out?
3. What reasons do they give for their positions on the issue?
4. What solutions do they propose?
5. After listening to others invested in my issue, what do I know about this issue now that I did not know before?

☛ **tip 6a**

Access Local Voices
Your local newspaper may have a search engine that allows you to search past articles and issues. Find the link to this search engine on your newspaper's home page, and then type in keywords connected to your issue.

Summarize Other Voices Fairly

To earn the trust of your audience, it is important that you treat your opponents fairly, and this means withholding judgment of opponents' views when you introduce them in your argument. Your evaluation of differing views can

bobbieo/Bobbie Osborne/iStockphoto.com

Figure 6.3 To a target audience, fairness is often measured by how an arguer treats those holding opposing views. It is essential that the arguer makes the effort to summarize the other side fairly.

and should occur *after* you summarize them in a neutral tone. In many cases, those holding other views are just as determined as you are to be heard and to influence local thinking. Review the following examples of writers' treatments of differing positions and the analysis that follows each summary.

Summary #1: By Linda Gonzalez

This writer is responding to the issue of illegal immigrants in the United States having driver's licenses and claims that immigrants should be allowed to obtain licenses under certain conditions. In the paragraphs that follow, the writer summarizes a view opposing her claim.

> Another point of view is the one held passionately by opponents of giving driver's licenses to illegal immigrants. These opponents argue that driving is a privilege and not a right. For instance, Republican Sue Myrick of Charlotte, North Carolina, says, "Our feeling is that a driver's license is a privilege for citizens and legal aliens and it shouldn't be something given to somebody who broke the law" (qtd. in Funk and Whitacre 2). Backers of Myrick agree by saying that issuing driver's licenses to undocumented people would attract more illegal immigrants to the country and it would then be easy for terrorists to come to the United States. Considering driving as a privilege, many politicians are completely against a plan that would allow illegal immigrants to obtain a driver's license. They believe that because people who have entered the country illegally have broken the immigration laws, they should not be allowed to receive any kind of benefits in this country. Moreover, a driver's license allows a person to be able to work, drive, and open a bank account; all these things make life easier for undocumented people in this country. One opponent argues that, "one legitimate kind of ID leads to more, leads to more, leads to more, and pretty soon, they've got an entire identity established" (Johnson 2). He also adds that having a legal document can give the idea of citizenship.
>
> Additionally, the government is taking stricter ways to keep the nation safe. One effective way is to not issue driver's licenses to illegal aliens so they cannot enter federal buildings, board airplanes, or use it as identification to give the impression of being legal. An illustration of this in their favor is that 8 of the 19 men in the terrorist attacks on September 11, 2001, got licenses in Virginia after presenting a simple notarized form saying they were state residents (Johnson).

Another example of illegal immigrants threatening the nation's safety is that there are drug dealers and criminals looking for easy ways to get licenses. "Driver's licenses are as close as we get to a national ID," says John Keely of the Center for Immigration Studies, a group in Washington that advocates limited immigration. "While the overwhelming majority of immigrants don't pose a national security threat," [Johnson said], "I don't think issuing driver's licenses to them affords protection to Americans, but hurts the efforts to shore up national security" (3). Authorities against a plan to provide driver's licenses to illegal immigrants do not take into consideration that undocumented people are not going to go away just because they do not have driver's licenses and that they will drive with or without it. Certainly, the arguments in favor of and against issuing driver's licenses to noncitizens are so strong that it is difficult to imagine an alternative position.

Discussion

This is a fair-minded summary of a position different from the writer's. The writer maintains a respectful, neutral tone in reference to her opponents. The writer identifies the opponent's claim of driver's licenses being a privilege of citizenship in the second sentence. Views of Myrick, Johnson, and Keely appear without judgment. The writer briefly disagrees with her opponents in the next-to-last sentence of the final paragraph, and her final sentence hints that her claim and support will occur later in the argument. The summary avoids brief, superficial treatment of opponents, and the writer is in no rush to dismiss them. This summary appears in a middle ground argument, as the last sentence suggests, where the writer will offer a practical position between what she views as two extreme positions. See Chapter 9, "Consider Middle Ground and Rogerian Argument, and Argument based on Microhistory," for a full treatment of middle ground argument.

Summary #2: By Brittney Lambert

This writer is responding to the issue of whether students on college campuses should be allowed to carry concealed weapons. She claims that students should be granted this right. She begins her paragraph by identifying a view opposed to hers.

One argument against the right to carry concealed weapons on campus is that students' protection and safety should be left to the police. This is because police have gone through four to five months' worth of training, but citizens who carry licensed concealed weapons have only gone through about a day of training. First of all, adults with concealed handgun licenses can protect themselves in most "unsecured places" already; they just lose that right when they step on campus. Secondly, police officers cannot be everywhere all of the time. In a study by the U.S. Secret Service, 37 school shootings were researched. Of the 37 school shootings, "over half of the attacks were resolved/ended before law enforcement responded to the scene. In these cases the attacker was stopped by faculty or fellow students, decided to stop shooting on his own, or killed himself. The study found that only 3 of the 37 school shootings researched involved shots being fired by law enforcement officers" ("Answers" par. 1).

Discussion

Although the writer has written an otherwise strong argument, there is room for improvement in her coverage of the opponent's position. This summary is not as strong as it could be because only the first two sentences of the paragraph address the opponent's position. The opponent's claim is clear, that campus safety is the responsibility of the police, but only one reason is given, that campus police have undergone training. The student's argument could have been stronger if she had included support for the opponent's claim-quotations, facts, or specific examples. Sometimes when an arguer glosses over an opponent's claim, it can strike an audience as unfairly brief, especially when the remainder of the paragraph is devoted to countering the opponent. By devoting only two sentences to another view, the writer might appear dismissive and unwilling to treat the opponent fairly. With some adjustments, this essay could become a strong, Toulmin-based argument, a kind of argument discussed in Chapter 8, "Consider Toulmin-Based Argument."

Summary #3: By James Guzman

In the following summary, the writer focuses on health care and whether it should remain privatized or change to a system with free services to all Americans. He argues a middle-ground position and claims that the answer to the health care question is to reform the present system. Prior to the paragraph below, the writer summarized the view of those opposed to free health care. He is now summarizing what he considers to be a second extreme position on health care.

On the other side are those who believe that our country should provide universal health care to all American citizens. The 46 million uninsured citizens are a disgrace on our country that is thought of as the land of opportunity for all. It's their opinion that this number alone is reason enough to warrant universal health care. It is hard to brag about equal opportunity when there are a huge number of low-income families that do not have a doctor or receive the necessary medical attention to maintain their health. Every other wealthy country has found it unacceptable to have portions of the populations uninsured and have implemented universal health care. Of all things that the government provides, health is surely up there with education and police protection in importance. It is true that this huge number of uninsured is alarming, but is it really *society's* responsibility to take care of those who choose not to buy health insurance? If a person truly is a hard-working citizen, we have tax credits designed specifically for those who buy their own health care. This argument could be easily interpreted as class envy. If this is another weapon in class warfare, then it would no doubt turn out to be another wealth-transfer system designed to punish the successful.

Discussion

This summary has both strengths and weaknesses. The first half of the summary identifies a claim and then refers to very clear reasons that support this claim. Brief support is included in the form of "46 million uninsured citizens" and "every other wealthy country." Yet this support would be even more compelling and trustworthy if documentation as to where the writer gathered this information were given. Proper documentation, examples, quotations, and other specific support for this opposing view would strengthen the summary and move the writer closer to earning credibility with his audience.

In your own arguments, include the strengths and avoid the weaknesses in the preceding summaries. Each of these writers crafted strongly worded claims and reasons and brought plenty of effective support to his or her argument, but only the writer of the first summary was fair and thorough in her treatment of an opposing view.

your turn 6c ▶ **GET STARTED** Evaluate Summaries of Differing Positions

Based on your treatments of opponents in an argument you are building, answer the following questions.

1. What does each opposing position claim? What reasons and support for opposing positions do you include in your summaries?
2. Do you document in parentheses the source of quoted and summarized material?
3. Is your audience likely to believe that you achieve a tone of fair play and mutual respect in your summaries of other positions? Explain.
4. In your view, would those holding the differing positions you summarize approve of these summaries? Would they feel they've been treated fairly and with respect? Explain.

Value Expertise over Advocacy

Make every effort to include opponents who support their claims with clear reasons and thorough support. In addition to local sources, bring to your argument opposing visews found in scholarly journals and periodicals gathered from academic databases and from search engines that allow access to scholarly and professional material. Avoid sources that are purely ideological, overly emotional, brief, and general. Referencing an advocate for or against universal health care, for example, who argues on primarily emotional grounds will weaken your argument. Your audience will have difficulty taking such an advocate seriously, and this will reflect on your willingness to treat

tip 6b

Search Thoroughly to Avoid Shallow Summaries

Many of us tend to default to mainstream search engines as a way to begin researching an issue. Avoid this habit! Instead, consult the academic search engines and databases to which your school subscribes, some of which are devoted specifically to particular fields, such as medicine, the environment, education, government, business, and specific academic disciplines like English, history, and computer science. See Chapter 4, "Evaluate and Engage with Your Sources," for additional sources housing scholarly material.

the opposition fairly. On the other hand, when you refer to an opposing view that is full of effective support and grounded in strong values, your argument becomes more credible and, importantly, challenges you to make your argument equally compelling in view of a well-informed opposition.

For example, during a prewriting activity in class you choose to share with your group a neighbor's complaint that universal health care is merely "welfare for the uninsured" and "rewards the lazy." The neighbor appears to offer no support for these claims. This is the kind of opposing view to avoid in an argument. Without substantial support, such claims become fallacies only. See Chapter 5, "Read Critically and Avoid Fallacies," for a full discussion of fallacies and how to avoid them in your writing.

internet activity 6b Connecting

Working with the online materials you gather for an argument, answer the following questions.

1. What specific research will you bring to your argument? How does this research go beyond mere advocacy along ideological grounds for a position and use facts and credible information as support?
2. While another position may include emotional appeals, is the position centered in primarily rational support? Explain.
3. Are the opposing views you bring to your argument found in reputable publications that include current facts and statistics? What are these publications?

Avoid Bias When You Summarize

Summarize positions of your opponents accurately, in your own words, and without a hint of judgment or evaluation. Your summaries should be so accurate that opponents approve of them. Consider the following paragraphs and the two summaries: one brief, inaccurate, and full of **biased language,** and the other accurate and objective. The paragraphs are from the article "Universal Healthcare's Dirty Little Secrets," by Michael Tanner and Michael Cannon, well-informed opponents of universal health care.

> Simply saying that people have health insurance is meaningless. Many countries provide universal insurance but deny critical procedures to patients who need them. Britain's Department of Health reported in 2006 that at any given time, nearly 900,000 Britons are waiting for admission to National Health Service hospitals, and shortages force the cancellation of more than 50,000 operations each year. In Sweden, the wait for heart surgery can be as long as 25 weeks, and the average wait for hip replacement surgery is more than a year. Many of these

individuals suffer chronic pain, and judging by the numbers, some will probably die awaiting treatment. In a 2005 ruling of the Canadian Supreme Court, Chief Justice Beverly McLachlin wrote that "access to a waiting list is not access to healthcare."

Everyone agrees that far too many Americans lack health insurance. But covering the uninsured comes about as a byproduct of getting other things right. The real danger is that our national obsession with universal coverage will lead us to neglect reforms—such as enacting a standard health insurance deduction, expanding health savings accounts and deregulating insurance markets—that could truly expand coverage, improve quality and make care more affordable.

Summary #1

Michael Tanner and Michael Cannon, both from the Cato Institute, argue the same tired conservative position we have heard for years. They provide only negative evidence from countries with free health care and want us to think that many people die before getting treatment because delays are so long. They view a competitive, free-market approach as better than guaranteeing that everyone receives health care.

Discussion

This brief summary is biased and inaccurate. Using words like "tired," "conservative," and "negative" establishes a narrow, judgmental tone. The summary ignores the factual support the writers bring to their argument. It also ignores the writers' call for specific reforms and their attention to those Americans who are now underserved. In general, the summary is not effective because it misleads and includes biased language.

Summary #2

Michael Tanner, Director of Health and Welfare Studies at the Cato Institute, and Michael Cannon, Director of Health Policy Studies at the Cato Institute, provide substantial data to argue against universal health care. They refer to other countries with established universal health care systems—Great Britain, Sweden, and Canada—and claim that large numbers of citizens have to suffer through long delays for hospital service and for operations. In Sweden, for example, the authors claim that some patients will die while waiting for heart surgery and hip replacement. Tanner and Cannon agree with their opponents that "far too many Americans lack health insurance" (par. 3), but they feel that reforming our present system is a more practical approach to this issue. Specifically, they want to see a deduction built into health insurance policies, an emphasis on health savings plans, and expanded deregulation of the health insurance industry.

Universal Healthcares Dirty Little Secrets, by Michael Tanner and Michael Cannon

tip 6c

Peer Edit Summaries
As a check against offering biased summaries, ask a peer to evaluate your summaries of differing views on the issue you're working with. Pay close attention to these peer responses, as they can point out biased language that can block fair representation of other views.

Discussion

This is a fair-minded, objective summary of an opposing viewpoint. The opposition's claim (first sentence), selected support (sentences two and three), and warrant (sentence four) are noted. The summary is free from biased language.

your turn 6d ▶ **GET STARTED** Avoid Bias

Based on your research of opposing views on an issue you're working with, answer the following questions.

1. Have you avoided judgmental or emotionally loaded language in your summary that could mislead an audience? Explain. What words might you replace to assure your audience that your summary is accurate and fair?
2. Are your summaries mostly in your words with only occasional quotations? Would your opponents agree with your summary of their positions, and would you feel confident presenting your summaries to your opponents? Explain.
3. When quoting or paraphrasing an opponent, do you document in parentheses appropriate page or paragraph numbers?

Find Points of Overlap

Although you may differ with your opponents, there likely are points in your argument where you overlap and share certain concerns and values. For example, you favor free universal health care and others oppose it, but in closely studying other views you'll probably observe that some of your values and the values of opposing views are quite similar. Often the best place to find shared values is at the level of the warrant in an argument, that is, the moral grounding on which an argument is based. For example, all players in the free health care debate may agree that:

- Quality health care should be available to those in need.
- Delivery of health care should be timely.
- Health care services should be run efficiently.

These shared values make rational communication possible and create a positive bridge between you and others at the discussion table. This bridge becomes possible because of your willingness to take in without judgment the views of others.

Identify Common Ground with the Opposition

The following issues are controversial because they elicit strong and often emotional responses. On the surface, it may seem that finding **common**

Figure 6.4 Acknowledging shared concerns and values is a strength in an argument.

ground would be impossible. But when you dig beneath attitudes and proposed solutions to our most controversial problems, you may uncover core
beliefs, values, and principles that reveal some common ground. To make
these revelations possible, be diligent in your research process and keep an
open mind to those who differ from you.

Example #1

Issue   Should water be publicly held or privately owned?

Description   This is a full-fledged issue in several western states and in
numerous countries. Proponents of classifying water as a privately held
commodity argue that, although water is a basic need, access to it should
not be a legally guaranteed right. This side also reasons that private companies are better at protecting water than the government, that innovation in the water industry springs from privately owned water companies,
and that competition among companies can drive down the price of water
for the consumer. On the other side, those who favor public ownership
of water claim that water is too essential for survival to let it be distrib-
uted by companies. This side also argues that the government is needed to
ensure that water resources are conserved, that water remains safe, and
that it is not subject to changes in an economic market, as this can work
against its availability to consumers.

Common Ground   Shared values among opposing sides on this issue
may include the recognition that, in recent decades, many water sources
have diminished and become tainted and that efforts to purify our water
are essential, that apparatus for distributing water be efficient, and that
any realistic assessment of our future must include water availability.

Example #2

Issue   Does homeschooling threaten American democracy?

Description   Many critics of homeschooling claim that homeschooled students may succeed as students but not as citizens. They reason that homeschoolers are trained to be more concerned about themselves than their communities, that they are subjected to educational agendas grounded in religious or ideological beliefs, and that the social isolation in which homeschooled students learn steers them away from civic involvement. On the other hand, many proponents of this movement argue that homeschooled students in fact make better citizens than students educated in public schools. As studies emerge following the first generation of homeschooled students in recent American history, these supporters note that homeschoolers contribute to democratic culture in greater percentages than graduates of public schools in the following areas: support of political parties, membership in civic organizations, voting, speaking out on public issues, and community service work.

Common Ground   Opponents in this issue may overlap in their belief that children deserve an education that prepares them for active citizenship and that this includes participation in civic and political activity.

Example #3

Issue   Is it fair to make birth records unavailable to adopted children?

Description   States vary in the laws that prohibit, limit, and allow access to the birth records of adopted children. Many claim that it is unfair to prohibit access to records on grounds that medical information of birth parents can reveal conditions that may affect adopted children and future generations. Another argument on banning access involves the regret and sense of loss that some women later feel after giving up their children for adoption, often at a young age. Others feel that laws protecting the privacy of biological parents should be honored, especially with regard to women who chose to give up their children with the understanding that confidentiality would be assured. Additionally, this side argues that the privacy of the adopted family would be compromised were adopted children given access to birth records.

Common Ground   Both sides on this issue have in common deep concern for the welfare of adopted children. This value alone can make communication possible when differing views are treated respectfully. Building on this shared value, this issue can reveal the importance of precisely crafted claims, those that avoid all-or-nothing approaches. For example, given that both sides want the best for adopted children, qualifiers can be built into claims that allow for access to birth records under certain conditions based on the needs of birth and adopted parents.

 tip 6d

Recognize Shared Values

Like yours, an opponent's public position on an issue and his or her problem-solving apparatus rest atop a set of values and core beliefs. This is where you can look to find common ground when none is immediately evident. Sometimes the opposition will spell out in direct language his or her values and beliefs; at other times, these values are implied or stated only indirectly. When researching other positions, remember to read carefully for the values that underlie a position.

your turn 6e GET STARTED **Find Common Ground**

Based on your understanding of views different from yours on an issue, answer the following questions.

1. What values and principles do you share with your opponents?
2. What reaction can you anticipate from your audience based on the shared values and common ground you establish with your opponents? How will audience reaction help your argument?

Respond to Other Views

This chapter is devoted to opposing points of view on an issue and how to present them fairly. But you should also plan to respond to differing views, and in general there are three approaches. First, based on your careful evaluation of another position, you may find yourself in disagreement with it, and your argument will be stronger if you spell out precisely why you disagree. Second, you may agree with another position, and this means that you should state why you agree. This view may not directly oppose your position, but it may approach your issue from a different perspective and bring in different reasons and support. Explaining the grounds on which you agree will add momentum to your argument. And third, you may choose to work with another view that you both agree and disagree with.

Whether you disagree, agree, or agree only in part with another view, it is essential that you respond immediately after summarizing the different view. This can occur in the same paragraph with your summary of another view or in the paragraph immediately following the summary.

Use the prompts in your turn 6f, 6g, and 6h to practice disagreeing, agreeing, and both agreeing and disagreeing with other views.

your turn 6f PRACTICE **Disagreeing with Another View**

To respond to a view you disagree with, answer the following questions. This will put you in a position to explain in specific terms the basis of your disagreement.

1. What are the limitations of this view; that is, what does it fail to acknowledge about the issue at hand and how do these omissions affect its credibility?
2. Does this view include overly general statements that do not stand up to close investigation? If yes, what research will you bring in to reveal the weaknesses in these statements?
3. Does this opposing view include the elements of good argument? For example, is support effective and free from fallacies, and does it include fair treatment of the opposition?

4. Is sufficient context part of this opposing view, and is the presentation of this context fair and objective?

your turn 6g ▶ **PRACTICE Agreeing with Another View**

To respond to a view you agree with, answer the following questions.

1. Are there values in this view with which you overlap? If yes, what are they, and why are these values appropriate in an argument on the issue at hand?
2. How does research validate this view?
3. What makes this view a practical approach to this issue? In your answer, identify how readers can benefit in practical ways by reflecting on this view.
4. In what ways does this view move beyond popular, less-informed responses to this issue?

your turn 6h ▶ **PRACTICE Agree and Disagree at the Same Time**

To respond to a view you both agree and disagree with, answer the following questions.

1. On what specific points do you agree with this view?
2. What keeps you from fully accepting this view?
3. How, precisely, does your view improve on, or add to, this view?
4. To what extent will you recommend this view to your readers?

Reflect and Apply

1. Based on an argument you plan to build, what opposing views will you include and how, specifically, will you be thorough and fair in presenting them?
2. What sources will you draw from as you gather research for your argument? Explain why an audience would consider them credible.
3. What common ground are you finding with other views in your argument? How will you make use of this common ground?
4. Your turn 6f, 6g, and 6h list ways of responding to other views in an argument. How will you respond to each differing view you bring to your present argument?

KEEPING IT LOCAL

As discussed in chapter 1, "Argue with a Purpose," and Chapter 2, "Explore an Issue that Matters to You," an issue exists because people have different points of view on something that affects them. Views different from yours need to be acknowledged. After all, if you want a seat at the discussion table in your community and in the classroom, it's essential that you acknowledge and validate others at the table. When you bring in differing views on an issue and do so with accuracy and a sense of fair play, you strengthen your argument and move yourself closer to winning the respect of an audience.

Returning to the matter that begins this chapter—a writer's concern with her elderly neighbor—you should now see why it's important to make plenty of room for the opposition in an argument; additionally, the exercises in the chapter provide you with a methodology for proceeding with others in a thorough, fair-minded way. The writer recognized that rallying those on her block to look in on John would not be enough. At this point, she began looking at her issue in broader, systemic terms, a choice that led her to advocate for free health care. The student who prepared this argument still looks in on John. The debate over free versus private health care systems continues. But because this student crafted an argument responding to a neighbor's circumstances and took in a range of other perspectives, she earned the right to be heard. A solid argument does not ensure change, but it does let us speak up on issues that matter to us and puts us in touch with others equally invested in local and, in this case, national issues.

● – – – – – – – – – ●

Based on the argument you're working with now, how will you make sure that your treatment of opposing views is fair and thorough? And if your issue affects the local community, how will you identify various positions that respond to the issue? Your answers to these questions will be the foundation for a major piece of your argument. Keep in mind as well that your treatment of the opposition can build your credibility with your target audience.

PART THREE

How to Plan, Structure, and Deliver an Argument

CHAPTER 7

Explore An Issue

As you stand in line to order a soda at a local fast-food restaurant, you notice a young mother with three children taking their food to a table. The trays Mom is juggling are piled with burgers and fries, even though healthier kids' meals are offered by the restaurant. You're puzzled. If healthy options are offered, why hasn't this mother taken advantage of them? You begin to think that maybe the mother just doesn't know any better. By offering healthy choices for children, fast-food restaurants are doing their part. But is there more that can be done?

You think about the family while you develop ideas for a nutrition course paper and wonder what your claim should be. Should you argue the causes of childhood obesity or the effects of children eating a fast-food diet? Should you work to discover the problems underlying childhood obesity and offer a solution? Along the way you will need to define terms and evaluate any solutions you propose. How can you use similar situations, maybe involving food served in school cafeterias, to compare with food served in fast-food restaurants?

COMMUNITY

School-Academic

Workplace

Family-Household

Neighborhood

Social-Cultural

Consumer

Concerned Citizen

TOPIC: Food Consumption

ISSUE: Fast Food and Health

AUDIENCE: Fast-Food Restaurant Owners

CLAIM: Fast-food restaurants should move beyond just offering healthy foods to encouraging children to eat healthier.

There are many argumentative writing tasks you may be asked to perform in your college writing career. In a business course, you may be assigned an evaluative essay that asks you to determine the feasibility of a new project. In a political science course, you may be asked to compare the governmental systems of two countries. Most frequently, you will be asked to argue a position. In Chapter 8, "Consider Toulmin-Based Argument," and Chapter 9, "Consider Middle Ground Argument, Rogerian Argument, and Argument based on a Microhistory," you will learn about formal types of argument (e.g., Toulmin, Rogerian). Here we will discuss the practicalities of presenting definitions, evaluations, causes and consequences, comparisons, and solution proposals.

Chapter 7 is designed to help you explore your issue from different angles, further solidifying your claim so that the argument's organizational structure becomes clear.

In this chapter you will work toward solidifying your claim as you:

- Develop an argument strategy based on:
  - Definitions.
  - Causes or consequences.
  - Comparisons.
  - Solution proposals.
  - Evaluations.
- Write an exploratory essay.

Arvind Balaraman/Shutterstock.com

Figure 7.1 Images like the above may inspire you to explore the issue of childhood obesity.

Use Definitions

Use a **definition** when an argument may benefit from an in-depth discussion of the terms involved. Throughout your college career (and very frequently in your professional career as well), you will be asked to define terms. Maybe you are developing a brochure for your clients and want your services to be clear. You would define each one. Maybe you are debating the outcome of a battle in a history course. Who won? That depends on the definition of *winning* that you use. Sometimes you will need to define terms within a paper in conjunction with other types of support; other times the definition will be the point of the paper.

Defining terms can be a useful way to begin your argument. But please do not begin every essay with "According to Webster's Dictionary ... " Supply a definition only under these circumstances:

- Your definition of a term is very different from that normally provided.
- There is a controversy surrounding the definition of the term, and it is important for your audience either to know about this controversy or to understand why you have settled on the definition you are using.

- Your term may have a multitude of meanings, and you need to clarify how you are using the term.
- Your term is often misunderstood.

For example, Brandon is working on an argument for his political science course. He is interested in the debate surrounding genetically modified foods, or biotech foods that are derived from genetically modified crops or organisms (GMOs). Brandon wants to argue that GMOs are safe, but will need to define some terms, particularly *GMO*, in order to specify how he is going to be using the terms. Here is his claim and two supports that provide two different definitions: one from the FDA and another from an anthropologist. These are then presented as an introduction and two body paragraphs.

CLAIM:	GMO foods are safe because they meet the standard of being substantially equivalent to their natural counterparts.
SUPPORT ONE:	The FDA's definition of *substantial equivalence*.
SUPPORT TWO:	The anthropologist's definition of *natural foods*.

The term *GMO foods* refers to foods that are made from genetically modified organisms. Specifically, this means organisms modified through the use of genetic engineering, or intentional manipulation of the organism's genetic material, its genes, or its DNA. Organizations that regulate food health worldwide use the concept of substantial equivalence to determine whether or not GMO foods are safe. If the modified food is substantially equivalent to its natural counterpart, it can be considered safe. Piet Schenkelaars, a biotech consultant, explains that the original definition of the term *substantial equivalence*, created in 1993 by the Organization for Economic Co-operation and Development, was that the GMO food in question "demonstrates the same characteristics and composition as the conventional food."

Some studies have found that genetically modified foods have more or less of certain important nutrients, therefore calling into question the idea that these foods are substantially equivalent. The whole usefulness of this safety standard depends on how we define the term *substantial*. Does it make a substantial difference if we eat soybean products that contain more lectin but less choline? The FDA specifically looks for substances that are new to the food and for different levels of allergens, nutrients, and toxins.

It may help to define *substantial equivalence* by comparison. There will always be differences between GMO foods and their natural counterparts. However, how great are these differences compared to the differences between other kinds of foods and their natural counterparts? After all, most of the foods we eat were genetically modified using traditional mutation and breeding techniques. One study even showed that these other differences were greater than those found in GMO soy. The study by Cheng, et al., was titled "Effect of Transgenes on Global Gene Expression in Soybean is within the Natural Range of Variation of Conventional Cultivars." If we accept some differences between the foods we eat and their natural counterparts, why should differences in GMO foods be especially worrisome?

Another issue is the context behind the definition of the term *natural foods*. No two varieties of conventional foods share the "same characteristics and composition," yet we readily accept these differences. In addition, virtually all of the foods we eat are very different than the original wild varieties. An anthropologist might define *natural foods* as those that human beings evolved to eat or those that were cultivated long ago. In prehistory and throughout our agricultural history, humans have selected and bred the plants that we preferred. Through this process of human intervention, the original ears of the teosinte plant have been transformed from the size of a slender finger to the foot-long ears of corn we know today. According to *Corn: Origin, History, Technology, and Production*, corn (officially "maize") allowed civilizations like the Mayans and Aztecs to flourish and is currently one of the most important food crops in the world (Smith). Which variety—conventional maize or the original teosinte—should be used as the "natural counterpart" for comparing with GMO maize to see if it is substantially equivalent? Are GMO strains natural counterparts of the foods we eat today, which have been created through techniques like mutation and selective breeding? Or should the GMO foods be compared with the original wild varieties that human beings evolved to eat, but which most of us have never seen, let alone eaten? These questions should be a part of any discussion of GMO food safety or the issue of substantial equivalence.

Works Cited

Cheng, K. C., et al. "Effect of Transgenes on Global Gene Expression in Soybean Is Within the Natural Range of Variation of Conventional Cultivars." *Journal of Agricultural and Food Chemistry* 56.9 (May 2008): 3057–67.

Schenkelaars, Piet. "Rethinking Substantial Equivalence." *Nature Biotechnology* 20.119 (2002): n.pag. Web. 19 Jan. 2013.

Smith, C. Wayne, Javier Betran, and E. C. A. Runge, Eds. *Corn: Origin, History, Technology, and Production*. Hoboken: Wiley, 2004.

Discussion: Notice that there are two definitions included in Brandon's supporting material: the definition of *GMO* and the definition of *natural foods*. Both definitions support the larger question of how to define *food safety*. His argument will undoubtedly include more terms to be defined because his audience will need to understand these terms in order to agree with his claim that GMOs are safe. In his argument, he will need to support each of these definitions with research.

Seven Types of Definition

There are many definition strategies that you can use in your academic writing. They may be combined as needed. An overview of seven of the types (Scientific, Metaphoric, Example, Riddle, Functional, Ironic, and Negation) follows.

Define with Science (Descriptive, Factual)

In this type of definition, whether the subject is scientific or not, you are answering questions such as, "How big?" "What color?" and "How old?" You are describing the subject systematically. Usually, you are describing those characteristics that make the subject what it is—a mammal, a poem, a weapon, a disease.

Bees are insects with six legs and two pairs of wings. Bees vary in size from roughly four millimeters to well over four centimeters in length, and weigh anywhere from ....

your turn 7a ▶ **Define with Science**

Define an issue that you are working on in terms of science. What are its component parts? Describe it accurately.

Define with Metaphor (Comparison)

Metaphors are not just useful in poetry and fiction. Metaphors provide a new way of looking at a subject and comparing it with other things. You may use metaphors and similes, and you might also include analogies and list synonyms for your subject term. Metaphorical definitions are very common. The following examples explain how metaphors can be used to define terms:

- A new diet, technology, or government program might be referred to as "a panacea." The real Panacea was a Greek goddess of healing. Now any time something seems like a cure-all, it will invariably be called a panacea.

- To convey that something is a burden, you might call it an "albatross." Here the reference is to the bird (an albatross) that was tied around a sailor's neck as a punishment in a poem by Samuel Taylor Coleridge.

- If you are defining something as a "red herring," you would be saying that it is irrelevant and out of place, like an actual red herring would be.

- An "anchor tenant" is a retail business that, like the anchor on a ship, provides stability for a shopping center or a mall. It consistently draws in customers who may or may not also shop in the smaller satellite stores. A store would be defined as a satellite if it is peripheral to the anchor tenant the way a satellite orbits the periphery of the earth.

your turn 7b   Metaphorical Definitions

Metaphorical definitions can be very effective in introductions. Write an introduction in which you define your term using a metaphor. What does this metaphor add to your introduction?

Define by Example

With this method, the writer provides examples that exemplify members of the category being defined. What are some examples of great athletes, poor drivers, early mammals? By describing the features of the individuals in the group, you will be defining the group as well.

> A great writer is someone like William Chaucer, Jane Austen, or Theodore Geisel, better known as Dr. Seuss.

your turn 7c   Define by Example

Use examples to define your issue. Why are these examples good representations of the category into which your issue falls?

Define with a Riddle

Riddles work well in introductions. The definition is given, but the reader has to guess what is being defined.

> If we allow these people to be integrated into the military, they will cause great harm to morale and discipline. They will cause dissension in the ranks and destroy unit cohesion. If unit cohesion goes, so will military readiness. If we lose military readiness, the defense of our country will be at risk. Our very survival is at stake. We must keep these people separate.
>
> Who are we talking about? Homosexuals? No. Women, then? No. This is a great example of misdirection. Keep going back in time to the first people the military tried to keep from integrating. Of course, the remainder of the argument can use any of the other definition methods to expand upon the answer to the riddle.

your turn 7d   Define with a Riddle

Write an introduction that poses your issue as a riddle. If you can mislead your reader, all the better. How is a riddle an effective strategy for introducing your issue?

Define by Function

When you are looking at your subject's function, you are explaining what it can (or cannot) do. The function of the space program is what? The function of a sphygmomanometer is what? The function of war is what? The essay then discusses these functions.

Functional definitions define things by what they do. To some people, a religion becomes different from a philosophy when it plays a psychological or sociological role. The social and legal definition of *family* was once biological, but that is now giving way to a functional definition.

- A family is a group of people who act as a family, with the bonds of family, or the behaviors or living arrangements of a family.
- A vegan is someone who doesn't eat any animal products.
- Functional definitions also help to classify things. Illicit drugs are classified according to their harmful effects on people. Whenever the government finds that people are using a substance to significantly alter their mood, no matter how natural that substance is, some officials will invariably call for that substance to be defined as a drug and outlawed. (The more harmful the substance, the higher its classification, with "A" indicating the most dangerous class of drugs.)

your turn 7e **Define by Function**

Define your issue in terms of its functions. Identify at least three functions related to your issue. Which may be the most important function and why?

Define with Irony

In an ironic definition, you are arguing that something is not necessarily what it seems, or you are arguing that it is something other than it seems, usually the least likely possibility. You are using ironic definition when, for example, you define a forest fire as the bringer of life. This statement seems counterintuitive, going against reason; after all, so much is destroyed in a forest fire. However, there are many important benefits that come from the destruction. One benefit is that the high temperatures of a fire allow certain pine cones to release their seeds.

your turn 7f **Define with Irony**

Irony is related to tone, so you do not want to push your irony to the point of sarcasm and put off your argument. Again, an introduction is a good place to provide an ironic definition. Write an introduction that defines your term in an ironic way.

Define by Negation

When you define a subject by what it isn't, you are setting up an interesting essay. For example, you could define *education* as NOT merely recall. You can use negation with description, example, function, and so forth. Philosophers say that you cannot define anything by using only negatives, but in fact, negative definitions are often quite useful.

- A virgin is a person who has not yet had sex.
- Parallel lines are a pair of lines on a plane that do not meet or cross.
- Candidate A is nothing like Abraham Lincoln. (Political candidates are often defined by negatives—i.e., they lack a certain quality, such as integrity, or they lack a qualification, such as military experience.)
- A manx is a certain breed of cat that originated on the Isle of Man, but it is also a cat without a tail.

your turn 7g ▶ **Define by Negation**

Sometimes it is easier to define your issue by what it is not, particularly if you are trying to highlight how your issue is lacking or approached differently in a different culture or situation. For example, you may define *democracy* by describing a country where democracy is not the standard way of life. Take a moment to define your issue in terms of what it is not.

Discover Causes or Consequences

A thorough examination of the causes or consequences of your argument (both good and bad) can help you select the best evidence to support your claim. What good would come if your argument is accepted? What bad? What might happen if your argument is not accepted? **Consequences (or effects)** look to the future; **causes** look back at the past. Together they create a chain of evidence that can be very convincing (as shown in Figure 7.2).

Figure 7.2 Cause and Consequence (simple)

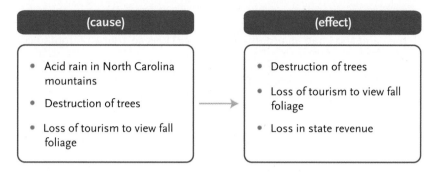

Figure 7.3 Cause and Effect (complex)

Are you interested in arguing based on causes or consequences (effects)? If you need to explain how something came about, you are arguing causes. Do you want to argue what the outcomes of a particular event will be? Then you're interested in presenting evidence of effects. But it's not as simple as it appears. In the example posed in Figure 7.2, we can see that a few of the causes of air pollution are on the left and some of the effects of air pollution are on the right. Air pollution is an issue that can be approached using both cause and effect. The effects themselves can go on to be causes of future events (as shown in Figure 7.3).

> **Claim:** Several factors are responsible for the acid rain destroying North Carolina's mountain trees.
> **Causes:** Factory smoke and car emissions cause acid rain.
> **Claim:** Acid rain in the North Carolina Mountains results in the loss of state revenue.
> **Consequences:** The destruction of trees will discourage tourists from visiting the mountains in North Carolina to view the fall foliage.

As you can see, each effect in turn becomes the cause of something else. And each one of these effects could be argued as being caused by factors other than the ones selected. Cause and/or consequence support can be useful, but very tricky. How far back do you need to research before you feel comfortable that you have reached the earliest cause? How far do you need to project into the future to feel confident that you have anticipated all reasonable consequences? Can you differentiate between primary causes and secondary causes?

A **primary cause** is the one that immediately precedes the effect. It can be very difficult to determine the primary cause of an event. As a humorous example of causal narrative, review this student example:

 tip 7a

Difference between *Affect* and *Effect*
One is a noun:
The <u>effect</u> of cutting back on welfare payments is that single mothers have to pay more for childcare.
One is a verb:
This <u>affects</u> their budgets adversely.

> This morning I broke my arm. This is how it happened. Last night my husband and I had an argument. Because I was so angry, I forgot to set the alarm clock before I went to bed. The next morning we all woke up late, so we were rushing around. As I went to leave, I realized I could not find my glasses. Figuring it was too late to search for them, I rushed out of the door and, to my dismay, stepped on the skateboard my son had left on the front steps. I fell and broke my arm.

The scenario may be silly, but an analysis of cause is not. Can we determine the primary cause of the student's broken arm? Was it the fight with her husband? Not wearing her glasses? The skateboard being in the wrong place? Actually, we could say that the primary cause of the injury was the contact of the cement steps with her arm bone! It is the one cause about which there can be no dispute. Concrete usually wins out over unprotected bone.

But what about secondary, sometimes called "peripheral," causes of the accident? **Secondary causes** are contributing factors. The list of factors contributing to the broken arm is quite long: an unset alarm clock, missing glasses, a misplaced skateboard. How far and wide should the net be cast when exploring secondary causes? It depends. Here are a couple of examples. The first is real, the second hypothetical.

> **Claim:** The rubella outbreak in the mid 1960s resulted in closed-captioning television.
> **Causes:** 1963–65 Rubella outbreak ⟶ high numbers of deaf children ⟶ as these children grew, they demanded closed-captioned TV.

Discussion: The link between the cause and effect could leave many scratching their heads. According to an April 1982 *New York Times* article, between 1963 and 1965 eight thousand pregnant mothers became infected by the rubella virus and gave birth to deaf children. As these children became adults in the early 1980s, they (along with other hearing-impaired individuals) demanded equal access to television programming. Closed captioning was developed in 1980 and spread quickly through the industry. At first, the claim—that the rubella outbreak led to the development of a technology that allowed deaf people to access television programming—seems unlikely. Yet, through a presentation of contributing factors, the connection is clear. Links such as these must be established with a chronology of events connecting the cause to the effect.

This next example involves a hypothetical plane crash. Note the different claims that are put forth by different participants in the scenario. The participants are

- Attorneys for crash victim's families
- Attorneys for the airline
- Attorneys for the Fancy School of Aviation Mechanics (FSAM)

> **Claim One** (made by attorneys for crash victims' families): A stress fracture (*effect*) in the plane's wing was the result of poor inspections by the airline (*cause*).
>
> **Support:** The inspectors were poorly qualified.
>
> **Claim Two** (made by attorneys for the airline): The stress fracture was missed (*effect*) because the inspectors were poorly trained by FSAM (*cause*), an accredited school from which we have been hiring inspectors for years.
>
> **Support:** Inspectors are trained by FSAM, not the airline.
>
> **Claim Three** (made by attorneys for FSAM): A lack of funding (*cause*) has led to the loss of quality instructors (*effect*).
>
> **Support:** FSAM's president embezzled millions of dollars affecting the school's budget.

Discussion: Plane crashes are always investigated, but not always for strictly humanitarian reasons. The primary cause of a crash can often be determined fairly quickly: a wing fell off, a bomb was detonated, the controls jammed, the pilot ignored the air traffic controller. The secondary causes, however, are often messier, and uncovering them is often a more protracted task. To determine the reason, blame has to be assessed. Who is at fault, and therefore, who must pay the cost of lost lives, cleanup, and so on?

How far back can we go to find contributing factors of a plane crash? Would it be unreasonable for the airline's attorneys to argue that the cause of the crash was the embezzlement of millions of dollars of school funds by the FSAM president? Follow the flowchart in Figure 7.4 to see how such a chain of evidence could evolve.

> **Claim Four** (made by the attorneys of the families): Because the airline hired the inspectors, the airline is responsible for the plane crash (*cause*).
>
> **Consequence:** The airline must pay restitution to the victims' families (*effect*).

Discussion: Obviously it is in the airline's best interests to argue that the cause of the plane crash originated elsewhere. After all, if the airline is held liable for the crash, all sorts of consequences could arise, including loss of revenue due to loss in reputation and millions of dollars lost in insurance claims. The immediate, primary cause of the plane crash may have been the wing falling off of the plane, but the secondary causes are more important in this argument. Most important in determining cause is to find the right one for the effect. Too often, arguments are based on flimsy cause–effect relationships, resulting in arguments that are not persuasive.

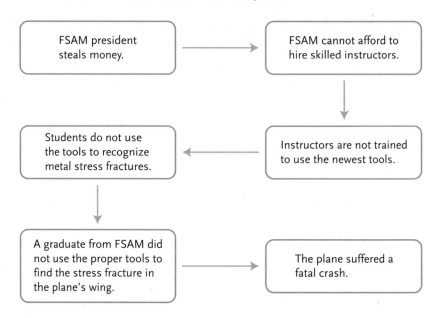

Figure 7.4 This flowchart depicts a chain of evidence.

How far in both directions (toward causes and toward consequences) do you need to go to be comfortable in supporting your claim?

your turn 7h   Explore Causes and Effects

Cast your claim in terms of causes. What is the primary cause of your claim? What are at least two secondary causes? Which of these causes would be most persuasive to your audience? What about effects? List at least three effects of your claim. Are they positive? Negative?

Present Comparisons

Comparisons can be very useful for establishing precedence and examining how similar situations have been handled. Perhaps your claim is one that is often lumped in with other topics. You may want to argue that compared with the other topics, your claim is significantly different and should be examined separately. Or you may be arguing that your claim is similar to other claims made and should be addressed in the same way.

Claim: Stop signs need to be installed at the intersection of Beadle and Poppin Streets, which is surrounded by a shopping center and a large neighborhood.

> **Support:** The intersection of East and West Streets, similarly situated between a neighborhood and a shopping center, has benefited from traffic signs.

Discussion: It can be useful to compare the intersection to another one in town that has the same shopping center/neighborhood configuration. Why does location B have a light, but location A does not? What is similar about the locations? What is different? Are the differences significant enough to allow B to have a light, but not A?

> **Claim:** The intersection of Beadle and Poppin Streets is being denied a traffic signal because it is in a lower income section of town.
>
> **Support One:** Of the requests for any improvements (roads, sidewalks, lights, etc.) in upscale Mayfair neighborhood, 80 percent are being granted; yet only 10 percent of requests from lower income Saxony neighborhood are being granted.

Discussion: What if there is no closely related situation? Then you should look for a situation that has similar characteristics. This type of comparison is larger in scope than an obvious comparison, such as one intersection and another, but it is helpful in shoring up your argument.

You can look for historically similar situations as well. This is called **precedence** and is one of the tools used by lawyers and judges in evaluating court cases. What past cases (in this town or in other towns) have been similar to this one? How were they handled? Knowing how previous problems were solved may be useful in arguing how the new problem can be solved. (See "Propose a Solution" in the section that follows.)

For example, a similar case of seeming discrimination was handled in Atlanta by the establishment of a citizen's group, which investigated all requests and routed them on to the correct departments after the investigations were complete. This group was composed of individuals from all areas of the city and therefore less likely to discriminate or show favoritism. Can such a solution be effective in Saxony? You may argue that it could.

One of the most frustrating experiences you can have in doing research is not finding anything on your particular subject. You know your issue is important, but you are just not finding any support that relates directly to it. Let's look at the issue of including extreme sports in the Olympic Games. We'll narrow the issue even further to target the inclusion of skateboarding. You have spent hours online and in the library but have found nothing really useful on skateboarding and the Olympics. Perhaps you need to do some historical research.

Maybe you can answer the question, "When were women first allowed to compete in the Olympics?" or the question "Why were women not considered athletic competitors in the first place?" Another question to research is "How did an obscure sport like curling become part of the Olympics?" Based on the answers to these questions, you may be able to argue by **analogy.** An analogy is a type of comparison. What about the history of curling is similar to the history of skateboarding? Can the same arguments for including one sport be extended to including the other? How can the answers to questions about including women and curling in the Olympics relate to including skateboarding, an activity that some people do not even consider a sport?

your turn 7i ▶ **Look for Comparisons**

In support of your claim, what can you use for comparison? How are the two situations similar? How are they different? Are there enough similarities that your audience would agree to entertain the comparison you are making?

Propose a Solution

As you continue to develop your argument, it may be useful to think in terms of problems and solutions. There are 13 exploratory steps that we suggest you consider in proposing a solution to a problem. You may find that you need to look at all 13 steps for your issue, or you may need to examine only a few. For example, you may already know the problem, such as when an instructor has assigned you a particular issue to research. Your goal may then be to find support for your claim, Section B. Or maybe you have a great solution but are not sure how to implement it; Section C would be the most useful for you. The chart below offers an overview of the 13-step problem–solution exploration process.

Section A: Exploring the Problem	1. Preparation and Persistence
	2. Understanding the Problem
	3. Ethical Considerations
Section B: Conducting Different Types of Exploration	4. Historical Exploration
	5. Process Exploration
	6. Creative Exploration
	7. Critical Thinking Exploration
	8. Metaphorical and Analogical Exploration
Section C: Exploring Implementation	9. Selecting Solutions
	10. Implementing Solutions
	11. Communicating Solutions
	12. Evaluating Solutions
	13. Future and System Considerations

These steps need not be followed in order, but by considering all of them, you will develop a clearer idea of what your argument is actually about, and you will know how to creatively find ideas and solutions that may elude you otherwise. As you skim over the list, you can see that it can lead you to ideas you had not considered, or that it may help you in solving a problem or implementing a solution (Section C). You may find that you are reinventing the wheel because you have not looked at how a particular problem has been solved historically (Section B). What has been done before and why did it not work? Or maybe you have to consider the ethical nature of a problem in determining fair and equitable solutions (Section A).

At the heart of this process is creative thinking. Ask yourself the question, "How can I approach my topic in a more creative way?" A wonderful book about creative thinking is Robert and Michèle Root-Bernstein's *Sparks of Genius* (Boston: Houghton Mifflin, 1999). The authors researched ways that creative people in varying fields and disciplines came up with ideas. They found, for instance, that a physicist might get

Figure 7.5 Using the science behind obesity and nutrition can help identify a process solution.

ideas by listening to a Bach concerto. A sculptor might discover a new technique by meditating. An engineer might find a solution to a problem while rowing a sea kayak in a storm. Creative thinking refuses to shut out possibilities and embraces ideas that can be found in all avenues of life. The most creative people do not close the door to ideas; instead, they find them in unexpected areas.

Our 13 items reflect many of the ideas that the Root-Bernsteins developed in their research. These steps are meant to be practical tools you can use to come up with ideas that strengthen your arguments. Let's follow the progress of a student, Lise, as she works through all 13 steps to develop a solution to the persistent problem of unhealthy fast-food meals and their link to childhood obesity.

Section A: Exploring the Problem

The steps in this section are very basic. What exactly is the problem at hand? Very often, problems can be challenging to solve because the exact cause is not clear; it can be difficult to find the causes of the problem, who it affects, and who is responsible for it. Moving through these steps can help you address these initial considerations.

1. Preparation and Persistence

What do you need to solve the problem? What are the necessary resources? Do you have enough assistance and persistence? Do you have the time, money, strength, and faith to continue toward a solution? Thomas Edison said that "Genius is one percent inspiration, ninety-nine percent perspiration." It is easy to be inspired, but it takes hard work to complete a task. What do you need to complete your task?

- Do you need to talk to people in relevant fields?
- Do you need research help from librarians?
- Do you need to start all over from scratch?

Lise's issue is one that she is arguing in her college health course, so the possibility of getting a high grade contributes to her motivation to find a solution. However, because she is studying to be a dietician, her motivation is professional and personal as well. Issues such as fast food and childhood obesity relate directly to her chosen career. In addition, she genuinely wants to help people eat better. A strong database of medical articles is available to her, making research easy. Lise's college's health program is linked to the local hospital which means she has access to faculty at the hospital as well. She envisions interviews with doctors at the hospital along with traditional library research.

2. Understanding the Problem

What exactly is the problem? Identify it. Define it. Define it scientifically; descriptively; metaphorically; by example; define the solution without naming it; define the problem by its function; ironically; by its negation; using elaboration; using evaluation.

- What exactly is the problem?
- Is it made up of several smaller problems?
- For whom is it a problem? For whom is it not a problem?
- What caused the problem?

Answering this set of questions will ensure that you are arguing about the real problem. In the student sample below, the problem is not the quality of the product, but the public's perception of the cost.

What does Lise really know about the problem of childhood obesity? Lise's reading so far indicates that there are both controllable reasons (e.g., diet and exercise) and uncontrollable reasons (e.g., genetics) for childhood obesity. Which of the controllable reasons are the biggest culprits for weight gain in children?

- Fast-food diets
- School lunches
- Lack of exercise at school and at home
- Too many unhealthy snacks

Lise will have to decide which problem to tackle. After witnessing the family ordering burgers and fries at the fast-food restaurant (as discussed in this chapter's first pages), she is leaning toward writing about the problem of fast-food diets.

3. Ethical Considerations

What are the rights and wrongs of solving your problem? In other words, how will solving your problem be right and wrong, and for whom?

- Should this problem even be solved?
- What will solving it do to the people involved?
- What will solving or not solving the problem do to the main purpose or core business of the problem-solver?
- What happens if the problem is not addressed or solved?

Solutions require us to expend resources, and they also affect future decisions and operations. Is solving the problem worth the costs, and to whom? Always consider the main purpose of the problem-solver. At our college, our main purpose is to serve students and our community. We consider our decisions ethical if they're good for students and good for our community.

But issues of right and wrong are often complicated. For instance, my purpose is to make a good living for my family. If the state of North Carolina raises instructors' salaries, where will the money come from? Higher taxes on other families who are already struggling with the economic downturn? Ethics can be a cloudy area.

> Lise is convinced that it is extremely important to solve the problem of unhealthy fast-food products being targeted at children. She feels restaurants have a moral obligation to improve their nutritional options for children and to provide encouragement and education through marketing programs or brochures. If the problem is not solved, those families who—by lack of better nutritional options or lack of education—frequently eat fast food will be raising an unhealthy generation of children who will develop health problems that will strain our medical system.

your turn 7j ▶ **Explore the Problem**

For Steps 1–3 above, explore your own issue, following Lise's example.

Section B: Different Types of Exploration

Now that you know what the problem is, where can you look for solutions?

4. Historical Exploration

Historical exploration answers the question, "How have similar problems been solved in the past?" Past cases and examples generate solutions. There is no sense in always starting from scratch. If we know how similar problems have been solved in the past, we may be able to adapt those solutions to fit our current needs. Looking to the past is often a very productive step toward a solution. Always start here.

- What have been some of the historical solutions to the problem?
- Why have they failed?
- Did they fail because the solution was a poor one or because it was not implemented correctly?
- Can an historical solution be used and improved upon with some newly available modifications?

> Of course there have always been overweight children, but studies show that the number of children considered overweight in this country is increasing at an alarming rate. In the past, most childhood weight gain was due to overeating and lack of exercise. The solution was considered simple: eat less and exercise more. Today, though, the childhood obesity problem is complicated by families eating out more, by the increased availability of cheap fast-food options marketed to children, and by skyrocketing food prices that encourage parents to buy cheaper, usually less healthy, foods. If families are having to cut back and are going to be eating out frequently, then one solution is to make sure fast-food restaurants have healthier options and that families know how to choose nutritious foods.

5. Process Exploration

How does the problem work? How do possible solutions work? When we explore processes, we are looking at how things work in order to generate solutions. Areas of exploration can be laws, policies, rules, or psychological and scientific theories. For example, advertisers market their products to younger people, even though older folks buy more products. The reason? They know that the older we are, the less likely we are to change brands, and that getting consumers to change brands is one main purpose for advertisements. Advertisements, then, target the audience that is most likely to be responsive. The idea is that if we know how things work, we can use known processes, theories, tendencies, and behaviors to help craft solutions.

Some processes are informal and more likely to change; they aren't written in stone. Whenever a new president comes into office or a new manager comes into a business, the staff has to figure out what the new person likes, dislikes, tolerates, expects, and so forth. These changing processes may depend on the new leader's personality, but the effect they have on people's lives is every bit as real as the law of gravity or criminal statutes.

- What processes are at work in relation to our problem?
- What are the existing theories in this field or area of activity?
- Which sciences are involved, and what do the experts tell us about our problem?
- What are some predictable behaviors surrounding our problem and its possible solutions?

How did fast-food restaurants begin serving such bad foods to children? When did kids' meals become popular? Lise suspects that fast-food advertising during Saturday morning cartoons began the craze for kids' meals and the toys they contain. By including toys that relate to popular movies, the restaurants and the kids' meals become even more attractive to children. Who makes the choices at the local level about what restaurants serve? For example, McDonalds has locations all around the world, and different foods are served in different places. To some extent, local decisions must determine which products are sold in each location; Lise needs to learn the processes that governs who makes these decisions.

6. Creative Exploration

This process allows you to explore and answer questions such as, "How else might the situation be?" and "What could we add to it or put in its place?" As important as it is to research historical solutions to similar problems, it is also important to use creative free-range thinking. For this step, ignore processes, past examples, and assumptions. If you could wave a wand to come up with any solution you like, what would that solution be? Then, once you've imagined the solution, no matter how far-fetched it is, work backwards to see how you might get there. Freeing yourself from logical thinking can often have amazing results. Perhaps you had a good idea all along, but your fears of looking foolish prevented you from committing the idea as a solution. Through creative exploration, you may discover that the idea may actually work! Here are some examples of creative problem-solving:

- When the Japanese invaded Okinawa, in 1607, the locals were forbidden to carry weapons, so they developed a form of open-hand combat called karate.
- According to legend, Irish step-dancing came about because dancing was outlawed but people wanted to dance anyway. They held their arms still and moved only their legs, which allowed them to dance behind stone walls without appearing to be dancing at all.
- When parents are desperate, they find creative ways to motivate their children to get good grades. Some of them even pay their children money for grades.

People have a long history of coming up with creative solutions to difficult problems. Climb out of the box for solutions. Read books or articles about topics that seem different from yours in order to see how other problems have been solved. For example, if your company has tried unsuccessfully to motivate employees with bonuses, try reading trade journals in other fields to see how different kinds of businesses motivate their employees.

Creativity shows up in the restaurant business frequently. "Thinking outside the bun" led to the creation of tortilla wraps. The focus on low-carb eating resulted in the introduction of ethnic cuisines, such as lettuce wraps.

> In the best of all possible worlds, children would be able to eat hamburgers and French fries that would actually be healthy for them. Fast-food restaurants are missing an opportunity to think outside the box about what healthy eating means. If a father insists on feeding his children a steady diet of burgers, then the burgers should at least be healthy. There are dozens of vegetarian versions of burgers that kids love. Potatoes are not inherently unhealthy, but frying is, so the fries could be baked instead. Apples can be served instead of apple pie; low-fat yogurt with granola can be served instead of full-fat yogurt with candy sprinkles. Problems that seem impossible at first can often be addressed with a little creative thinking.

7. Critical Thinking Exploration

How else might the situation be? What could we take away from the problem or from each possible solution? Question your basic assumptions to generate solutions.

- Do you even need to solve the problem?
- Are the rules governing the problem mandatory?
- Did past solutions work for the reasons you thought they worked?

At a local pizza shop, customers who pay with plastic have a long wait-time. In order to process credit card transactions, the cashier has to ring up the order at the register, swipe the card, walk across the store and around a shelving unit, wait to gather the receipt once it prints, come back, and only then complete the transaction. The manager's explanation of the problem was, "Our credit card machine runs through the computer, which is across the store." Hasn't she considered moving the systems closer together? A little critical thinking could make credit card processing more efficient.

It often pays to ask, "What if the accepted 'truth' is not actually true?" What if there really is no gravity? What if we don't have to die? What if the earth *isn't* round? The weird people who ask these odd questions end up discovering new things. In fact, our latest theory of gravity (Einstein's) is being questioned and may soon be replaced with a new theory. In fact, science may find a solution to the dying process in your lifetime. In fact, the earth is bulgy, not round.

> Is fast food really the problem? Isn't lack of exercise just as important a factor in childhood obesity? The assumption is that children are getting too many "bad" calories from burgers and chicken fingers, but do we know that is true? Perhaps the number of times a week a family stops at Burger Barn is a bigger factor than what is actually consumed. Lise asks questions that seem obvious but need to be addressed. She also needs to examine the products that popular fast-food chains actually offer children. Have the restaurants tried to provide healthy options in the past? Were these attempts profitable? What could they do to increase the profitability of healthy options?

8. Metaphorical or Analogical Exploration

Metaphorical thinking asks us to see the connections and similarities between seemingly different things. Analogies involve seeing similarities between seemingly different situations. It can be helpful to think more creatively about your issue. For example, Lise was having difficulties untangling all the threads of her issue to determine which one to present as her claim. She could concentrate on fast-food advertising, the types of kids' meals restaurants serve, the types of families that eat in fast-food restaurants frequently, and the cost of the food. Until the image of a tree with branches came to her, Lise couldn't see that her argument had one "trunk" and that the different areas of her argument could be organized into "branches." Her metaphorical thinking yielded an organizational format that she couldn't see before: one main problem with smaller problems branching off from the main trunk.

- What is the problem like?
- What are possible solutions like?
- Can a metaphor be created?
- Is an analogy better?

Example of Metaphor:

Let's say I sell used cars and I'd like to double my sales. I can cast about in my mind to answer the question, "What else doubles?" and come up with the answer, "Bread dough." "How?" "Yeast." "What's the yeast in sales?" "Energy, charisma, good looks, manipulation, reciprocity, value, compassion—whatever is needed." One of these ideas might prove to be an important part of the solution, no matter what an expert consultant might say. My car lot might well need sprucing up. Or my cars might not seem to have much value. Or my staff might smell bad. Textbook solutions (historical and scientific) are wonderfully important in many cases, but in this case the metaphor might be useful because thinking of my sales as bread dough sent me looking for the "yeast" that might be missing.

Example of Analogy:

I had a problem keeping all of the leaves and debris out of my pool. I live in the country, surrounded by nature's abundance, and a lot of stuff gets in the pool. It is almost an everyday affair to keep it cleaned. I could clean it myself, but doing so would take up immense amounts of my time and energy. While I was watching a show about animals whose teeth and bodies are cleaned by other animals, I thought of my pool-cleaning problem. In order to clean themselves, the animals would expend energy and time, just as I would do if I cleaned my own pool. They would have the impossible task of growing new appendages, just as I would have the impossible task of creating more time. I decided to invest in an automatic pool cleaner—just as the animals have "automatic" teeth and body cleaners.

If a solution has been found to a problem that is similar to yours, perhaps you can apply or adapt that solution.

What object, issue, or situation does the problem of childhood obesity resemble? The more Lise read, the more the issue seemed to branch off into other issues. Before long, her issue had become as tangled as tree branches. The metaphor of a tree worked for Lise. She could see the different types of problems (poor nutrition, lack of family time, the low cost of fast food) as branches of a tree (fast food). Chopping the tree down is not an option, but leaving it alone only allows it to continue growing wildly in any direction it chooses. Lise started to think about ways that the branches could be pruned and shaped so as the tree continues to grow, the branches (the issues) will be directed. How can specific foods offered by fast-food restaurants be modified to become healthier?

your turn 7k ▶ **Look for Creative Answers**

For Steps 4–8 above, explore your own issue, following the student models of Lise.

Section C: Exploring Implementation

Maybe your problem is not coming up with solutions, but identifying which potential solution would be the best choice. Or maybe you have settled on a solution but don't know whom to address in your claim or how to implement your solution.

9. Selecting Solutions

Which proposed solution should be chosen? Often, a given problem will have several potential solutions. Deciding which one to choose is difficult. If it's your problem, you have to satisfy yourself, right? What if it satisfies you but makes your family mad? Or your boss? Or what if you can't afford it?

- Which is the best solution?
- Which is the simplest solution?
- Which solution best fits your goals?
- Which solution is the most ethical?
- Which solution is the cheapest?
- How will you decide which solution to propose?

As Lise continued her research, she saw solutions that companies in other industries had used, and she began thinking of how to apply those solutions to the problem of fast-food meals for children. But which of these solutions should be present in her argument? Some solutions would be expensive because they would involve introducing new products, and passing this cost on to the consumer would drive lower-income parents to search out cheaper types of fast food. Some solutions would involve developing clear nutritional guidelines for kids' meals. Some of the less expensive solutions might not offer the same degree of success. Cost and effectiveness were the two variables that Lise decided to use as her guide in crafting solutions that would please both fast-food restaurants and families.

10. Implementing Solutions

How can the solution best be implemented?

- What resources will the solution entail?
- What process should we put in place?
- Will it involve monitoring and enforcement?
- Who should do the implementing?

I went to a discount store the other day and encountered a problem. When I asked the cashier to ring up six bags of dirt, she told me I needed to go outside and make sure it was there. I said it was probably there and asked her to go ahead and ring it up. She was very nice but refused to let me pay for the dirt until I had gone personally to verify that it was in stock. I looked at the long line behind me and left the store. The store had a problem: How could they make their products convenient to buy? In other words, how could they save their customers time and money? The first solution they tried didn't work in my case: they wanted employees to remember what the store had in stock and not ring-up anything else. This solution relied too much on training employees to remember which products were in stock.

The next time I purchased dirt at the discount store, a new solution was in place. The manager had checked the stock and covered the bar codes on the scan sheets to show items not in stock. That way no one could ring up something they didn't have. The second solution was easier to implement, a lot cheaper than training, and a lot more reliable than a busy clerk's memory. They solution had been possible all along, they just hadn't identified it.

Lise comes to realize that fast food causes big problems for children struggling to maintain a healthy weight. When children eat a steady diet of fast food, they do not thrive physically. Issues contributing to the problem were food cost and fast-food convenience. Lise decides that issues of time and money are not as easily addressed as food quality. Since restaurants can be required to provide nutritional information for the foods they sell, then surely they can be required to provide nutritious food for children. School lunch programs have become healthier by providing options that do appeal to children; fast-food restaurants can do the same.

11. Communicating Solutions

Very often, solutions are devised at the very top of an organization, and the steps required to implement the solution are communicated quite efficiently throughout the organization. Unfortunately, the reason for those steps often does not filter down, diminishing the effectiveness of the solution. How, then, can the solution best be communicated?

> Lise's argument has to be presented as a researched paper to a college professor. However, if she were working for a particular restaurant desiring to provide healthier foods, she would probably have several choices in how to communicate her findings to her boss. Here are two of her choices:
>
> • A formal report may be the best choice in response to a request by the boss for a study of the issue
> • A memo may be appropriate if she is the one bringing up the topic with her boss and wants to do so informally

12. Evaluating Solutions

How can the effectiveness of the solution be evaluated? Was it really the best solution? Although it is most often thought of as occurring after a solution is implemented, evaluation is actually part of every step: before, during, and after implementation. At each of these stages, the key to good evaluation is to understand the real values we need to measure the results against.

> To determine whether a solution is effective, Lise will have to implement it and develop a tool to evaluate its effectiveness. What would such a tool look like? To whom should she propose her solution and how might it be implemented? Lise's research led her to believe that in addition to submitting her argument to her professor, she could pitch her problem–solution argument at the fast-food restaurant in her neighborhood, a locally owned eatery. She develops a new policy to encourage children to lose weight and get fit using a "fat-to-fit" program that will result in increased sales. She now has a narrower perspective on the issue, and this narrows the type of research she needs to do. A narrow angle can really benefit an argument by allowing the writer to focus on specifics.

13. Future and System Considerations

Now that we've solved the problem and evaluated the effectiveness of the chosen solution, what is the next step?

• Should we consider the process closed? Or has our solution created another problem to solve?

• Has the solution eliminated our argument's reason for being?

• Has it changed the nature of our core business?

• What are the unintended consequences of the chosen solution?

• How has the solution changed the internal or external organizational system?

A positive example of evaluation of a solution is provided by the G.I. Bill. After World War II, huge numbers of young men came back from the war and enrolled in college using money from the G.I. Bill. That gave them the skills they needed to compete for good-paying jobs. In turn, that boosted our economy, which in turn helped people make more money and buy houses and pay more in taxes, so that the government had even more money to give the next generation of soldiers to go to college. It helped the whole system.

> After using the problem-solving process to evaluate her topic, Lise now has a claim that she can research and a solution she can propose. She may even be able to evaluate the solution if it is implemented in her community. If successful, a change in a small local restaurant may spark interest in the larger chains, prompting them to implement similar changes. Lise is ready to tackle her research in earnest, and her argument will be more effective and focused, using specifics instead of abstractions.

your turn 7I **Implement Your Solutions**

For Steps 9–13 above, explore your own issue, following the student models of Lise.

Evaluate Your Claim

An **evaluation** should be used when you are attempting to persuade your audience that one thing is better (more efficient, more feasible, etc.) than another. As long as you clearly explain your evaluation criteria, evidence that provides an evaluation of your problem and solution can be important in persuading your audience. When presenting your evaluation, you will sometimes be asked to offer a single solution or to offer several solutions and indicate which is best based on the indicated criteria. For example, in a humanities course, you may be asked to which category, genre, or movement a work of art, a text, or a piece of music belongs.

> The Problem: *Madonna and Child with Angels and St. Jerome* by the Italian artist Parmigianino (see Figure 7.6), is an example of what style of art?
> The Solution: *Madonna and Child with Angels and St. Jerome* is an example of Mannerist art because ...
> The Criteria: ... it exhibits the following characteristics of Mannerism:
>
> - Elongated figures and forms
> - Garish color combinations
> - Exaggerated body positions
>
> Parmigianino's painting is an example of Mannerist art because it exhibits all three characteristics of that art style.

Madonna with the Long Neck, 1534–40 (oil on canvas), Parmigianino (Francesco Mazzola) (1503–40)/Galleria degli Uffizi, Florence, Italy/Alinari/The Bridgeman Art Library

Figure 7.6 Parmigianino, *Madonna and Child with Angels and St. Jerome*

In an evaluation, you will:

- Select the criteria or characteristics that you will use to evaluate your subject.
- Discuss your selection of criteria.
- Present an evaluation of your subject based on that criteria.

your turn 7m **Evaluate Your Solution**

From your exploration of your issue from the 13-step problem–solution perspective, evaluate the solution you decided upon. Make sure to select the criteria you will use, and evaluate the solution based on those criteria. Alternatively, develop three solutions and use your criteria to determine which solution best fits the problem.

Write an Exploratory Essay

An exploratory essay is a useful way to examine both a) what you know about your topic so far, and b) what directions you may still need to pursue before putting your argument together.

What do you know about your issue? An exploratory essay usually is undertaken after you have completed some research on the issue, maybe after you have worked through some of the prewriting methods or the problem-solving items. Don't narrow your research too soon. At the beginning, read enough on the subject to be conversant with the players involved, about the problems and different points of view. You can then sift through your materials and decide what parts of the issue you are now comfortable with. What you do know may include:

- Historical or cultural background on the issue.
- The players involved in the issue.
- What claims you may want to make.

Once you have seen what you do know, it is time to examine what elements about your issue that are confusing or that require further research. As you tackle what you do know, you may often find more questions that need to be answered.

What you don't know may include:

- Support for your claims.
- Where to look for materials such as statistics, interviews, articles, and so on.
- Possible solutions.

Your essay should present the reader with a clear idea of what your questions are, what you have learned so far, and what you still need to do to complete your argument.

▶ Exploratory Essay Checklist

Have you included the following elements in your exploratory essay?

☐ Claim

☐ Background that includes context and all those involved

☐ What you know so far (research and common knowledge)

☐ What you still need to research

☐ Types of support you will need (see Chapter 11, "Support an Argument
with Fact (Logos), Credibility (Ethos), and Emotion (Pathos)")

Sample Exploratory Essay

Below is Lise's exploratory essay, along with her instructor's comments.

Lise Holt

Health 232

Professor Smith

4 September 2013

Exploratory Essay

What is the specific claim to be made? What organizational strategy would best be employed?

Fast-food restaurants have been around for quite a while now. They have not traditionally been known for their healthy foods; they are popular for their ability to get hungry, busy people in and out fast. Can't the two goals, health and speed, be combined? In particular, can't healthy foods and a healthy eating program be combined to help families eat healthier? I am arguing that fast-food restaurants should add nutrition-education programs, using their websites and brochures, to explain their healthier kids' menus. My primary strategy will be to offer a solution with a fat-to-fit program at Mama Maya's Italian Eatery in town. The program will be both healthy and cost effective.

Who are the players involved in this issue?

Who is involved in the issue? Families with children who eat at fast-food restaurants are the focus of my claim; they would be the beneficiaries of any educational programs and the improvements that restaurants make to their kids' menus. The restaurant owners themselves are the second interested parties. Their motivation is keeping businesses. How would they be motivated to change their menus? Are they receiving any complaints now? If not, what would be their motivation to offer education and new menu selections?

By selecting a topic that generates personal interest, Lise will be able to begin forming opinions about the issue and selecting research that is more focused on her particular claim.

I became interested in this topic when I was standing in line at Mama Maya's ordering dinner. It occurred to me after seeing several parents ordering food for their children that they were ignoring the healthier options on the menu. In my health class, we are currently debating the issue of obesity in children and I immediately thought of the kids at the restaurant.

What is there still to be done? Lise has now identified a claim that will help her direct her research and gather appropriate support.

My next step will be to research the argued causes of childhood obesity. I will also need to find out why some restaurants have begun offering healthier options for kids and others haven't. Finally, I will develop a fat-to-fit program to accompany Mama Maya's menu.

Write an Exploratory Essay

Address these items in an exploratory essay about a topic you are researching.

- What is the historical or cultural background to the issue?
- Who are the players involved in the issue?
- What tentative claims do you want to make?

Include what you do not know that needs more research. What you don't know may include:

- Support for your claims.
- Where to look for materials (statistics, interviews, articles, etc.).
- Possible solutions.

Reflect and Apply

1. As you explore your issue, you will need to make some choices about how to arrange your argument. Explain your decision to use one of the following organizational strategies: define, compare, evaluate, or evaluate causes and effects. Why did you select your organizational strategy? How would your argument be different if you selected a different strategy?

2. Once you have identified which sections of the exploration process you need to apply to your issue, work through them carefully. Explain what these processes add to your thinking about your issue. What solutions do these processes suggest?

3. Your exploratory essay is an opportunity to take a step back from your issue and consider what you have discovered and what more needs to be done. How are you articulating your ideas to your reader in your exploratory essay? Are there any questions that your reader may still have after they read your exploratory essay? How would you answer those questions?

KEEPING IT LOCAL

IN EVERY TOWN there is at least one popular local restaurant that everyone flocks to after football games, soccer practice, even church on Sunday. For as diverse a culture as we have in the United States, the offerings of these restaurants are surprisingly similar. Most menus will include hot dogs, hamburgers, fried fish or shrimp, chili, ice cream or shakes, and cakes and pies. Even those eateries that offer veggie plates usually fry their okra or boil their field peas with fat back. If we want our children to eat better, we cannot rely on fast-food restaurants to magically begin putting healthier foods on the menus. By using different argument strategies, we can compare restaurants' offerings in parts of the country where people are considered healthier with those in parts of the country where people are not so healthy. We can define what healthy food choices mean to us and outline processes to meet these definitional goals. We can campaign against bad food choices based on their effects on our children's lifestyles and health. By examining the restaurant issue, or any other issue important to us, through multiple lenses, we can discover powerful methods of developing solutions to seemingly insurmountable problems.

●‑‑‑‑‑‑‑‑‑‑●

What issue is important to you? Start the exploration process by asking yourself the questions in the "Propose a Solution" section. Where are these questions taking you? Sometimes you may find that these questions are opening avenues that you had not considered. Are you ready to go down those avenues and learn something new?

CHAPTER 8

Consider Toulmin-Based Argument

During a class activity, a student spoke intently about the political climate at our community college. He was born in the United States, and his native language is English. His parents moved to the United States from another country 25 years ago, bringing his two sisters—who were very young at the time—with them, so that he and his siblings could enjoy more opportunities and the promise of better lives. Ever since he can remember, his parents have contributed to the civic and religious life of our community. Both hold full-time jobs, and his mother has been promoted several times at work. This student has earned top grades, and his sisters plan to attend the same college in the next few years. But last spring, just after the end of the semester, our state—North Carolina—became the first in the country to recommend that children (who do not have lawful immigration status) of illegal immigrants be barred from attending community college. While the student will complete his degree next semester, he worries about his sisters not being able to attend community college, which will mean that college will be delayed for them. He reveals that he is caught in a swirl of emotions and is not sure what to do. Motivated by concern for his sisters and others in the community who had planned to take advantage of the reasonable tuition and convenience of the local community college, he wants to make his point of view known on this important issue.

The student decides to contact two instructors at the school and ask if they would be interested in supporting him. Together, the three decide to aim an argument at the State Board of Community Colleges, an organization in a position to ensure that the community college system continues its original open-door policy.

All Illustrations by iStockphoto.com/A-digit

COMMUNITY

School-Academic

Workplace

Family-Household

Neighborhood

Social-Cultural

Consumer

Concerned Citizen

TOPIC: Children of Illegal Immigrants in the Community College System

ISSUE: Admission Policy for Children of Illegal Immigrants

AUDIENCE: State Board of Community Colleges

CLAIM: Children of illegal immigrants should be allowed to attend community colleges.

This chapter introduces you to Toulmin-based argument and the ways this structure can serve your purpose as you argue an issue that matters to you. As discussed in Chapter 2, "Explore an Issue that Matters to You," an argument should be a practical response to an issue, especially when you have a good sense of your audience, what it values, and why this issue is important to this audience. In the example that opens this chapter, the writers have made a practical decision to target the State Board of Community Colleges as the audience for their Toulmin-based argument.

You should construct an argument so that all its pieces serve your purpose. If your purpose is to convince an audience of the rightness of your own claim, as opposed to differing claims on an issue, then working with a Toulmin-based approach can serve your purpose. As you'll see in Chapter 9, "Consider Middle Ground Argument, Rogerian Argument, and Argument Based on a Microhistory," there are other argument structures that may be appropriate for your purpose. For example, if your intention is to argue for a practical position between two extreme positions, then a middle-ground strategy can serve your purpose. But if your purpose is to create productive dialogue and common ground on a testy issue with an individual or group whose perspective differs sharply from your own, then a Rogerian approach is practical. And if your purpose is to examine closely a largely forgotten individual, place, or event from the past, then an argument based on a microhistory can work for you.

In this chapter, you will learn how to:

- Structure a Toulmin-based argument to fit your purpose.
- ...ly the features of Toulmin-based argument to an issue.
- ...oulmin-based argument.

Construct an Argument to Fit Your Purpose

Once you've decided what you want to accomplish with a Toulmin-based argument, make sure you (as discussed in Chapter 2, "Explore an Issue That Matters to You"):

- Deliver your argument at a time when your audience is invested in the issue at hand.
- Center your argument in what is practical and possible.
- Know what your audience values.
- Let your audience know what it has to gain from your argument.
- Earn credibility early in the argument by establishing your knowledge of the issue and by defining your relationship to your audience.

For example, the narrative that opens this chapter addresses an issue getting a lot of attention in our state these days. The issue originates with the attorney general's recommendation that children of illegal immigrants be barred from pursuing degrees in the state's community colleges, a recommendation that the president of the community college system has chosen to follow. Because this student attends a community college and because his coauthors teach at the same college, writers of this argument have firsthand knowledge of this issue, and this may establish their credibility with their audience. The issue is generating much discussion across the state based on the news media's regular attention to it. Thus, the argument will be delivered at a decisive moment in the state's struggle with the immigrant presence in schools and other publicly funded institutions. The writers' decision to use a Toulmin-based approach is practical for their purpose—to convince their audience that "children of illegal immigrants should be allowed to attend community colleges." Consider how an argument centered in this issue might take shape using a Toulmin-based approach.

Terms of Toulmin-Based Argument

Contemporary British philosopher Stephen Toulmin has shaped the way we think about argument today. Where classical argument is centered in a three-part structure called a syllogism (major premise, minor premise, and conclusion), Toulmin renames these terms, adds three additional terms to the model, and moves argument from an exercise in logic to a practical scheme geared toward audience acceptance. Toulmin's six terms can be used as a checklist for writing effective arguments when your purpose is to persuade an audience of the rightness of your position. Those terms, defined in the following section, are *claim, support, warrant, backing, rebuttal,* and *qualifier*.

When you build an argument based on the Toulmin model, it's helpful to think of each term as a question that you must answer. With regard to the term *claim*, the question you must answer is, "What is my point?" or "What am I trying to prove?" For the term *support*, the question is, "How will I prove

Ozgurcankaya/E+/Getty Images

Figure 8.1 Close attention to audience and what it values is the hallmark of a Toulmin-based argument. The need to convince an audience of the rightness of a claim depends in large part on the range of support, or evidence, the arguer brings to an argument.

my point?" For the term *warrant*, the questions are, "Will my audience believe me based on values we share?" and "How can I justify my claim?" For the term *backing*, be prepared to answer the question, "What additional support for my warrant will I need in order to persuade my audience?" The term *rebuttal* requires that you ask, "What points of view different from mine should I bring to an argument?" And for the term *qualifier*, you must ask, "How can I modify the language in my argument, especially with reference to my claim and reasons, to make an argument more acceptable?"

But we must add a seventh and vital term to the Toulmin model, and this term is *reasons*. A reason falls between a claim and the specific support you bring to an argument. A reason supports a claim, and in turn, a reason requires support to make it believable. For example, focusing on the issue of children of illegal immigrants being barred from attending community colleges, if you claim that children of illegal immigrants should be allowed to enroll, you will need to provide reasons in support of this claim. One reason the coauthors can address beyond moral or financial arguments is that a skilled workforce is better for the state's economy. This reason requires specific support. So, while the term *reasons* is not among the terms usually used to develop a traditional six-part Toulmin argument, this seventh term is important, especially when you use a Toulmin approach to build a practical response to an issue affecting you.

Claim

A **claim** organizes your argument. It is the single statement to which every-thing else in an argument connects. It focuses your audience on what you want to achieve. It's the point you want to make. For example, a few years ago, a student new to her city made this claim in her first argument: "Links to websites that promote dangerous, antigay propaganda should not be posted on official community websites." Her online search for gay organizations at one point led her to a site stating that same-sex relationships were mor-ally wrong and that counseling was available for those struggling with their sexual identity. The fact that a link to the site appeared on the Chamber of Commerce website motivated her to argue.

Key Questions:
What is my point? What am I trying to prove?

Reasons

Reasons are direct support for your claim. Reasons often function as topic sentences, which you studied in earlier writing courses: they many times begin paragraphs and announce a paragraph's main idea or focus. As a way to begin working with reasons in an argument, think about immediately following a claim with the word *because*. Thus, the claim "Links to websites that promote dangerous, antigay propaganda should not be posted on official community websites" was supported with these reasons:

Key Question:
What comes after *because*?

- Because sites that promote "recovery" from homosexuality are just as harmful as explicitly hateful sites, such as "godhatesfags.com," a site promoting lies and cruelty
- Because not only is the information from such "recovery" sites harmful, it is also inaccurate
- Because the dangers of antigay propaganda are vast, the most visible occurring in antigay battery and assault

Support

Bring in specific **support** to defend your reasons. As we will see in Chapter 11, "Support an Argument with Fact (Logos), Credibility (Ethos), and Emotion (Pathos)," support can be logical (e.g., facts, statistics, data), ethical (e.g., scholarly articles, credible publications, examples from your own and oth-ers' experiences), or emotional (e.g., examples and startling information that can cause an audience to react emotionally). Vary the support you use, but remember that logical support is proof to an audience that you've done your research and that you're prepared to defend your claim on rational grounds. In most arguments, your goal is to have your audience accept your claim, and the thoroughness of supporting evidence is often what sways an audience. Consider the support this writer brings to her argument.

Key Question:
How will I prove my point?

- Logical support includes numerous examples drawn from antigay web-sites; the FBI's *Uniform Crime Report*, which reveals the annual number of hate crimes based on victims' sexual orientation; and an academic study focused on gay teens and suicide.

- Ethical support includes quoted and paraphrased commentary on homosexuality from the American Psychiatric Association and the dean of the Georgetown University Medical Center, along with examples—from the writer's experience and those of her friends—of antigay violence, including slurs, bullying, beatings, and property damage.
- Emotional support includes reference to Matthew Wayne Shepard, a gay man beaten and left for dead in Wyoming (an example that opens the argument) and personal examples of her experience with those in her new community who offer "love and guidance" as "solutions" to her sexual orientation.

Warrant

Key Questions:
Will my audience believe me
based on values we share?
How can I justify my claim?

Use a **warrant** to identify the values and beliefs you share with an audience. The warrant grants you permission to address your audience with your argument because you share at least some moral principles. A warrant justifies a claim; as a writer, you must make clear to your audience that the moral principle in your warrant justifies your claim. This is the warrant the writer used to argue against antigay websites: "I do not want any person to suffer the harm and injustice that so many GLBT (gay, lesbian, bisexual, transgender) persons suffer on a daily basis." This writer connects warrant and claim. The principle in her warrant—not wanting people to suffer harm and injustice—justifies her claim of not wanting her local Chamber of Commerce, a publicly funded organization, to support an antigay website.

Backing

Key Question:
What additional support
for my warrant will I need
in order to persuade my
audience?

Backing supports a warrant. Bring in backing when you sense that an audience will need additional convincing of your warrant. In support of the warrant that centers on the need to avoid harm and injustice, the writer explains why sexual orientation should not be cause for discrimination. She brings in compelling examples from individuals who have suffered harm and injustice as well as examples from individuals who live in communities where sexual orientation is not an issue.

Rebuttal

Key Question:
What points of view different
from mine should I bring to
my argument?

A **rebuttal** argues against a claim. It presents a different or opposing point of view on your issue. It is helpful to anticipate objections to an argument for several reasons. First, when you summarize a differing view fairly, you become credible to your audience—because you can be trusted to describe without bias another view. Second, countering a rebuttal to your claim gives you the chance to demonstrate to an audience that your claim (or solution) is more practical than the one proposed by the opposition. A rebuttal needs to be countered, with an eye toward why an audience might consider a position different from yours. In the issue we're working with, the writer brings in two rebuttals. One claims that choosing a gay lifestyle is abnormal and unhealthy. The second argues that homosexuality is "wrong, immoral, and dangerous" and should be corrected. The writer counters both rebuttals by claiming that sexual orientation is not about choice; rather, she explains, sexuality is a "precognitive aspect of personality developed even before language skills." Additionally, she counters both rebuttals by referring to the American Psychiatric Association and the scientific view that homosexuality is not a psychiatric illness and that the only disorder in this context has to do with not accepting one's sexuality.

Qualifiers

Key Question:
How can I modify the language in an argument, especially with reference to my claim and reasons, to make an argument more believable?

The great strength of Toulmin's system is its focus on audience. A claim is your position on an issue, a position that must be delivered to an audience open to hearing it. The support you bring to an argument will be of three kinds—logical, ethical, and emotional—and each kind should appeal to your audience in a practical way. Your warrant ties you to your audience based on shared or similar values, beliefs, and feelings. Backing allows you to elaborate on your warrant in order to appeal more specifically to your audience's value system. A rebuttal (or rebuttals) in an argument lets you anticipate audience objections to your claim, objections that you can then counter. **Qualifiers** prevent you from making absolute statements because they involve words such as *often*, *typically*, and *in most cases* (instead of words like *always*, *only*, and *for certain*). Collectively, wise application of these qualifying terms centers an argument in practical—rather than idealistic, unrealistic—appeals.

As you can see, Toulmin-based argument is about arguing before an audience that is invested in your issue and therefore willing to listen to what you have to say. This kind of argument is also about each part of an argument supporting another part—a warrant that supports a claim, backing that supports a warrant, specific support that strengthens reasons, and reasons that support a claim. The seven strands of a Toulmin argument are knit together to form a single garment, a single argument. Each part serves the next with no room for filler. With reference to any single strand, a question helpful in building a Toulmin argument can be, "How does this part of my argument move my audience closer to accepting my claim?"

> **your turn 8a ▶ GET STARTED A Toulmin-Based Argument**
>
> Answer the following questions as a way to begin working with the Toulmin model.
>
> 1. What issue will you argue on? Why is it important to you? What might you claim?
> 2. What reasons can support your claim?
> 3. What support will you use to prove your reasons? Specifically, what kinds of logical, ethical, and emotional appeals will you use with your audience?

4. What values and beliefs connect you to your audience? Explain how you will build on this connection during your argument.

5. Describe the rebuttals you'll bring to your argument. How will you counter these differing views?

6. In addition to your claim, would other statements in your argument benefit from the addition of qualifiers? If yes, what are the statements, and what qualifiers will you use?

7. Bring to class an example of a Toulmin-based argument. Find this argument in an online or print newspaper or magazine.

Map a Toulmin-Based Argument

Below are outlines for two arguments that use the Toulmin system. Figure 8.2 on page 197 provides a visual reminder of the way Toulmin argument works. Note that the term *reasons* is given separate treatment and lies between *claim* and *support*.

COMMUNITY

School-Academic

Workplace

Family-Household

Neighborhood

Social-Cultural

Consumer

Concerned Citizen

TOPIC: Food Consumption

ISSUE: Traditional vs. Fair Trade Bananas

AUDIENCE: Church Social Action Group

CLAIM: Consumers should buy organic, fair trade bananas because of the high humanitarian and environmental cost of marketing traditional bananas.

Reasons

- Most workers on traditional banana plantations labor under unsafe conditions.
- Low wages prevent the majority of workers from improving their living conditions.
- The absence of child labor laws means that children, many of whom are more susceptible to dangerous pesticides than adults, are often made to work on these plantations.
- Workers who do manage to organize and strike for better conditions often are threatened with violence if they do not return to work.

- Many banana producers blatantly violate environmental laws.
- Local ecosystems can suffer due to the intensive use of pesticide and antifungal chemicals.

Support
- Logical support includes facts, figures, statistics, and commentary that describe the banana trade and conditions for workers, as well as definitions for the terms *organic bananas* and *fair trade practices*.
- Ethical support can include scholarly articles and research drawn from credible online and print sources that focus on conditions of banana production and marketing. It can also include personal examples that motivate readers to buy fair trade bananas.
- Emotional support can focus on your decision to switch to organic, fair trade bananas; descriptions of working conditions; and examples drawn from the experience of workers, families, and children associated with traditional banana production.

Warrant
The fair treatment of workers and good stewardship of the environment are important for the global economy.

Backing
Support for this warrant can include examples of the increasing number of importers that will buy bananas only from companies that guarantee worker rights and environmental standards. It can also include the commentary of economists who view fair trade as essential to the global economy.

Rebuttals
The following rebuttals will need to be countered.

- Major banana exporters argue that they comply with the "Social Accountability 8000" labor and human rights standard.
- Major exporters also claim 100 percent compliance with the Rainforest Alliance's "Banana Certification Program," designed to protect workers from excessive exposure to pesticides and to protect the environment from pollution and deforestation, among other requirements.

Qualifiers
Note that in the first reason, the qualifier *most* is used, and that in the second reason the phrase *the majority of* functions as a qualifier. The third reason includes the qualifiers *many* and *often*; the fourth reason also uses the qualifier *often*; and the final reason uses the qualifier *can*.

COMMUNITY

School-Academic

Workplace

Family-Household

Neighborhood

Social-Cultural

Consumer

Concerned Citizen

TOPIC: Relationships

ISSUE: Online Dating Sites and Advertising Practices

AUDIENCE: Members of My Writing Class

CLAIM: Some high-profile online dating companies use extreme and unfounded claims to attract clients.

Reasons

- Some companies, though they do not openly deny access to gays and lesbians, nevertheless deny options for people seeking same-sex matches.
- Other companies seem to require a religious preference and will not pursue matches for clients falling outside this invisible guideline.
- As a way to lure clients, a number of companies create false profiles representing potential matches; then, after the prospective client pays the joining fee, the enticing profiles disappear.

Support

- Logical support can include factual information from online dating companies, such as questionnaires, application materials, and promotional language and images; statistics drawn from scholarly articles; and surveys conducted by reliable sources and by you.
- Ethical support can include personal experience with online dating; the experience of others with online dating; the use of credible, agenda-free research on online dating companies; and proper documentation of your research, including quoting and paraphrasing.
- Emotional support can include brief, powerful anecdotes drawn from your experience with online dating; the testimony of others with regard to online dating; and examples drawn from your research that appeal to your audience's values and emotions.

Warrant

What I want to stress most is that no one should become a client of companies that discriminate.

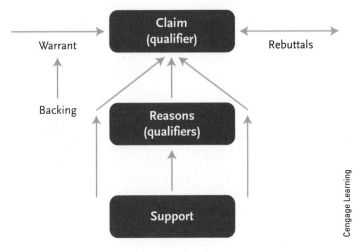

Figure 8.2 The Toulmin model of argument

Backing

- Everyone deserves to be happy and find special love, regardless of faith, sexual orientation, or race.
- These companies need to reevaluate their policies and realize that today gay couples raise families and in most cases experience no ill will from their communities.

Rebuttals

- If these complaints about online dating companies are taken seriously, it can lead to overregulation of a successful industry, and this will damage profits.
- Many companies have successful histories matching their clients.

Qualifiers

Note the qualifiers used in the claim and reasons above. Do they make these statements more believable than if they were left out? Note also the absence of qualifiers in the warrant and backing. Are these statements acceptable as they are, or would they benefit from qualifying language?

your turn 8b ▶ **PRACTICE Map a Toulmin-Based Argument**

Map a Toulmin-based argument for each of the following five issues. Specifically, in response to each issue, draft a claim, two reasons that support this claim, two or three specific examples supporting each reason, and a warrant along with backing for the warrant. Then identify one or two rebuttals you might encounter.

1. The term *food dumping* refers to the practice of industrialized countries providing free food to developing countries. Some critics claim that this practice hurts rather than helps, because the injection of free product into local markets causes small farmers in developing countries to go out of business and thus fall further into poverty.

2. Promotions and higher pay at your job are based strictly on seniority. In your view, your job performance exceeds the performance of some coworkers with more seniority.

3. Because of increasing development in your community, air and water quality have declined. Laws are in place to monitor and respond to these declines, but local officials claim that hiring an adequate number of trained inspectors will raise local taxes.

4. Pharmaceutical companies defend targeting their research at markets that will generate profitable returns. Returns from drugs for Alzheimer's, male enhancement, and cancer, for example, allow research to continue. Some argue that pharmaceutical companies are without social conscience for neglecting the many devastating tropical diseases that affect poor people.

5. The prevailing attitude of many local school board members is that the history of slavery, especially as it concerns the treatment of the enslaved, is an inappropriate subject for public school students.

 tip 8a

Use Visualization with Toulmin-Based Argument
Visualize yourself as an attorney defending an unpopular client. Know that your case must be painstakingly researched, that you must answer the opposing attorney's claims, and that you must use varied appeals to sway the jury.

Student-Authored Toulmin-Based Argument

In the following example, a student is using a Toulmin-based approach to advocate for a school voucher system in his community. As a home-schooled student, the writer is intent on proving the advantages of an education apart from public schools. His audience includes members of his writing class, especially those who defend public schools and regard home-schooling as ideological and prescriptive. Strengths of this argument are the writer's application of the Toulmin approach, his effective research, and his inventiveness to offer and defend an original idea.

Ben Szany

ENG 112-04

Professor Phillips

March 18, 2013

Although the title does suggest the subject of the argument, opening with a question often is not effective. An assertive title, one that hints at a writer's claim, is a good strategy.

Vouching for Our School System?

Our public school system is our country's biggest and most inefficient monopoly, yet it keeps demanding more and more money.—*Phyllis Schlafly*

A monopoly is defined as exclusive control of a product or service ("monopoly" Def. 1). Public schools may not possess *exclusive* control of education in Charlotte, but for low-income families there are no real alternatives. Private schools cost several thousand dollars a year per child. Home-schooling is very difficult to nearly impossible in single-parent households or in situations where both parents must work. The problem would be lessened if the public schools provided a good education. However, in 2011, only 72.2% of Charlotte-Mecklenberg high school students earned a diploma (Chesser par. 4). How can we give families more options for their children's education? By giving parents vouchers for education, we can create an opportunity for parents to send their children to the private school of their choice. The Charlotte Mecklenburg School system and local government must allocate vouchers—which can be exchanged at public schools, private schools, and home-schools—to parents.

In a school voucher system, the money follows the student. A month before school enrollment opens, families would receive a voucher for every school-aged child in their family. Each student could only redeem a voucher in his or her name. Vouchers could not be stockpiled, saved from year to year, or reused. When the time came to enroll in school, the student could redeem the voucher for a given amount of money at any qualified private school and receive a credit toward the cost of enrollment. At a public school, the cost of enrollment after a voucher would always be $0, just as the cost of enrollment in public school is currently $0. If used toward a private school, the voucher's value would vary based upon income of the family. Poorer families or children with disabilities would receive vouchers worth more than vouchers for children of the middle or upper classes. This would make private school significantly more affordable for lower-income families. For those parents who home-school, the vouchers would have a value dependent upon the income of the family. Home-schooling families would turn in the vouchers when filing their taxes; the money would be given in the form of a tax refund. The amount would be worth 15% of the voucher's value at a private school. If the voucher was worth $1,600 because of the family's income level, they would receive $240 if they home-schooled. This money could be spent on school books, supplies, computers, or other educational items.

All families, regardless of income, can benefit from a school voucher program. Lower-income parents gain access to a wider range of educational

The quotation orients the reader as to what will follow and sets a decisive emotional tone.

A qualifier, such as *some* or *many*, in front of *parents* would make the writer's assertion more believable.

The final two sentences of the first paragraph are the writer's warrant and claim. The warrant is grounded in values of "opportunity" and "choice."

The paragraph opens with a reason that directly supports the writer's claim.

options. Often these parents are forced to leave their children in failing or low-performing schools. As Harvard University Professor Paul E. Peterson explains, "I would say the results on parent satisfaction are overwhelmingly conclusive. If parents are given a choice, they're very happy. They're much happier with their private schools" ("The Case for Vouchers"). A school voucher program would greatly aid these parents, who are desperate to give their children the educational opportunity to succeed. Wealthier families' tax dollars would continue to fund the public school system as they do now, and they too would receive educational savings from the vouchers if they choose to enroll their children in private schools or home-school, although these savings would be modest at best. Thus, the vouchers do not ignore the needs of the poor nor do they swindle the wealthy; they are fair to both.

Making private schools and home-schools more affordable offers another advantage to parents; it forces the public school system to become more competitive. Currently in Charlotte, the public schools have something of a monopoly, especially regarding the education of children from lower-income families. By providing the opportunity for these parents to more easily remove their children from the public school system, we level the educational playing field. The Charlotte Mecklenburg school system will have no alternative but to improve performance in schools that consistently score below average. If they do not, children will leave the failing schools in favor of local private schools. This has already happened in Milwaukee, a voucher-using city that is comparable to Charlotte in both population and ethnic diversity. After 11 years of the voucher program, a study conducted by Harvard's Caroline Hoxby showed increased scores from children who used the vouchers to enroll in private school *and* from the children in local public schools. Public school test results jumped by 8.1% in math, 13.8% in science, and 8% in language (Stossel 135–136). The number of private schools in Milwaukee had increased to meet the demand of parents who opted out of the public schools (Koch 15). "The public schools," wrote John Stossel, host of ABC's *20/20*, "didn't want to lose their students to voucher schools, so they tried harder. They did a better job" (136). There is no reason why a school voucher program in Charlotte would not provide a similar improvement in results.

There is some concern that a school voucher program would greatly weaken Charlotte's public school system. Sandra Feldman, president of the American Federation of Teachers, stated, "[School vouchers mean]: Give up on public education in America; stop investing in it, siphon off as much funding as you can" (qtd. in Koch 5). A school voucher system would lessen the public school's monopoly on education, but it would not mean abandoning the public school system. The Charlotte Mecklenburg school system would still be expected to teach a majority of local students. Presently, public schools are responsible for the education of 90% of American children. With a universal school voucher program, that number is estimated to drop to 60 or 70% (Hood par 9). Despite this shift, Charlotte schools would be able to spend more money per pupil than without a voucher system. How is this possible?

In Milwaukee, the average cost per voucher is $4,894 (Koch 11). That figure is several thousand dollars less than the $7,155 that Charlotte schools spend per pupil (Roberts 29). In other words, if the Charlotte school system would spend $7,155 to educate a child for one year, and that child instead uses a $4,894 voucher to go to a private school, the public school system nets $2,261 per voucher, which can then be spent on other students. "What's more," said Virginia Governor Tim Kaine, "for every few hundred students who accept vouchers, the district saves itself the expense—tens of millions of dollars—of building a new school to accommodate rising enrollment" (Hinkle par 9). It isn't just theory. In 2001, Scott Greenberger, a staff writer at the *Boston Globe*, wrote that, "In Milwaukee, which has the nation's oldest and largest voucher program, even voucher opponents now acknowledge that no public school has been decimated by a loss of money or pupils. Furthermore, many public school principals and teachers here say the voucher program has pushed them to improve" (par 7). A school voucher program would not signal abandonment of the public school system but a desire within the community to improve the educational system as a whole.

Opponents of a Charlotte Mecklenburg school voucher system claim that such a program would be unconstitutional because many private schools have religious affiliations. Elliot Mincberg, of People for the American Way, argues, "Voucher programs that include sectarian schools grossly violate the constitutional separation of church and state" (qtd. in Koch 16). However, children are not ever required to use the voucher at a religious private school. Only their parents can decide where they go to school. In other words, if a parent does not want their child in a religiously oriented setting, there is nothing that can force their child into such a school. The decision is entirely up to the family. It must also be noted that public funds often support students in religious schools. Students receiving federal grants are free to attend sectarian universities such as Brigham Young University (Mormon) or Notre Dame (Roman Catholic) (Koch 9). Federal child care funds can be used by parents to send their toddlers to religiously affiliated day care centers. Finally, the Wisconsin Supreme Court ruled that Milwaukee's school voucher program was well within the bounds of both the state constitution and the U.S. Constitution (Koch 7). A voucher system that permits enrollment in religious schools does not violate the rights of any citizen, and the decision to send a student to such a school can only be made by that student's parents.

The Charlotte Mecklenburg school system holds a monopoly on education in Mecklenburg County. Breaking this stranglehold with a school voucher program would give parents more educational options and force the public and private schools to compete. This healthy competition would provide a better and more fruitful learning experience to students currently stuck in the public school system.

This conclusion can be stronger. Ideas in the writer's claim and warrant are repeated, but some attention here and earlier in the argument is needed to address why this competition would be "better and more fruitful" for students. Backing for the writer's warrant would be effective.

Works Cited

Chesser, John. "The Highs and Lows of High School Graduation Rates." *UNC Charlotte Urban Institute*. 24 Aug. 2011. 17 Mar. 2013. Web.

Greenberger, Scott S. "Voucher Lessons Learned." *Boston Globe*. (2001). *NewsBank*. 8 Mar. 2013. Web.

Hinkle, A. Barton. "The Governor Makes a Pretty Good Case for School Vouchers." *Richmond Times—Dispatch*. (2006). *NewsBank*. 15 Mar. 2013. Web.

Hood, John. (2007). "Spend a Lot to Teach a Little." *The (NC) Laurinburg Exchange. NewsBank*. 16 Mar. 2013. Web.

Koch, Kathy. "School Vouchers." *CQ Researcher* 9.13 (1999): 281-304. *CQ Researcher Online. CQ Press*. 16 Mar. 2013. Web.

"monopoly." *Dictionary.com Unabridged (v 1.1)*. Random House, Inc. 16 Mar. 2013. Web.

"The Case for Vouchers." *Frontline*. PBS. UNC-TV, Research Triangle Park, 23 May 2000. Television.

Roberts, Cheryl and McCracken, Lee. *Charlotte's Education System: Measuring Up?* (2004). Charlottechamber.com. 8 Mar. 2013. Web.

Stossel, John. *Myths, Lies, and Downright Stupidity: Get Out the Shovel— Why Everything You Know Is Wrong*. New York: Hyperion, 2006. Print.

Reflect and Apply

Answer the following questions as a way to review the purpose of a Toulmin-based argument.

1. Based on the argument you're presently building, why is or isn't a Toulmin-based argument appropriate to your purpose?

2. Map a Toulmin-based argument based on an issue you're struggling with in daily life. Where would you place the rebuttal and how would you respond to it?

3. Stephen Toulmin believed that argument should have a practical function and that an effective argument could be modeled, in part, on sound courtroom practice. Given a Toulmin-based argument you intend to build and with a courtroom setting in mind, how will you balance the support you bring to your argument; that is, will you balance evenly logical, ethical, and emotional support, or will you emphasize some kinds of support more than others? Explain.

KEEPING IT LOCAL

THE COMPELLING NARRATIVE that begins this chapter responds to a local and personal issue with a Toulmin-based argument. It is the kind of argument the writers consider most practical when they want to prove the rightness of their position and when they want action taken in response to their claim. The student bringing this issue to the table is motivated by deep concern for his siblings, by his parents' efforts to create opportunities for their children, and by others in his community who happen to be children of illegal immigrants. Had this writer elected not to respond to the state's recommendation to bar children of illegal immigrants from attending community colleges, then the public debate over this issue would be missing the informed position of a stakeholder in this important controversy. When we fail to speak up on an issue that matters to us, we let others make decisions for us, and this means that our position on an issue may be left out of the conversation. And because the writers want immediate action taken on this issue, they aimed their argument at the State Board of Community Colleges, an audience in a position to act. They are careful to identify values they and board members share and then build their arguments based on these values. Toulmin-based argument gives these writers, and us, a way to respond to important personal issues. This kind of argument and the kinds of argument discussed in Chapter 9, "Consider Middle Ground Argument, Rogerian Argument, and Argument Based on a Microhistory," are created using practical skills that can be deployed before audiences we want to influence and inform. Learn these skills and you'll be in a position to represent yourself with integrity and with a sense for what is practical on issues that matter to you.

●‑ ‑ ‑ ‑ ‑ ‑ ‑ ‑ ‑ ‑ ‑ ‑ ‑ ●

As you work through your argument, consider the following questions: At what audience will you aim your Toulmin-based argument? How did you narrow to this audience?

A common complaint about arguments is that they're too theoretical and not practical enough. What, exactly, will make your Toulmin-based argument practical?

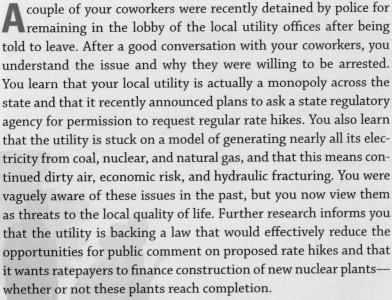

CHAPTER 9

Consider Middle Ground Argument, Rogerian Argument, and Argument Based on a Microhistory

A couple of your coworkers were recently detained by police for remaining in the lobby of the local utility offices after being told to leave. After a good conversation with your coworkers, you understand the issue and why they were willing to be arrested. You learn that your local utility is actually a monopoly across the state and that it recently announced plans to ask a state regulatory agency for permission to request regular rate hikes. You also learn that the utility is stuck on a model of generating nearly all its electricity from coal, nuclear, and natural gas, and that this means continued dirty air, economic risk, and hydraulic fracturing. You were vaguely aware of these issues in the past, but you now view them as threats to the local quality of life. Further research informs you that the utility is backing a law that would effectively reduce the opportunities for public comment on proposed rate hikes and that it wants ratepayers to finance construction of new nuclear plants—whether or not these plants reach completion.

You decide that the state Utilities Commission is the most practical audience for your argument because it is the organization with the power to regulate the powerful utility. More specifically, the commission can approve, reject, or call for modifications on the utility's policies and activities. This choice of audience seems practical because the Utilities Commission is charged with being on the look-out for any economic hardship that the utility might cause citizens of your state. The stated values of the Utilities Commission must overlap considerably with the values of ratepayers like you who may suffer from rate hikes and other utilities-related issues.

All Illustrations by iStockphoto.com/A-digit

COMMUNITY

School-Academic

Workplace

Family-Household

Neighborhood

Social-Cultural

Consumer

Concerned Citizen

TOPIC: Utility Company's Proposed Rate Hikes and Other Potential Dangers

ISSUE: Regulation of utility company

AUDIENCE: State Utilities Commission

CLAIM: The Utilities Commission should announce a moratorium on requests from the utilities for rate hikes and changes to public hearing requirements.

The chapter introduces you to three approaches to argument: Middle Ground, Rogerian, and Argument Based on a Microhistory.

Each of these approaches is uniquely different from Toulmin-Based Argument, the focus of Chapter 8, "Consider Toulmin-Based Argument." Collectively, the four kinds of argument provide you with options when you approach a given issue.

To distinguish in a general way among these approaches, it can be helpful to think about audience. In a Toulmin-based approach, the idea is to persuade an audience of the rightness of your position by using convincing support and effective handling of the opposition, much like the arguments created by competent trial attorneys. A middle-ground approach allows you to offer an audience a reasonable middle position between two relatively extreme positions. A Rogerian approach challenges the arguer to demonstrate common ground among sharply divergent positions on an issue; Rev. Martin Luther King, Jr. takes up this challenge in "Letter From Birmingham Jail" (excerpted in sections that follow). Finally, an Argument Based on a Microhistory lets you step into the shoes of a historian as you work with primary sources: in this kind of argument, you are making sense of the past in a new way, one that can let an audience view a particular event, for example, from different perspectives. Let the approach you choose to work with complement your goals with your audience.

In this chapter, you will be introduced to three approaches to argument:

- Middle Ground Argument
- Rogerian Argument
- Argument Based on a Microhistory

Middle Ground Argument

A **middle ground argument** argues a moderate, practical claim between two extreme positions (see Figure 9.2, p. 212). Middle ground arguments often are used with political, business, religious, and even personal issues and can provide a practical position when two sides of an issue are far apart. When aimed at an appropriate target audience, the middle-ground approach offers a practical, more moderate alternative to two more extreme positions. When an audience is uncertain, unaware, undecided, or silent on an issue, arguing for a practical middle position—or what you *perceive* to be a middle position—can be an effective strategy.

Make a Middle-Ground Position Practical

Importantly, a middle-position approach is used when you believe your solution to be between two extreme positions, but you still must *prove* that your middle-ground position is practical. Do this by discussing why the other positions are extreme and by providing your audience with persuasive reasons and support for your position. As with a Toulmin approach, you will include a claim, reasons, support, warrant, backing, and qualifiers. But compared with the Toulmin approach, middle ground argument requires much more attention to the opposition, or the two extreme positions you argue against. In Toulmin argument, attention to the opposition is called "rebuttals."

A sensible approach to middle ground arguing is first to introduce an issue and explain why a middle position is appropriate at this time. This introduction can then be followed by substantial and accurate summaries of each extreme position, with

© Kablonk/SuperStock

Figure 9.1 Middle Ground argument means arguing for a position between two extreme positions. This photo reveals a thoughtful third party who may be ready to argue for a more practical solution to an issue.

special emphasis on what makes each position impractical. These summaries first should be accurate and objective; second, each summary must be followed by your evaluation of each position, in which you identify the shortcomings of each view. The remainder of your argument should prove why your position is more practical than the two positions you have identified as extreme. In contrast with the Toulmin structure, you will devote up to half of your argument to the opposition before you get to your own position. (See Chapter 6, "Work Fairly with the Opposition," for tips on presenting the opposition fairly.)

your turn 9a ▸ **PRACTICE Recognize When a Middle-Ground Approach Is Practical**

Respond to the following questions as a way to begin thinking about how a middle-ground approach can offer practical choices on tough local and global issues.

1. Identify three issues—a personal issue, a community issue, and a global issue—that are polarizing or that set two clear positions against one another. For each issue, describe the two positions.
2. Focusing on one of these issues, does each group seem extreme or impractical in its position? Why?
3. What middle-ground position can you offer? Why would your position be more practical than either of the other positions?

Recognize Where Middle Ground Arguments Are Possible

Consider the following three issues, the two extreme positions for each, and then the claims that argue for middle-ground solutions. With each issue, the two extreme positions are far apart; this can open the door to a more practical middle position.

Issue #1: "Brain drain" of health care workers from poor to rich countries

- Extreme Position A: Doctors and nurses from poor countries have the right to pursue opportunities in rich countries.
- Extreme Position B: Doctors and nurses from poor countries have an obligation to serve people from their home countries.
- Middle-Ground Position: Groups such as Human Rights Watch should recommend that doctors and nurses from poor countries serve people in their native countries for a minimum five-year period.

Issue #2: Flying the Confederate flag in our community's public cemeteries

- Extreme Position A: The Confederate flag should be flown daily as a way to honor our ancestors who died during the Civil War.
- Extreme Position B: The Confederate flag should not be flown at all because it symbolizes a way of life that kept many of our ancestors oppressed.
- Middle-Ground Position: The Confederate flag should be flown on national holidays only.

Issue #3: Reducing carbon emissions in our state

- Extreme Position A: The best way to reduce carbon emissions in our state is to make a complete switch to alternative fuels in the next 10 years.
- Extreme Position B: Because laws are now in place to protect our air and water quality, we simply need to hire more inspectors and regulators.
- Middle-Ground Position: The governor needs to appoint a committee that allows consumers to work with public policy experts and energy companies in order to create a realistic plan to lower carbon emissions.

Let's say that the arguer targets students in her nursing classes as an audience for the "brain drain" issue. For the Confederate flag issue, the arguer aims at readers of the local newspaper. And for the carbon emissions issue, the governor is the target audience. Because there are strong views on all of these issues, it will be vital that arguers offer middle-ground positions that appear reasonable and well thought out. But remember that the audience might not agree with the arguer's opinion that the middle position offers a compromise or that it presents the middle ground between two extreme positions. Your best chance at having your middle position accepted is to know what your audience values and then craft appropriate appeals based on these values. Because writers of middle-ground positions regard other positions as extreme, they will need to specify why the extreme positions are less practical than the proposed middle position. Furthermore, while the writer's middle-ground position differs from the other positions, the writer must nevertheless respect the differing views and acknowledge points of overlap. It may be that underneath the differences all groups want a similar outcome, but the methods each extreme position advocates are less practical than your approach. In general, you will need to earn credibility from your audience by appearing fair-minded in your summaries and critical in your evaluations. Use Your Turn 9c as a guide to setting up middle ground arguments.

Map a Middle Ground Argument

An outline for a middle ground argument addressing the contentious issue of extra credit work and whether it should be allowed in college classes appears in the following section. To many students and teachers, extra credit is an important issue because it touches one's sense of fairness. In fact, the following positions, labeled "extreme" by many, may not seem extreme to readers of the college newspaper, the writer's intended audience. If the middle-ground position is to be convincing, it surely must acknowledge—and, when possible, honor—the range of school newspaper readers and their values. This will be challenging work for this writer because research demonstrates that most students favor the chance at extra credit work, especially when their grades are low or some of their required work is missing. The support this writer uses with his reasons must be compelling and reveal the practicality of his position.

EXTREME POSITION #1: No! It's unethical.

CLAIM: Extra credit work rewards students for being irresponsible; therefore, it is unethical.

Reasons

- Extra credit work rewards students for failing to learn course content, as reflected in poor exam scores.
- Final course grades should reflect performance only and not be based on extra credit work.
- Extra credit usually is not available in the real world, especially in the workplace.
- Extra credit opportunities are unfair to responsible students.

EXTREME POSITION #2: Yes! It's practical.

CLAIM: With so much pressure on students to complete a college degree and transition into the workplace these days, teachers should allow extra credit opportunities.

Reasons

- Extra credit gives students a second chance.
- Denying extra credit can be a roadblock to success.
- Demands of family and job get in the way of preparing for class.
- Extra credit rewards effort.

MIDDLE-GROUND POSITION: Yes, extra credit work should be allowed, but only when it leads to deeper knowledge of the content area.

CLAIM: Extra credit should be allowed for students who want to pursue a question or problem that falls outside requirements of a course but within the content area.

Reasons

- Extra credit assignments can be designed to create deeper familiarity with course content.
- Extra credit is one way to encourage research and critical-thinking skills.
- This kind of extra credit is a way to reward genuine effort beyond what is expected.
- Establishing and maintaining a single standard for extra credit work is one way to keep grading policies consistent and without exception.

COMMUNITY

School-Academic

Workplace

Family-Household

Neighborhood

Social-Cultural

Consumer

Concerned Citizen

TOPIC: Grading Policies

ISSUE: Extra Credit

AUDIENCE: Readers of School Newspaper

CLAIM: Extra credit should be allowed for students who want to pursue a question or problem that falls outside requirements of a course but within the content area.

Based on the middle-ground position this writer will defend, Position #1 is considered extreme because it shuts the door on the possible benefits of extra credit work. It makes a dangerous assumption that extra credit work encourages irresponsible behavior. It does not allow for the chance that some students may want to pursue deeper work with a topic. It ignores the conditions for extra credit that some teachers set, such as limits on how extra credit can affect a final grade or that all required coursework must be completed before extra credit assignments can be pursued. This position also assumes that students seeking extra credit did not put forth effort in a class. Finally, it neglects to consider circumstances such as illness and family duties, which can get in the way of a student's preparation for exams and assignments.

Position #2 assumes that students need second chances in order to succeed. The argument assumes that teachers—not students or the circumstances of students' lives—can be roadblocks to student success. Implicit in the reasons for this claim is the attitude that students are naturally under duress and unable to keep up with requirements of their courses.

With these extreme positions summarized for the audience, the writer must now aggressively support his claim and prove that his middle position is more practical. The writer is a teacher who has struggled during his career with the idea of extra credit. For the past five years, he has settled on the position defended below. Claim and reasons were noted in the previous section under "Middle-Ground Position."

Support

Support will be drawn primarily from the writer's experience with extra credit work over a 20-year teaching career. References to published scholarly research addressing extra credit in the college classroom also will be included.

Warrant

Providing opportunities for students to pursue a problem or topic connected to course content rewards intellectual curiosity.

Backing

- Intellectual curiosity is important because it complements critical-thinking skills, a core competency at our college.
- Intellectual curiosity is important because it respects a student's interest in a course and the questions that follow from this interest.

Qualifiers

The claim does not make extra credit work available to all students under unspecified conditions; instead, it limits extra credit work to students who want the chance to pursue a question or topic not covered in class. Reason number one includes the qualifier *can*; reason number two includes the qualifier *one way* (as opposed to *the only way*); reason number three includes the qualifier *a way*, and reason four includes the qualifier *one way*.

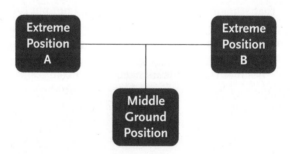

Figure 9.2 The middle ground model

> your turn 9b ▶ PRACTICE **Middle-Ground Thinking**

Based on the following descriptions of six different issues, along with the two extreme positions noted for each, write a claim for each issue that offers a middle position. Below each claim you offer, list two or three reasons that support your claim.

1. Executive compensation—salaries and bonuses paid to executives in American companies—has come under fire recently. Some argue that a top executive in a company should not be allowed to earn more than 25 times what the lowest paid employee in the company earns. Others believe that attractive compensation packages are needed to attract top talent and should not be regulated.

2. Plagiarism occurs in our schools and colleges at alarming rates. One possible response is to institute a campus-wide honor code that mandates a single standard: expulsion. Another view claims that a more practical approach would be for writing classes to provide more comprehensive attention to the issue of plagiarism and how to avoid it.

3. Undocumented workers in the United States are the subject of a long-standing debate. The center of this debate is whether or not penalties should be levied on employers hiring undocumented workers. Several political action groups have formed to protest the hiring of undocumented workers, arguing that these jobs should belong to American workers and that penalties should be levied on employers. Another side claims that most American workers don't want these low-paying jobs and that employers are left with little choice other than to hire undocumented workers.

4. *Digital divide* is a term that refers to the gap between people who have access to the Internet and people who do not. Some people believe that Americans whose annual income falls below the poverty line should be given inexpensive laptops and access to the Internet. Others hold that the this provision is unnecessary because Internet technology has become available to almost everyone through schools, libraries, and a range of social programs.

5. The local newspaper's recent series of stories on poultry processing plants revealed horrific worker conditions that have resulted in many chronic injuries. Some concerned parties advocate for union representation for workers; others argue that laws are already in place to protect workers and that hiring more inspectors to enforce these laws is the solution.

6. Tipping in local restaurants, a concern for servers whose income depends on tips, generates two extreme positions: first, that a mandatory 15 percent tip should be noted on restaurant menus; or second, that tipping should be at the discretion of customers, who presumably base the tip amount on the professionalism of the server.

tip 9a

Identify Local Models of Middle-Ground Positions

In many ways, we are trained to look to leaders beyond our immediate communities for practical solutions to pressing issues. But this need not be our first line of inquiry. Identify practical middle-ground positions offered to address local issues. These solutions might be offered by friends, fellow students, coworkers, or family; they might also be found in the local newspaper, on your favorite blogs, or on social networking sites. What makes the middle-ground positions more practical than the extreme positions?

your turn 9c ▶ GET STARTED Set Up a Middle Ground Argument

Answer the following questions to set up a middle ground argument.

1. Identify the issue you plan to address and describe the specific context you bring to your argument. How far back in time will you need to go to reveal the roots of this issue? What are these roots?
2. Why, exactly, is this issue deserving of our attention now? What specific present conditions make this issue important?
3. What does each extreme position claim? What is the history of each group with regard to this issue? Why is each group so deeply invested in its position?
4. How does each group justify its position? What is the warrant for each group's claim? What support does each group use?
5. What values and beliefs do you share with each group?
6. What are the limitations and potential damages you see with each position?
7. What is your claim on this issue? Why is it more practical than other positions?
8. What reasons will you use to support your claim? What major examples, statistics, and personal experiences will you use as part of your support?
9. What does your audience have to gain by accepting your position? How will the community benefit?

Student-Authored Middle Ground Argument

Illegal immigrants, mostly Hispanics, are employed extensively in the community in the construction, landscaping, and food and beverage industries. The writer of the following argument is responding to the issue of whether illegal immigrants should be eligible for driver's licenses. This issue has been a matter of public concern for several years and is reported on regularly by local media. The writer perceives the need for a more practical approach, so she has chosen to write a middle ground argument, one that (in her view) offers a practical middle position between two positions that the author considers extreme. The writer's purpose is to generate awareness of the importance of driving privileges for illegal immigrants in the community. Her audience is her writing class, most of whom are U.S. citizens. The first paragraph introduces the issue, the next two paragraphs present the two extreme positions, and the fourth paragraph presents the writer's claim. The remaining paragraphs, not included here, support the claim with reasons and plenty of support. Also not shown here is the Works Cited.

Linda Gonzalez

English 112

Professor Phillips

19 November 2013

Driving to a Reasonable Solution

Millions of illegal immigrants live in the United States. Most of them drive to work every day without a driver's license. Before 9/11, illegal immigrants in North Carolina could get a driver's license if they presented a foreign legal document to the Department of Motor Vehicles (DMV). Some of the documents accepted at the time were passports, birth certificates, voting cards, and driver's licenses from applicants' countries of origin. Then, the DMV stopped accepting foreign documents and asked for a document issued by the US Government. Originally the W-7 form was among the US-issued documents that could be used to obtain driver's licenses. The W-7 form, used in order to apply for an Individual Taxpayer Identification Number, used to be provided to people regardless of their migratory status by the Internal Revenue Service. According to DMV commissioner George Tatum, 25,957 undocumented people applied for a W-7 in 2004, fewer than the 41,977 applicants in 2003 (Funk and Whitacre 2). Today, Maryland is one of the states that still issues driver's licenses without asking applicants to prove their migratory status. Some state authorities want to adopt a plan to issue driver's licenses to undocumented immigrants while others are totally against it.

Those in favor of providing driver's licenses to illegal immigrants think the roads would be safer because driver's licenses would bring people out of the shadows and allow them to obtain insurance. The proponents of this solution would issue driver's licenses that distinguish illegal immigrants from U.S. citizens by noting the driver's migratory status. This driver's license would be strictly for driving purposes (i.e., it would not allow the holder to board airplanes or enter federal buildings). John Madden, a New York planning consultant, supports the plan and says, "Most illegal immigrants drive without driver's licenses anyway. You might as well make them legal drivers" (qtd. in Crawley 2). In every U.S. State, one must pass a written test and a driving test in order to get a driver's license. Because illegal immigrants would need to read the driver's handbook in order to pass these tests, allowing illegal immigrants to get driver's licenses would make them more aware of the rules of the road and thus make them safer drivers. Immigrants also would be able to get insurance at the same rates as other drivers. According to New York's State Department of Insurance, expanded license access would reduce the premium cost associated with uninsured motorist coverage by 34%, which would save New York drivers $120 million each year (Crawley 3). Additionally, people would get out of the shadows. Jack Schuler, a reverend of Our Lady of Guadalupe Catholic Church in Cool Valley, California, says, "It is a matter of accepting that illegal immigrants are here; it is a reality, and they are an integral part of the state" (Johnson 1). He claims that not only do these people exist, but that they are simply trying to make a living and that others cannot pretend they do not exist. What they fail to see is that illegal immigrants would not want to have a driver's license showing their immigration status. They fear being deported; therefore, many would prefer to remain without a license than risk police finding out that they are in the country illegally.

Another point of view is held passionately by opponents of giving driver's licenses to illegal immigrants. They argue that driving is a privilege, not a right. For instance, Republican Sue Myrick of Charlotte, North Carolina, says, "Our feeling is that driver's license is a privilege for citizens and legal aliens, and it shouldn't be something given to somebody who broke the law" (qtd. in Funk and Whitacre 2). Backers of Myrick agree, claiming that issuing driver's licenses to undocumented people would attract more illegal immigrants and make it easier for terrorists to come into the United States. Considering driving as a privilege, many politicians are completely against a plan that would allow illegal immigrants to obtain driver's licenses. They believe that because people who have entered the country illegally have broken the immigration laws, they should not be allowed to receive any kind of benefits in this country. Moreover, driver's licenses allow people to work, drive, and open bank accounts, thus making life in this country much easier for undocumented people. According to Johnson, "One legitimate kind of ID leads to more, leads to more, leads to more, and pretty soon, they've got an entire identity established" (2). Johnson adds that having a legal document can give others the impression that a person has citizenship. Additionally, the government is seeking stricter means to keep the nation safe from terrorists; one effective way to do so is to deny driver's licenses to illegal aliens, thus preventing them from entering federal buildings, boarding airplanes, and using the licenses as identification to give the impression of being in the country legally. Most readers will consider it relevant that 8 of the 19 men in the terrorist attacks on September 11 got licenses in Virginia after presenting a simple notarized form saying they were state residents (Johnson 2 par 11). Another example of illegal immigrants threatening the nation's safety is that there are drug dealers and criminals looking for easy ways to get licenses. "Driver's licenses are as close as we get to a national ID," says John Keely of the Center for Immigration Studies, a group in Washington that advocates limited immigration. "While the overwhelming majority of immigrants don't pose a national security threat, I don't think issuing driver's licenses to them affords protection to Americans, but hurts the efforts to shore up national security" (Johnson 3). Authorities against the plan to provide driver's licenses for illegal immigrants do not take into consideration that undocumented people are not going to go away just because they do not have driver's licenses and that they will drive with or without licenses. Certainly, the arguments in favor of and against issuing driver's licenses to illegal immigrants are so strong that it is difficult to imagine an alternative position.

However, there is another position, one held just as passionately by its proponents as those just described. I agree with many people who think that driver's licenses should be given to illegal immigrants. If that cannot be accomplished, then at least licenses already obtained by people without legal status who have no major traffic violations should be renewable. Individuals who hold this point of view say that issuing driver's licenses to illegal immigrants would help the police do their job better. In addition, they believe allowing immigrants to get driver's licenses would help the economy because then this population will be paying taxes; in addition, this plan would lower the use of false documents.

Rogerian Argument

Rogerian argument is a way to establish **common ground** between a position you hold and positions that one or more other parties hold on an issue. It is a kind of argument built on fair, compassionate presentation of differing views, and it highlights the strengths of each, along with points of overlap with your view.

Listen Closely to the Opposition

Rogerian argument is centered in good listening and in close, respectful consideration of points of view different from your own. It is an argument strategy adapted from the work of psychologist Carl Rogers, who was interested in factors that help or hinder good communication. He theorized that good communication requires that each position on an issue is fully acknowledged—without judgment. Rogers believed that a careful, empathic listener can clarify differing positions and create space for productive interaction. This approach to an issue asks that a writer listen and respond with charity in order to create common ground based on shared values and a shared sense of purpose. Rogers believed that, although on the surface of a contentious issue the sides may seem far apart, on a deeper level warring sides may in fact

Figure 9.3 Taking in fully another view and then presenting it fairly is at the center of the Rogerian approach.

Bruce Ayres/Stone/Getty Images

share some values and beliefs. However, before such commonalities can be identified, we must first take the time to cool our emotions and really listen to each other.

For example, when Martin Luther King, Jr. reaches out to white clergymen in his famous "Letter from Birmingham Jail," he refers to his audience—the same clergymen who helped put him in jail—as "men of genuine good will," and as "Christian and Jewish brothers." In addition, throughout the letter he emphasizes their common faith and adherence to religious principles. In this letter, King responds to a moment of intense racial and political separation by studying with compassion the values of his opposition, who vigorously oppose the nonviolent demonstrations supported by King and the Southern Christian Leadership Conference. He identifies a desire on both sides for negotiation, but he also embraces the need for a "constructive, nonviolent tension which is necessary for growth."

Over the years, many students have claimed that Rogerian argument is a practical approach to controversial issues, especially in the workplace and in local politics where compromise is essential. They reason that when things need to move forward—for example, a company's projects, production, and sales; decisions affecting local schools; help for the increasing number of homeless people; crime prevention in the community—it becomes essential to listen closely to individuals deeply invested in their positions. While resolution of every issue cannot be guaranteed, many businesses practice Rogerian methods, simply because when a positive dialogue is created production and efficiency improve. Dispute-resolution programs used by large community organizations, such as local post offices and city governments, value Rogerian strategy because it emphasizes listening and mutual respect, allowing disputing parties to better understand each other. And when understanding and respect are built, better communication often follows.

Writers of a Rogerian argument are similar to mediators, people who facilitate settlements among two or more disputing parties. In a closed mediation, a mediator often asks each party to restate the other party's position; in this way a sense of understanding and trust can begin to develop. Sometimes a resolution of the issue can result; almost always, parties understand each other better. Your job as a writer is to adapt this process of close listening to a written argument as you respectfully and accurately present positions that differ from yours. Usually during the second half of a Rogerian argument the writer steps out of the mediator role and brings in his or her claim and support for an issue, creating common ground with other views.

Rogerian strategy replaces rebuttal of opposing views with efforts to understand them. Because the foundation of Rogerian argument is an accurate, bias-free description of an opposing view, make sure you restate accurately for readers other positions on issues you address. Strategies for fairly negotiating with the opposition are discussed in Chapter 6, "Work Fairly with the Opposition."

In brief, Rogerian argument requires the arguer to see an issue from other points of view, emphasizing points of overlap, or common ground, among differing positions. (See Figure 9.4 for a representation of Rogerian argument.) A successful Rogerian argument allows your audience to judge for itself whether or not your claim is practical. And along the way you do much to earn credibility with an audience through your compassionate and accurate restatement of opposing views.

Identify Common Ground

The following two issues recently were addressed successfully with a Rogerian approach. Note the common ground that each writer creates.

Issue #1: Living at home while attending college

This writer fully acknowledges her parents' position that, because she has completed high school, living at home is no longer an option. Her parents content that they can no longer afford for her to live at home, that they plan to downsize to a smaller home, and that she should take on the responsibility of paying for things herself. The writer honors her parents' position by describing it fairly and without judgment. She offers these reasons for wanting to remain at home: she will be able to devote more time to her courses and earn her degree sooner, she won't have to work a second and possibly third job to cover costs of living on her own, and she will be there to help with chores around the house. But before delivering her reasons, the writer first creates common ground with her parents by identifying certain shared values and beliefs tied to this issue. For example, both parties value the importance of a college degree, professional competence, financial independence, and the ability to provide for one's family.

In this example, the writer's audience (her parents) is also her opposition. To earn credibility with this audience, the writer completes the two essential steps in Rogerian writing: she describes without bias her opponent's position and locates common ground. Rogerian strategy is more about reaching into opponents' camps and representing their views fairly; it is less about achieving a desired outcome. Rogerian argument extends the olive branch of peace and fair play.

Issue #2: Homelessness in the community

With the recent downturn in the economy, the number of homeless people in the community—including children who attend local public schools—is increasing. Area shelters provide beds for less than 25 percent of the homeless population, and it is uncertain when new shelters will be available. At a recent county commission meeting, a coalition of local organizations working with homeless people rolled out a 10-year plan to end homelessness in the area. The plan was unanimously approved by commissioners, but more than a year later, no funding has been approved. Last week your teacher invited the volunteer coordinator from the city's largest shelter, along with an expert on affordable housing, to speak to your class, motivating you to act. You want to argue that funding the 10-year plan is the community's best hope for addressing the homelessness crisis. Based on what you learned during the presentations, you know that your opposition is not a single individual or a single group but an attitude that is held by many local citizens who would rather not deal with the issue because it is uncomfortable and without a clear solution. Additionally, many people in this silent majority believe that homeless people do not make the same kind of effort as those who work hard to pay for their homes and that the homeless are gaming a system that will allow them to get by without assuming the responsibilities of citizenship.

You choose as your audience members of your communications class, and you plan to deliver your argument as a speech due in this class in a few weeks. You choose a Rogerian approach because you know that if the 10-year plan has any chance of being funded those on opposite sides of this issue must begin listening to each other. You identify and honor values of citizenship that you share with those reluctant to fund the plan: making positive contributions to the community, paying taxes, sustaining employment, and renting or owning a home. These points of overlap become clear when you converse with your opposition. You are now in a position to build on the common ground you have created by paying close attention to another perspective on homelessness. Because you have established this common ground and validated your opposition, you can argue your claim without rebutting.

Furthermore, you now have a chance to provide some education on the issue of homelessness. You recognize that many citizens opposed to funding the 10-year plan may not have a clear sense of the causes of homelessness, such as mental illness, physical disability, job loss, natural disasters, divorce or break up, and a full range of unforeseen events that throw an individual off balance. By listening closely to your opposition, you have earned the chance to deliver your argument on homelessness. Whether your claim is accepted is another matter, but you have put your best foot forward by building your argument on a foundation of shared values and beliefs.

The issues discussed above—one personal and the other local and national—involve parties that at first are far apart and aggressive defending their positions. Toulmin-based arguments might produce rhetorical victories, but a Toulmin approach would miss the common ground of the disputing parties. Similarly, a middle-ground approach would miss chances to work with shared values and instead emphasize the failures of the opposition on these important issues. Rogerian argument, however, can bring sides closer together. Its aim is to identify values that the disputing parties share. In turn, these shared values can make clear for all sides a common ground, where strategies for resolving issues can be discussed openly and without fear of judgment.

your turn 9d ►**PRACTICE Rogerian Thinking**

For each of the following issues, provide your claim and one or two claims made by differing points of view; then identify common ground. Plan to research issues with which you are not familiar.

1. Campaign finance reform in your state: This movement seeks to limit the amount of monetary contributions that can be made by individuals and groups to the campaigns of political candidates.
2. Affordable housing and homelessness: The term *affordable housing* refers to housing that does not exceed 30 percent of the household or family income. The term is often used in the discussion of home-lessness in the United States.
3. Stem cell research focuses on scientists' ability to reproduce cells from living organisms. Some argue that this kind of research has important medical and reproductive benefits for humans; others feel it unfairly manipulates human life and that it can be used for cloning.
4. Course evaluation and instructor performance surveys are common in U.S. colleges. They are often used as a performance measure dur-ing an instructor's annual review.

Map a Rogerian Argument

The earlier examples about living at home and homelessness, both rooted locally, suggest ways to build arguments based on Rogerian strategy. The key to the success of this kind of argument is your ability to understand and honor differing views. The following section presents a fuller treatment of another local issue, this one related to the workplace. The writer is frustrated with a pay scale based on seniority; her supervisor is the audience for her argument.

Supervisor's View

CLAIM: Increases in salary should remain tied to the seniority system.

Reasons

- The seniority system has been in place for many years and has been proven to help with employee morale.
- A clear standard for pay raises supports consistency and prevents favoritism.
- Our company values employee loyalty and years of service, and the seniority system is a way to reward employees who share these values.
- Many of our senior employees are hard working and productive.

SUPPORT:	Because the supervisor has been at the company for many years, she can attest that few complaints have been filed with regard to the seniority system, loyal and productive employees, or the company owners' commitment to fair treatment.
WARRANT:	The seniority system is effective because it maintains an ethical standard that employees are aware of from the beginning of their employment.

Backing

- Consistency and fair play are important in the workplace.
- A predictable reward system can mean fewer complaints from employees and greater worker satisfaction.

Writer's View

COMMUNITY

School-Academic

Workplace

Family-Household

Neighborhood

Social-Cultural

Consumer

Concerned Citizen

TOPIC: Compensation

ISSUE: Pay Scale and Seniority

AUDIENCE: Supervisor

CLAIM: Our company should award salary increases based on production and efficiency.

Reasons

- Efficient, productive employees can generate more profit for this company.
- Regular effort and productivity should be rewarded with regular salary increases.
- Pay raises based on productivity can elevate morale and foster loyalty to the company.

SUPPORT:	Much of this writer's support should be drawn from her experience as a productive, hard-working employee. Examples can reveal her contributions to company expectations and beyond. Additionally, research drawn from professional and academic journals can reinforce her pay-based-on-productivity request. Personal

examples can also speak to the writer's ability to maintain good work habits while pursuing her college degree.

WARRANT: Ethical standards should be maintained in the workplace.

Backing

- Consistency and fair play are important in the workplace.
- A fair, predictable reward system can lead to increased worker satisfaction.

COMMON GROUND: Listening closely to her supervisor, the writer is able to pin down common values and goals. They include shared concerns for employee morale, avoidance of favoritism, company loyalty, and hard work and productivity. In the summary of her supervisor's position, the writer can validate these concerns and then build on them as she delivers her argument. Often, common ground among disputing parties is established at the level of the warrant, and this should be clear in the mapping of this argument. Ethical standards, consistency, a sense of fair play, and predictable rewards are common values the writer shares with her supervisor.

Note that the writer avoids at every turn rebutting her supervisor. From her experience with this company, it likely would be easy to rebut with plenty of specific examples. But she has chosen a Rogerian approach to this sticky problem, and this means making her best effort to demonstrate that she understands and honors her supervisor's reasons and values. In practical terms, a Toulmin-based approach might have produced a solid argument, but it could have left the writer out in the cold in terms of getting her supervisor to acknowledge her position on salary increases. When your audience is your

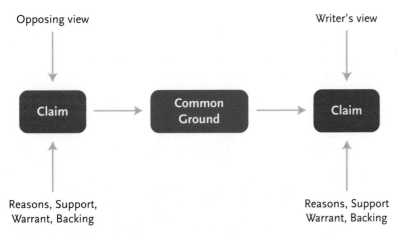

Figure 9.4 The Rogerian argument model

tip 9b

Acknowledge and Validate the Opposition

Put yourself in the frame of mind to build a Rogerian argument by recalling a time in your life when others put you first and listened closely and without judgment to your opinion on a given issue. What might have motivated these individuals? What might motivate you to behave this way with an opponent?

opposition, as is frequently the case in Rogerian writing, make the effort to dignify the other view, honor its strengths, and point out shared values; this can indicate that you are less interested in dueling and more interested in a serious, mutually respectful conversation.

your turn 9e   **GET STARTED** **A Rogerian Argument**

In introducing an issue, what historical context will you provide? What specific information will you use to orient readers to the issue? Answers to these and the following questions will help you start your Rogerian approach.

1. When sides are far apart, a Rogerian approach often works best. Are you working with an issue that is sufficiently controversial to generate distinctly different sides? Explain.

2. What is the claim, what is the warrant, and what are the main reasons for each view on this issue? What beliefs and values do each of the parties hold?

3. What measures will you take to avoid judging or rebutting your opposition? How will you establish and maintain a neutral, objective, fair-minded attitude toward each opposing view and those who hold it?

4. Would each party with a stake in this issue be comfortable with how you present its position? Explain.

5. How will you maintain a neutral tone toward other parties? Explain how your tone calms rather than ignites emotions.

6. What is your claim? Describe your warrant. What are the main reasons and kinds of support you bring to your position?

7. What specific values and beliefs do you share with each party? What values does your audience hold regarding this issue? Establish common ground by describing overlapping values among the opposition, your audience, and your own view.

8. Is your audience likely to accept your claim based both on your accurate, fair-minded presentation of other views and on the reasons and support you build into your position? Explain.

Sample Rogerian Argument

Martin Luther King, Jr. wrote his "Letter From Birmingham Jail" in the margins of a newspaper and on scraps of paper, the only materials he could obtain. This document contains effective examples of Rogerian writing. King aims his letter at white clergymen during a time of racial segregation and profound differences over tactics appropriate in the struggle for racial equality. The paragraphs included below demonstrate King's ability to reach out in positive ways to his opposition. These few paragraphs are part of a long letter to the very clergy who recommended his incarceration: remember that a Rogerian approach is often practical when opposing parties are deeply divided. Note below how the writer finds common ground and uses it to both respect his opposition and deliver his ideas.

PARAGRAPHS FROM "LETTER FROM BIRMINGHAM JAIL"

By Martin Luther King, Jr.

MY DEAR FELLOW CLERGYMEN:

[Paragraph #1] While confined here in the Birmingham City Jail, I came across your recent statement calling my present activities "unwise and untimely." Seldom do I pause to answer criticism of my work and ideas. If I sought to answer all the criticisms that cross my desk, my secretaries would have little time for anything other than such correspondence in the course of the day, and I would have no time for constructive work. But since I feel that you are men of genuine goodwill and that your criticisms are sincerely set forth, I want to try to answer your statements in what I hope will be patient and reasonable terms.

[Paragraph #3] But more basically, I am in Birmingham because injustice is here. Just as the prophets of the eighth century B.C. left their villages and carried their "thus saith the Lord" far beyond the boundaries of their home towns, and just as the Apostle Paul left his village of Tarsus and carried the gospel of Jesus Christ to the far corners of the Greco-Roman world, so am I compelled to carry the gospel of freedom far beyond my own hometown. Like Paul, I must constantly respond to the Macedonian call for aid.

[From Paragraph #31] But though I was initially disappointed at being categorized as an extremist, as I continued to think about the matter I gradually gained a measure of satisfaction from the label. Was not Jesus an extremist for love: "Love your enemies, bless them that curse you, do good to them that hate you, and pray for them which despitefully use you, and persecute you." Was not Amos an extremist for justice: "Let justice roll down like waters and righteousness like an ever-flowing stream." Was not Paul an extremist for the Christian gospel: "I bear in my body the marks of the Lord Jesus." Was not Martin Luther an extremist: "Here I stand; I cannot do otherwise, so help me God." And John Bunyan: "I will stay in jail to the end of my days before I make a butchery of my conscience." And Abraham Lincoln: "This nation cannot survive half slave and half free." And Thomas Jefferson: "We hold these truths to be self-evident, that all men are created equal . . ." So the question is not whether we will be extremists, but what kind of extremists we will be. Will we be extremists for hate or for love? Will we be extremists for the preservation of injustice or for the extension of justice? In that dramatic scene on Calvary's hill three men were crucified. We must never forget that all three were crucified for the same crime—the crime of extremism. Two were extremists for immorality, and thus fell below their environment. The other, Jesus Christ, was an extremist for love, truth and goodness, and thereby rose above his environment. Perhaps the South, the nation and the world are in dire need of creative extremists.

[Final paragraph] I hope this letter finds you strong in the faith. I also hope that circumstances will soon make it possible for me to meet each of you, not as an integrationist or a civil rights leader but as a fellow clergyman and a Christian brother. Let us all hope that the dark clouds of racial prejudice will soon pass away and the deep fog of misunderstanding will be lifted from our fear-drenched communities, and in some not too distant tomorrow the radiant stars of love and brotherhood will shine over our great nation with all their scintillating beauty.

Argument Based on a Microhistory

An argument based on a **microhistory** allows you to comment on a particular part of our past, especially if what you have to say differs from the conventional understanding of a person, event, or place you are studying.

Focus on the Local and Specific

Microhistory is a relatively recent approach in the field of history. Traditionally, history sought to record the accomplishments of a few individuals in positions of power, sometimes called "the history of great men." Or traditional history was focused on military and political histories of a country or culture. Social histories focus on emerging social movements and what caused these movements, and they can include economic, legal, and labor histories. Common to these traditional approaches to history is the attention they give large social and political institutions, group behavior, and, in general, central and mainstream features of a society.

In contrast, a microhistory narrows the scope, focusing on:

- A person, a certain event, or a particular place.
- The margins or fringes of a certain culture or society, the ordinary people and events that typically are considered unimportant and that often are left out of larger histories.
- Precise, or "thick," description of the everyday details of an individual's life, a place, or an event.
- Primary documents and materials created by or connected to an individual, an event, or a place.
- Connecting the microhistory to the larger culture as a way to reveal trends, forces, pressures, and expectations acting on an individual or place.
- Filling gaps created by broadly focused histories so as to acknowledge and honor common people *and* to reveal the effects of economic and political forces on the common people.

Building this kind of argument requires that you work as a historian and then use the microhistory that you prepare in order to deliver an argument. Writing an argument based on a microhistory means that you will:

- Introduce to your audience the subject of your microhistory and the light you hope to shed on its significance.
- Explain your interest in your subject and the questions you hope to answer by compiling your microhistory.
- Provide extensive context for the individual, event, or place you will study. This means accessing as much primary source material as you can—court and public records, diaries and journals, letters and correspondence, articles and information drawn from local newspapers, newsletters, special-interest publications, maps, and in general any materials that clarify the daily realities of your subject.
- Draw conclusions for your audience that reveal how a close study of the individual, place, or event reveals something about the larger culture. This will mean background reading in secondary documents to get a sense of what the culture values and how its rules and regulations affected the lives of everyday people.
- Deliver at or near the end of your argument a claim based on your microhistory.
- Give voice to the questions and uncertainties that remain for you at the end of your argument.

Make Room for Local Histories

Delivering an argument based on a microhistory can be a powerful experience for a writer. It is a chance to collect and analyze primary historical material and then argue a claim based on that analysis. The ideas you bring to the conclusion of your argument as you make sense of the historical information can bring to light some of the challenges everyday people weathered during an earlier time, challenges that often are missing in broader histories. Your research and the conclusions you draw can add to our "public memory" of a certain time and place, and this is no small contribution.

But what role can argument play in a microhistory? Based on the primary materials you're working with and the sense you make of them, you are in a position to make a claim that argues against the generally accepted understanding of a particular time and place in history. For example, if you choose to dig into that box of letters your great-grandmother wrote three generations ago, you may find information that contradicts our general notion of women's roles during your great-grandmother's time. Suppose you learn that your great-grandmother was active in civic life, spoke up at town meetings, and wanted women to be allowed to enter the fields of law, medicine, and finance. You learn that in some letters she wrote to a friend about religion and spirituality, marriage, and food and diet. At the end of your work with these primary documents, you know that your great-grandmother's life differs from our culture's general understanding of women's civic and intellectual lives during your great-grandmother's time. Based on your work with the letters, you are in a position to make a claim that argues against the limited understanding of women's lives three generations ago.

Two additional examples might help clarify the value of forging an argument based on a microhistory. Recently, a student and passionate baseball fan crafted a compelling argument focused on the integration of Major League Baseball in 1947. Mainstream history represents this event as a victory in American race relations, with much of the credit going to an executive with the Brooklyn Dodgers, the team that penciled Jackie Robinson into its starting lineup. The student moved outside this perspective by reading the columns of an African American sportswriter for the black-owned *The People's Voice*, a weekly newspaper published from 1942 to 1947. In these columns, the student uncovered a new perspective, one that told a very different history than the formerly accepted "history." The sportswriter revealed that integrating Major League Baseball was not completely positive: as a result of the integration, the Negro Leagues were dead a few years later, leaving the players and employees for these teams out of work. Having studied this primary material, the student was motivated to claim that integrating Major League Baseball in 1947 was a partial victory only. He supported his claim with evidence from the sportswriter's columns. The opposing point of view in this argument is the more general and common history of baseball's integration.

The second example involves a writer's work with a historical monument erected in 1929 next to what is now a college campus. The monument commemorates a reunion of Civil War veterans and reads as follows:

GLORIA VICTIS
IN COMMEMORATION OF THE 39TH ANNUAL REUNION OF THE UNITED CONFEDERATE VETERANS AT CHARLOTTE, NORTH CAROLINA, JUNE 4–7, 1929.
A STATE AND CITY'S TRIBUTE OF LOVE; IN GRATEFUL RECOGNITION OF THE SERVICES OF THE CONFEDERATE SOLDIERS WHOSE HEROISM IN WAR AND FIDELITY IN PEACE HAVE NEVER BEEEN SURPASSED.
ACCEPTING THE ARBITRAMENT OF WAR, THEY PRESERVED THE ANGLO-SAXON CIVILIZATION OF THE SOUTH AND BECAME MASTER BUILDERS IN A RE-UNITED COUNTRY.
VERITAS VINCIT

Language on the monument motivated the student to research events associated with the reunion—a large parade, social activities, reports and editorials in the local newspaper, and so forth—and it motivated the student to understand how ideas grounded in racial inequality could be memorialized. Interestingly, in her research, this writer also learned much about African American political life in the community in 1929, and this information allowed her to think about the monument in much broader terms. She argued that the marker must be contextualized to include differing ideas in the community regarding notions of "civilization" and a "reunited country." Specifically, editorials in the community's black newspaper and references to sermons delivered by African American ministers provided a much different history for the monument, one not grounded in "tribute" and "love."

Work with Primary Materials

A first step in preparing a microhistory is locating **primary materials.** Local and college libraries often hold special collections and archived material. This material can include letters, various other kinds of correspondence, court and legal records, diaries, journals, bills of sale, and business records. Local museums, churches, and historical societies are also depositories for this kind of primary material. Communities always keep records of their past in one way or another, and sometimes this information is kept by families and individuals. It may be that members of your immediate or extended family are keeping such records and that some of those records may inspire you to prepare a microhistory and offer a claim based on what you learn. Think of yourself as an archaeologist uncovering neglected artifacts at the site of a dig. Your job is to describe and make sense of your findings.

There are many excellent, book-length microhistories. All are built on very specific information that reveals more complete pictures of a culture. Subjects of microhistories have been far ranging and include people, products, places, and facts that fall outside the scope of mainstream history: the natural ice industry in nineteenth-century North America; the final Civil War

Hank Frentz/Shutterstock.com

Figure 9.5 Primary documents, like this collection of old photographs, and their interpretation are the center of arguments based on a microhistory. The ways in which these documents argue against common and more general treatments of a historical period can reveal the complexity of our past and steer us away from damaging stereotypes.

battle at Gettysburg in 1863; cadavers; the cockroach; and products including Spam, sugar, coffee, coal, and cotton. Sometimes microhistories consider community institutions whose histories have been overlooked, such as local businesses, social service organizations, hospitals, schools, and government-related agencies. Of course a microhistory that you prepare for an assignment will be shorter than book length, but the narrative you piece together and the conclusions you draw can be just as compelling as longer projects.

Subjects and Materials for Microhistories

Subjects practical for arguments based on microhistories can include but are not limited to the following.

Individuals

- A family member or relative
- A member of your community whose life experience is not part of public knowledge
- A local employee, official, coach, clergy, teacher, neighbor, or police officer
- Any other person, living or dead

Events

- An event that affected your family, such as a marriage, a divorce, a hiring or firing, a birth or death, a dispute, or a relocation
- An event in your community, such as a business closing and the resulting loss of jobs, a celebration, a battle, or a natural disaster

Places

- Neighborhood
- Natural area
- Home
- Factory, warehouse, place of employment
- School
- Church
- Government building

Sources

Primary materials to consider when preparing a microhistory can include:

- Letters
- Journals
- Diaries
- Family histories
- Business records

- Court documents
- Legal documents
- Photographs
- Church records
- Newspapers and newsletters
- Sermons
- City and community histories
- Oral histories

Map an Argument Based on a Microhistory

Following is an outline for an argument based on a microhistory. Note that the structure of this kind of argument differs from Toulmin-based, middle ground, and Rogerian arguments.

COMMUNITY

School-Academic

Workplace

Family-Household

Neighborhood

Social-Cultural

Consumer

Concerned Citizen

TOPIC: Justice

ISSUE: Murder of a Female Slave

AUDIENCE: Members of Writing Class

CLAIM: Evidence like this court transcript suggests that in some areas of the slave South justice was applied across the color line.

Support

- Primary documents: Transcript of 1839 Iredell County, North Carolina Superior Court decision. The transcript recounts the trial of a slave-holder who, with "malice aforethought," murdered his female slave. The transcript is lengthy and full of details about owner–slave relations.
- Secondary documents: Scholarly books and articles about justice regarding slaveholders and slaves.

What the Microhistory Reveals about the Culture

The court records document the court's decision to execute the white slaveholder for murdering his slave. This decision in many ways reveals that some communities delivered justice when and where it was due, regardless of color and status.

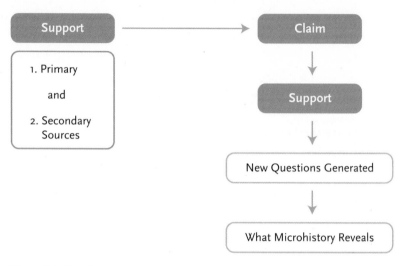

Figure 9.6 The Microhistory model

Claim

Evidence like this court transcript suggests that in some areas of the slave South justice was applied across the color line.

New Questions Generated from the Microhistory

Based on work with these primary documents, findings can move readers away from thinking about justice in the slave South in common and stereotypical ways. New questions might focus on how justice was carried out in a particular community or on a particular plantation, how this kind of information can be incorporated into public school curricula, and what factors from the local culture influenced this court decision.

 tip 9c

Think of Microhistory as Archaeological Work

Writing a microhistory means working outside the mainstream. Your work will involve digging into mostly unrecognized corners of our past and bringing to light a person, place, or event. Your job is to uncover, dust off, and interpret the primary materials you identify and review.

your turn 9f ▶ GET STARTED Set Up an Argument Based on a Microhistory

1. What is the subject of your microhistory? What motivates you to study this subject?
2. What do you hope to learn from this project?
3. What primary source materials will you use as you prepare your microhistory? Where will you find these materials?
4. What secondary sources will you use to establish cultural context, or background, for your subject?
5. What does the larger culture's history seem to value about the time period you are examining? For example, were there acceptable and unacceptable kinds of behavior and attitudes during this time, and does your microhistory contradict these ideas?

6. What does your subject reveal about the culture? For example, if your subject is an individual, how does he or she fit into or not fit into the norms and expectations of the culture? If your subject is an event or place, what does it tell you about how the larger culture functions, about behavior the larger culture approves or disapproves of, about behavior the larger culture encourages or discourages?

7. Based on this close study of your subject and its time period, do you now think differently about this period? Explain.

8. Based on your microhistory, what will you claim?

9. What additional questions do you have about your subject and the time period of your microhistory?

10. How can your argument based on a microhistory make us think more realistically about the period, individual, event, or place that it addresses?

The questions in Your Turn 9f are challenging, and because you have made a careful study of your primary documents, you can answer them in order to prepare a sound argument. While the other approaches to argument that are discussed in this chapter—MIDDLE GROUND and Rogerian—devote much attention to support for the claim, an argument based on a microhistory requires that you devote most of your project to support. Bring your claim in at or near the end of an argument based on microhistory, after you establish credibility with readers based on your work with primary source material. A warrant and backing are addressed when you discuss how your subject reveals something new about the culture and what we can learn from your subject today.

The microhistory you prepare will be original and unique to you. While this project likely will be submitted as a class assignment, the work you do and the insights you generate will help fill gaps in our culture's collective memory and widen the window to our past. Furthermore, because your subject in all probability has been left out of conventional histories, you bring in from the margins of a culture an additional perspective that can help us better understand our past and our present.

Sample Argument Based on a Microhistory

In the following microhistory, what this New York City writer considers is the integration of Major League Baseball. The writer's primary material is an extensive archive of columns written by area sportswriters. The writer's claim, appearing in the argument's conclusion, is that while Jackie Robinson and Branch Rickey should be honored as the player and executive who broke the barricades preventing Black ballplayers from entering the Major Leagues, the real heroes of this civil rights victory are the sportswriters because they did the hard work of building support for integration over many years. The idea for the microhistory originated in columns found in family scrapbooks. The writer then accessed research libraries, including the Schomburg Center for Research in Black Culture, which houses many columns written during the run-up to April 15, 1947, the date when Jackie Robinson was penciled into the starting lineup of the Brooklyn Dodgers. The writer's careful research allows him to argue against our limited public memory of this seminal historical event; that is, the research allows the writer to focus attention on the heroic work of these sportswriters, figures all but lost in our overly generalized understanding of Major League Baseball's integration. The first paragraph introduces the writer's project, and the other paragraphs focus on primary materials.

Baseball, Integration, And Militant Rhetoric:
The Pioneering Work Of New York City Sportswriters

Jackie Robinson and Branch Rickey are American heroes, and everybody who knows even a little about baseball respects them. They are heroes because they had the courage to cross the color line and integrate our national game. They should always be heroes. But if we want to really understand why Black ballplayers were finally allowed to compete alongside whites, it is essential that we honor the work of sportswriters who fought over many years to convince readers of the moral rightness of integrating the game.

As a nation, we focus our eyes on April 15, 1947, the day when Robinson started at first base for the Brooklyn Dodgers. A 2013 movie, *42*, was made and many books have been written about this day and about Robinson's career, about the regular taunting from opposing players and hostile fans and about his incredible determination and strength to keep going. I probably would have walked away and hoped to take some of my dignity with me.

Making all this possible were mostly Black sportswriters like Joe Bostic, Dan Burley, and Romeo Daugherty, who toiled for Black-owned dailies and weeklies. Perhaps the greatest praise should be heaped on a white sportswriter, Lester Rodney, who began campaigning for integration of baseball in 1936 as sports editor for the *Daily Worker,* the newspaper of the Communist Party. If we want to know about the difficult work of creating social change, we must study the historical columns of these brave sportswriters.

Joe Bostic was sports editor from 1942 to 1945 for the militant *The People's Voice*, a Black-owned newspaper published in Harlem. Bostic often called out the white baseball establishment for its racist practices. He also questioned the presumed superiority of white players and whether or not integration would mean a step up for Black players. In a July 11, 1942 column, he writes, "We're not convinced that the baseball played in the organized leagues necessarily

represents the best caliber of ball played per se, and therefore, the Negro players would not be moving into faster company than that in which they were
already playing" (Reisler 85). One has to wonder how Bostic flipping the "superiority" mindset might have influenced readers. Bostic also knew that while
integration might be a social victory, it would also be a financial defeat for the
Negro Leagues, a predominately Black-owned industry.

In what some view as the most aggressive challenge to Major League
Baseball's segregationist policy, Bostic arranged a tryout at the Dodgers'
spring training camp in April of 1945 for two Negro League players, Terris
McDuffie and Showboat Thomas. Bostic appeared at the camp uninvited and
knew that he'd cause trouble. He was challenging Dodgers' President Branch
Rickey to make practical his contention that he favored integrating the game.
Rickey was furious and never spoke to Bostic again. The players were not
signed. Bostic wrote about the tryout, embarrassed Rickey, and added a few
more soldiers to the march against segregation.

After reading all of Bostic's baseball columns, I am convinced that he should
be in the Baseball Hall of Fame for his efforts. Mostly I see him as a man ahead
of his time. He knew that the game would be integrated, especially after
Commissioner Landis died, but he wanted the world to know that the Negro
Leagues were successful in their own right and that Black players were unlikely
to find "faster company" in white leagues. He also exposed Branch Rickey, a
powerhouse in the baseball establishment, for wanting to integrate the game
on his terms only. For me, Bostic's militancy distinguished the Negro Leagues
and, ultimately, contributed to the work of integrating the game.

Lester Rodney is not exactly a household name, but it should be. Rodney
was sports editor for the *Daily Worker* from 1936 to 1958 and spent much of
his first decade with the paper working aggressively to promote the integration
of baseball. Rodney believed that a Communist critique of a capitalist system
could occur on sports pages as well as anywhere, and that these pages were
good places to appeal to workers. Rodney was different from most Communist
Party hard-liners in that he believed that workers' passion for their teams was
genuine and not something manufactured by the system. On a personal level,
Rodney describes his drive for integration this way: "I was in it because I wanted
the damn ban to end, to bring elementary democracy to the game I loved and to
see the banned players get their chance to show they belonged" (qtd. in Tygiel x).
Rodney's many columns on the issue spurred the *Daily Worker* to conduct
petition drives in which more than one million people signed in support of
the integration of baseball. Rodney and writers at some Black papers regularly shared information in a concerted drive to build momentum.

Rodney did not hold back in his criticism of American racism. Of April 15,
1947, he writes: "It's hard this Opening Day to write straight baseball and not
stop to mention the wonderful fact of Jackie Robinson. You tell yourself it
shouldn't be especially wonderful in America, no more wonderful for instance
than Negro soldiers being with us on the way overseas through submarine
infested waters in 1943" (qtd. in Silber 98).

Sometimes Rodney's columns issued challenges. For example, in an interview Rodney recalls a conversation he had with the great Negro Leagues pitcher Satchel Paige in 1937 in which Paige had suggested that the winner of that year's Major League World Series play an all-star team of Negro League players:

So I say to him, "What makes you so sure you'll win?" And he replies, "We've been playing teams of major league all-stars after the regular season in California for four years and they haven't beaten me yet. . . . Must be just a few men who don't want us to play Big League ball. The players are okay and the crowds are with us. Just let them take a vote of the fans whether they want us in the game. I've been all over the country and I know it would be one hundred to one in favor of such a game (qtd. in Silber 62).

Like Joe Bostic, Rodney used various strategies to push the integration movement forward. He is a hero, more than deserving of a prominent place in our public history.

Works Cited

Bostic, Joe. "In Re Negroes in Big Leagues." *Black Writers, Black Baseball: An Anthology of Articles from Black Sportswriters Who Covered the Negro Leagues.* Ed. Jim Reisler. Jefferson: McFarland, 2007. 84–86. Print.

Silber, Irwin. *Press Box Red: The Story of Lester Rodney, the Communist Who Helped Break the Color Line in American Sports.* Philadelphia: Temple UP, 2003. Print.

Reflect and Apply

Answer the following questions as a way to determine the kind of argument practical to your purpose.

1. Identify a few issues in your personal or public life that seem especially appropriate for middle-ground approaches. If you were to argue on these issues, how would you reconcile their extreme positions with more practical claims?

2. How does the approach to the opposition in Rogerian argument differ from the approach to the opposition in Toulmin-based argument? Reflecting on issues in your life as a student, worker, consumer, and concerned citizen, explain why some issues are appropriate for a Rogerian approach.

3. Regarding your family or your community, what part of history do you want to know more about? Why? What primary documents available to you could lead you into a deeper understanding of an earlier time period?

KEEPING IT LOCAL

THE NARRATIVE that opens this chapter—a writer's burgeoning awareness of how a big utility impacts citizens' daily lives and the writer's task of crafting a Middle Ground argument in response—provides a strong lesson in audience awareness. Because the writer aimed at the state Utilities Commission, and not the utility, the general public, or elected officials, the writer could emphasize the commission's dual role to both protect ratepayers and ensure that the utility brings in sufficient profit to continue operating. Had the writer aimed the argument at the utility, then a Toulmin-based approach would have been appropriate because of the writer's concern for ratepayers. Or, had the writer aimed the argument at the Chamber of Commerce, a group representing the interests of local businesses, then a Rogerian approach may have been practical because of business owners' sensitivity to the utility as a business not only providing an essential service but also vulnerable to economic risk. In a middle-ground approach, the writer identified the two extreme positions as (1) the utility's request for regular rate hikes in the midst of a tough economic cycle, and (2) some ratepayers' demands that the utility reduce rates and cross over to renewable energy sources in the next few years. The writer's claim: "The Utilities Commission should rule that yearly rate hikes are unacceptable and mandate an energy portfolio standard that includes increasing percentages of renewable energy sources."

It's important, always, to decide early in your writing process whom you want to influence and inform on an issue. Knowing what an audience values—profit, public service, or both—makes it easier to choose the best approach to your argument. Your choice of approach begins with a sense of your local community: who holds the reins of power, who looks out for everyday people, and where openings for change can be found.

● – – – – – – – – – – – – ●

When our opinions on an issue differ with others' opinions, we tend to think in "I'm right, and you're wrong" terms. In many ways, that is how we have been trained to think. In everyday life you have choices about your thought process in situations where you differ with others on an issue that's important to you. How will you remind yourself that these choices exist?

Now identify the single most difficult issue in your life, the one you'd most like to avoid. Now that you have learned four ways to approach an issue, which approach to argument would you choose for this tough issue? What would you claim?

CHAPTER 10

Build Arguments

The current assignment in your argument class asks you to argue on an issue that affects the local environment. Your teacher advises the class that extensive research will be essential to forge a persuasive argument because environmental issues are usually evaluated in terms of the factual evidence supplied by each side. A brief conversation with your neighbor, who opposes the construction of a nearby coal-burning plant, compels you to do some preliminary research, and the issue motivates you to argue a position. The two sides are clear: for and against. Each side supports its position with scientific studies, personal testimony, and a lot of economic data and projections.

To date, opponents of the plant have been unsuccessful in their efforts to halt construction, even though protests and public hearings have received substantial media coverage. On the other side, the private utility provider building the plant argues that jobs created by the new plant are essential to the local economy and that improved technology will limit emissions of coal dust into the air.

With the plant's construction already underway, you decide that your argument must generate local awareness of the health risks the plant poses to your community. With its extensive circulation, the local newspaper seems to be a practical place to present your argument, especially because twice a week, the paper provides space for editorials that address local issues.

All Illustrations by iStockphoto.com/A-digit

COMMUNITY

School-Academic

Workplace

Family-Household

Neighborhood

Social-Cultural

Consumer

Concerned Citizen

TOPIC: Air Quality

ISSUE: Construction of Local Coal-Burning Facility

AUDIENCE: Readers of Local Newspaper

CLAIM: Concerned citizens in our community should be aware that completion of a coal-burning plant will create health risks for the next 50 years.

A powerful local issue like this one calls for a practical response. When an argument contains a clear center that an audience recognizes as thoughtful, direct, and fully supported, it presents such a response. In Chapters 8, "Consider Toulmin-Based Argument," and 9, "Consider Middle Ground Argument, Rogerian Argument, and Argument Based on a Microhistory," you learned about kinds of argument, that is, approaches to an issue that can serve your purpose. But any of the four kinds of argument treated in these chapters require some or all of the following parts: claim, reasons, support, qualifier, warrant, backing, and reservations. This chapter teaches you how to use each of these parts to build your argument and in this way fleshes out the four kinds of argument discussed in Chapters 8 and 9.

At this point, it may be helpful to think about a complete argument as having two major parts. (See Figure 10.1.) Part one is built around a claim, its support, and the qualifiers that make your argument realistic. Part two is built around a warrant, backing, and reservations, elements that justify your claim. With both parts of an argument, pay close attention to your audience and let your argumentative strategies appeal both to your audience's values and to your audience's reservations.

In this chapter you will learn how to:

- Understand the function of a claim.
- Choose the kind of claim appropriate to your purpose.
- Recognize the function of reasons.
- Use qualifiers to make your claim believable.
- Use your knowledge of your audience to build a warrant.
- Use backing to support a warrant.
- Address audience reservations to make your warrant believable.

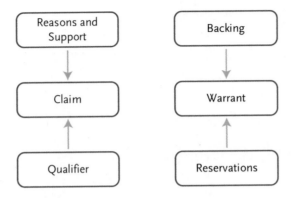

Figure 10.1 The two major parts of a complete argument

How a Claim Functions

The following sections explain why a claim must be the center of an argument. It is the single statement that your readers, including your teacher, refer back to in order to stay focused on your purpose and position in an argument. Unlike a thesis that explains, summarizes, or confesses, a claim is a type of thesis that argues. It identifies an issue, takes a position, and addresses those who hold differing views.

Claim: The Center of Your Argument

A **claim** is the center of an argument and is a kind of thesis. It is your position on an issue, the idea or belief that motivates you to argue. From the perspective of you, the arguer, a claim answers the following questions:

- Where do I stand on this issue?
- What point of view do I want my audience to accept at the end of my argument?
- What is my purpose in delivering this argument?

A claim is also a position you are prepared to defend with reasons and support. The effectiveness of a claim always depends on your ability to convince an audience of its truthfulness. A claim is the single statement that members of your audience, including your teacher, regularly revisit in order to confirm that you remain focused on your claim.

An audience may agree with a claim, it may agree in part with a claim, or it may be skeptical of a claim and require substantial convincing. In all cases, careful study of your audience will put you in a position to craft a claim practical to your purpose. As you begin building an argument, it will be helpful to review the Chapter 2 section titled "Define and Target Your Audience" (page 32) regarding the importance of aiming an argument at an appropriate audience.

AP Photo/Robert Mecea

Figure 10.2 In this photo a New York University student is addressing the media during a student-led protest. The setting and her expression reveal three elements of a successful claim: the arguer knows where she stands on the issue at hand, she knows what she wants her audience to accept, and her purpose is clear.

From the perspective of an audience, a claim should answer these questions:

☐ Where does the arguer stand on this issue?

☐ What is the arguer trying to prove?

☐ What are we being asked to accept or consider?

A claim is often most effective when placed at the beginning of an argument, in your introduction or in an early paragraph. But depending on your purpose, sometimes a claim is effective at or near the end of an argument, especially when it is important for you to first fully inform an audience about an issue. Consider the issue below and how the writer builds a focused, clearly worded claim that is aimed at a specific audience.

COMMUNITY

School-Academic

Workplace

Family-Household

Neighborhood

Social-Cultural

Consumer

Concerned Citizen

TOPIC: Discrimination in the Health Care Field

ISSUE: Promotion Practices

AUDIENCE: Director of Hospital Services

CLAIM: Competent, qualified nurses of color in our hospital are often passed over for better-paying positions.

In response to this issue of promotion practices at a local hospital, the arguer has chosen a claim of fact (defined in Table 10.1) as the center of her argument. She makes clear her position, or what she wants her audience to accept, and implies that she wants her claim acknowledged as objective fact in the hospital where she works. In terms of audience, the arguer makes it clear where she stands, and she implies that she intends to prove that this kind of discrimination exists. Then she must sway her audience using convincing support. The arguer plans to target the individual who oversees promotions and disputes as the audience. The arguer's purpose is to make this person aware of her claim of fact. Later arguments on this issue may require different kinds of claims, such as a claim of cause or a problem-based claim, especially if the arguer intends to argue for something to change. This claim is strong because it is direct and because it targets an appropriate audience.

Connect Claim with Purpose

Choose a claim based on what you want to accomplish with an audience. If your aim is to rally an audience to action based on your solution to a current problem, then a problem-based claim would be appropriate. When you determine that confusing or ambiguous language characterizes an issue, you can isolate a key term or word and offer a precise meaning in a claim of definition. If you are motivated to argue an issue on moral grounds, choose a claim of evaluation in which you can center your argument in the particular moral principle in question. When you prove that something is factual that is not regarded as factual by everyone in your audience, a claim of fact forms the foundation of the argument. And when you are compelled to reveal the history of an issue and thus to connect the past with the present, a claim of cause can be effective. Use Table 10.1 to determine the kind of claim that best fits your goals with your audience.

All three kinds of support—logical, ethical, and emotional—can be used effectively in any type of argument. The category "Primary Support," in Table 10.1, identifies the *essential* support required in each kind of claim.

your turn 10a ▶ GET STARTED **Determine Your Purpose before Writing a Claim**

Answer the following questions to determine the kind of claim that fits your purpose in an argument. Use Table 10.1 as a guide.

1. On what single issue are you motivated to argue?
2. What is the audience for your argument? Why, exactly, is this audience a practical target?
3. What do you want to accomplish with this argument?

Five Kinds of Claims

Practical arguments require clearly worded claims directed at specific audiences. When your goals with your audience are clear, choose the kind of claim that matches your purpose. Kinds of claims are discussed in the following sections.

Table 10.1 Finding an Appropriate Claim

Purpose of Argument is to . . .	Appropriate Kind of Claim	Essential Support

Prove something as true
Prove that something happened
	Fact	Logical
		  facts
		  examples
		  credible research

Define
Clarify
Identify characteristics
	Definition	Logical and Ethical
		  facts
		  personal examples
		  credible research

Prove a problem exists
Prove a problem needs attention
Offer a solution
Rally audience to action
	Problem-Based	Logical, Ethical, and Emotional
		  facts
		  credible research
		  personal examples
		  emotional example

Make a judgment
Prove relevance of a principle
	Evaluation	Logical and Ethical
		  personal examples
		  credible research
		  facts

Establish cause and effect
Identify relationships
Position an issue in history
	Cause–Effect	Logical
		  facts
		  credible research

Claim of Fact

A **claim of fact** argues that something is a fact—an event or series of events, a trend, an attitude, or a part of history—that may not be considered a fact by everyone. When you argue a claim of fact, you argue that something is truthful and can be proven objectively in the real world. Your responsibility in this kind of claim is to bring enough support to make your claim believable. Review the following examples of claims of fact.

- Although many local businesses claim to be green, problems with air, water, and waste continue and, in some cases, have gotten worse.
- Despite the complaints of many students about online courses, I gain a lot from these courses: I interact more effectively with my teachers than in the classroom, I get more thorough feedback, and members of my group are more responsible.
- Bailing out big banks helps the banks but not everyday Americans.